Love, Friendship and Faith in Europe, 1300–1800

Love, Friendship and Faith in Europe, 1300–1800

Edited by

Laura Gowing

Michael Hunter

and

Miri Rubin

First published 2005 by
PALGRAVE MACMILLAN
Houndmills, Basingstoke, Hampshire RG21 6XS and
175 Fifth Avenue, New York, N.Y. 10010
Companies and representatives throughout the world

PALGRAVE MACMILLAN is the global academic imprint of the Palgrave Macmillan division of St. Martin's Press, LLC and of Palgrave Macmillan Ltd. Macmillan® is a registered trademark in the United States, United Kingdom and other countries. Palgrave is a registered trademark in the European Union and other countries.

ISBN-13: 978–1–4039–9147–8 hardback
ISBN-10: 1–4039–9147–2 hardback

This book is printed on paper suitable for recycling and made from fully managed and sustained forest sources.

A catalogue record for this book is available from the British Library.

Library of Congress Cataloging-in-Publication Data
Love, friendship, and faith in Europe, 1300–1800 / edited by Laura Gowing, Michael Hunter & Miri Rubin.
   p.   cm.
Includes bibliographical references and index.
ISBN 1–4039–9147–2 (cloth)
1. Friendship—Europe—History.   2. Love—Europe—History.
3. Homosexuality—Europe—History.   4. Interpersonal relations and culture—Europe—History.   5. Religion and culture—Europe—History.   I. Gowing, Laura.   II. Hunter, Michael Cyril William.
III. Rubin, Miri, 1956–
HM1161.L68 2005
306.76′6′094—dc22   2005047733

10   9   8   7   6   5   4   3   2   1
14   13   12   11   10   09   08   07   06   05

Printed and bound in Great Britain by
Antony Rowe Ltd, Chippenham and Eastbourne

Contents

Notes on Contributors   vii

Introduction   1
Laura Gowing, Michael Hunter and Miri Rubin

1   Friendship's Loss: Alan Bray's Making of History   15
    Valerie Traub

2   Sacred or Profane? Reflections on Love and
    Friendship in the Middle Ages   43
    Klaus Oschema

3   Friendship in Catholic Reformation Eichstätt   66
    Jonathan Durrant

4   A Society of Sodomites: Religion and
    Homosexuality in Renaissance England   88
    Alan Stewart

5   'Swil-bols and Tos-pots': Drink Culture and
    Male Bonding in England, c.1560–1640   110
    Alexandra Shepard

6   The Politics of Women's Friendship in
    Early Modern England   131
    Laura Gowing

7   Friends and Neighbours in Early Modern England:
    Biblical Translations and Social Norms   150
    Naomi Tadmor

8   Tricksters, Lords and Servants: Begging, Friendship
    and Masculinity in Eighteenth-Century England   177
    Tim Hitchcock

9   Spinoza and Friends: Religion, Philosophy and
    Friendship in the Berlin Enlightenment   197
    Adam Sutcliffe

Index   221

Contents

Notes on Contributors

Jonathan Durrant is Lecturer in Early Modern History at the University of Glamorgan. He has published on witchcraft and gender in the German prince-bishopric of Eichstätt, and is now working on masculinity and the military during the Thirty Years' War. He is a co-convenor of the Forum on Early Modern Central Europe and editor of the Witchcraft Bibliography Project Online (www.witchcraftbib.co.uk).

Laura Gowing is Reader in Early Modern History at Kings College, London. She works on sex, gender, the body, and crime in early modern England. Her books include *Domestic Dangers: Women, Words and Sex in Early Modern London* (1996) and *Common Bodies: Women, Touch and Power in Seventeenth-Century England* (2003).

Tim Hitchcock is Professor of Eighteenth-Century History at the University of Hertfordshire, and has published widely on the histories of eighteenth-century London, poverty and sexuality. His most recent book, *Down and Out in Eighteenth-Century London* (2004) describes how to beg and live poor on the streets. His previous books include *English Sexualities, 1700–1800* (1997); with Michèle Cohen, *English Masculinities, 1660–1800* (1999); and with Heather Shore, *The Streets of London from the Great Fire to the Great Stink* (2003). He is also the co-director, with Robert Shoemaker, of the Old Bailey Online (www.oldbaileyonline.org).

Michael Hunter is Professor of History at Birkbeck, University of London. He has been one of the convenors of the seminar on 'Society, Culture and Belief 1500–1800' at the Institute of Historical Research since founding it with the late Bob Scribner in 1979. He has written or edited many books on the history of ideas and their context in late seventeenth-century Britain, and is the principal editor of the *Works* (14 vols, 1999–2000) and *Correspondence* (6 vols, 2001) of Robert Boyle.

Klaus Oschema studied Medieval History, Philosophy and English Literature and Linguistics at the Universities of Bamberg and Paris X – Nanterre. In 2004 he received his PhD from the Technical University of Dresden and the École Pratique des Hautes Études at Paris. Since 2002 he has been teaching Medieval History at the University of Bern (Switzerland). Publications include articles on the 'Idea and Concept of Europe in the High and Late Middle Ages' and the 'Paradoxical Attitude of Chivalry towards Death'; his thesis on 'Friendship and Proximity in Late Medieval Burgundy' is forthcoming.

Miri Rubin is Professor of Early Modern History at Queen Mary, University of London. She studies social relations in the religious cultures of Europe between 1100 and 1600: charitable activity in *Charity and Community in Medieval Cambridge* (1987), sacramental religion in *Corpus Christi: The Eucharist in Late Medieval Culture* (1991), anti-Jewish narratives in *Gentile Tales: The Narrative Assault on Late Medieval Jews* (1999). Her most recent book, *The Hollow Crown: A History of Britain in the Late Middle Ages*, appeared in January 2005 and she is working on a cultural history of Mary.

Alexandra Shepard is a Lecturer in History and Fellow of Christ's College at the University of Cambridge. She has written several articles on masculinity and gender in early modern England, and her publications include (edited with Phil Withington) *Communities in Early Modern England: Networks, Place, Rhetoric* (2000) and *Meanings of Manhood in Early Modern England* (2003).

Alan Stewart is Professor of English and Comparative Literature at Columbia University. His publications include *Close Readers: Humanism and Sodomy in Early Modern England* (1997); *Hostage to Fortune: The Troubled Life of Francis Bacon* (with Lisa Jardine, 1998); *Philip Sidney: A Double Life* (2000); *The Cradle King: A Life of James VI and I* (2003); and, with Heather Wolfe, the exhibition catalogue *Letterwriting in Renaissance England* (2004).

Adam Sutcliffe is Lecturer in Early Modern History at Kings College, London. He is the author of *Judaism and Enlightenment* (2003) and the co-editor (with Ross Brann) of *Renewing the Past, Reconfiguring Jewish Culture: From al-Andalus to the Haskalah* (2004). He is currently working on a study of the evolution of concepts of friendship in European Enlightenment thought, and also on an investigation of approaches to nationhood, ethnicity and Jewishness in late eighteenth- and early nineteenth-century political radicalism.

Naomi Tadmor is a Lecturer in History at the University of Sussex. Her research is focused on the history of social relations and the history of language and texts. Her book *Family and Friends in Eighteenth-Century England: Household, Kinship, and Patronage* was published in 2001 by Cambridge University Press. She is currently studying the language of social relations in early modern English biblical translations. She has published several articles, and was co-editor of *The Practice and Representation of Reading in England* (1996).

Valerie Traub is Professor of English and Women's Studies at the University of Michigan. She is the author of *The Renaissance of Lesbianism in Early Modern England* (2002), which won the Best Book of 2002 award from the Society for the Study of Early Modern Women. Author of *Desire & Anxiety: Circulations of Sexuality in Shakespearean Drama* (1992), and co-editor of *Feminist Readings of Early Modern Culture: Emerging Subjects* (1996), she has written widely on the history of sexuality and early modern literature.

Introduction

Laura Gowing, Michael Hunter and Miri Rubin

Over the twenty-three years since the publication of Alan Bray's first, ground-breaking book, *Homosexuality in Renaissance England* (1982), his work has had its greatest influence in the field of the history of sexuality. Bray's work provided the starting point for an emerging field, in which scholars began to study the texts and histories of Renaissance England and Europe with an ear to the fluctuating, transforming meanings of sodomy and homosexuality. Importantly, Bray's work put the whole category of homosexuality in Renaissance England in question, and those who followed him took inspiration from the questions he had asked.

Over the subsequent twenty years, Bray's own scholarship took a somewhat different route. The logical conclusion of his own redefinition of homosexuality and its place in early modern society and culture led him to think about the components of and the challenges to relationships between men in a much wider sphere than the purely sexual – a category which itself, he argued, made little sense in the pre-modern world. His subsequent researches engaged him with the noble household; the early modern family; the world of scholars; the networks of patrons and clients; and the letters of kings and their favourites. He began to write a history that examined friendship, intimacy and love, and that put those relations into the contexts that gave them meaning: kinship, families, and faith. The end result was *The Friend*, published posthumously in 2003.

The writing of *The Friend* coincided with Bray's more formal membership of a world of historical scholarship. His honorary fellowship at Birkbeck College, University of London; his editorship of *History Workshop Journal*; and his role as a convenor of the Institute of Historical Research's seminar on 'Society, Culture and Belief 1500–1800' brought him into

1

continual, formal and informal contact with early modern and modern historians and literary critics who were, often, asking related questions from very different starting points. Alan was a great talker, a wonderful listener and conversationalist, and we want, in this book, to continue some of his conversations. The essays collected here relate very much to three of the themes prominent in Alan's late work: love, friendship, and faith in the early modern world. But they also reflect his intellectual journey from the beginnings of his scholarship, on the history of homosexuality.

*   *   *   *   *

Alan Bray's early work revolutionised the history of homosexuality. It did so from a perspective that combined activist commitment with academic rigour: the result was a new story of homosexuality in Renaissance England. Histories of homosexuality had, by the 1980s, become of central importance to gay politics. They began from the point that was fundamental, through much of the twentieth century, to homosexual liberation movements: homosexuality has a history. That history, for years, was understood as a mirror for the present. Lists and studies of notorious, mostly male, homosexuals of the past made it possible to argue for present liberation. To read A.L. Rowse's *Homosexuals in History* (1977) alongside Bray's work, published only five years later, is to begin to comprehend how huge a leap Bray was making when he asserted that homosexuality, and above all sodomy, meant something quite different to the early modern mind.[1] He was saying, as so many subsequent scholars argued, that there was no such thing as homosexuality before it was invented. Instead, he traced the lineage of an idea of sodomy which allied it with heresy, blasphemy, and popery. That idea, he suggested, made it almost impossible for ordinary people to recognise the homoerotic nature of relationships and acts in their midst. At the same time, Bray began the historical work of reconstructing a world in which such homoeroticisms were taken for granted. From the shared beds of apprentices and masters, to the powerplay of patrons and clients, intimacies between men were, he demonstrated, central to the fabric of early modern society. Michael Rocke, writing about Renaissance Florence, cites the 1476 explanation of a carpenter's erotic relationship with a grocer's son: 'This he did out of great love and good brotherhood, because they are in a confraternity together, and he did as good neighbors do.'[2] The meanings of sodomy were worked out between the idea and the practice.

This framework, with its insistence on the power and the failure of representation, laid the foundations for some of the most innovative work in early modern studies and in the history of sexuality. At first, and in England, Bray's approach lent itself more readily to the study of literary texts than to the archival project. Bruce Smith, Jonathan Goldberg, Alan Stewart, Mario DiGangi, and many others found in Bray's work a language and a framework with which to do queer readings of early modern texts: to look at what was named and what was not, to historicise the closet, to read between the lines of verse and prose for the erotics of friendship.[3] Yet as Valerie Traub points out in chapter 1, one of the lasting achievements of Bray's work was to give a unique historical specificity to the idea that 'heterosexuality' is dependent on its homosexual other. Even without the tools of queer theory or deconstructive criticism, Bray's work demands a new and promising history of emotion.

At the heart of Bray's argument, as he later acknowledged, lies an apparently inescapable essentialism. There are still 'homosexual' acts, their nature unidentified and largely unproblematised; it is the meanings of sexual acts that are contested.[4] Yet Jonathan Goldberg reads this more flexibly. Bray's book, Goldberg suggests, searches for (and finds) 'homosexuality' without 'locating a discourse that identifies persons as homosexual'. At once, this insures against prescriptive definitions of homosexuality and usefully supports a 'universalising' view of homosexuality.[5] As Traub's essay demonstrates, the diverging interpretations of Bray's arguments suggest a persistent tension in his thought between intimacy and friendship.[6]

If Bray's early work could be read as giving 'homosexuality' a history, his later work did a good deal to break the most superficial connections of intimacy with sexuality. The shift, first evident in his published work in the essay 'Homosexuality and the Signs of Male Friendship in Elizabethan England' in *History Workshop Journal* in 1990 marked a transition towards a reading of male intimacy that looked not for the signs of homosexuality, but for the signs of something else: friendship.[7] With the later publication of 'The Body of the Friend', written with Michel Rey, the project of re-imagining early modern male intimacy began to come into focus.[8] It was, perhaps paradoxically, a more physical, more embodied project than *Homosexuality in Renaissance England* had been: it required readers to think about touch, about brushes of the hand, about crowded courts and shared beds. It encouraged, too, a reading of texts by and between male friends where intimate words were overlaid just as bodies might be, and where the line between the great ideal of friendship and the whisper of suggested sodomy could move swiftly and dangerously.

So far, social and cultural historians have been slow to take up the challenges of taking friendship seriously. Historians of masculinity have focused on the outward forms of politeness and the transformation of manners; the affectional transactions that underlay the gestures of civility are much harder to excavate.[9] The study of masculinity has also been anachronistically heterosexual in its orientation; the shadow of homosexual intimacies that Bray delineated, and the wide-ranging manifestations of the erotic that featured in early modern men's lives have not yet been the subject of substantive study. And where, like Bray, historians have examined the power of anxiety in shaping male identities, they have tended to look at economic and social insecurities, rather than the sexual ones which come to the fore in Bray's work on the New England Puritan Michael Wigglesworth.[10]

Bray's interests also encompassed a more rhetorical realm: the friendships that were dreamed of by Montaigne, Bacon, and their many contemporaries, imagining Aristotle's model of two souls in one body. For them, friendship was a flow of affect between two equals, a current of, as Jeffrey Masten astutely identifies, 'sweetness' – an almost tangible, edible affect. As humours flowed in the Galenic body, so the currents of friendship ran between men, binding them in equality and interdependence.[11] Modernity, Bray argued with Derrida, destroyed this pre-Enlightenment dream.[12] Historians' attention to it might bring ethical inspiration, as well as deeper understandings. Frances Harris's work on the friendship of John Evelyn and Margaret Godolphin – a heterosexual Platonic relationship whose participants felt it to be unique, like the friendships of men idealised by Montaigne – explores some of the possibilities of such dreams for seventeenth-century people.[13] In a world where some were beginning to see conventional marriage as, in Montaigne's formula, 'a covenant which hath nothing free but the entrance', friendship suggested another, more liberal, intimacy.[14]

'Friend' had copious and special meanings for early modern people. It brought economic obligations: friends helped the young make marriages, carrying an interest in their future. To ask one's friends, in a society where many young adults had no living parents, was an act of trust, of confidence, of obligation. In the flexible families of early modern Europe, friends were also kin.[15] The study of friendship necessarily bears on the history of the family. In the narrowest sense, early modern friends were family. Lawrence Stone's overpowering narrative of the development of modern heterosexual family forms leaves behind the complex kinships of pre-modern households: step-children, relatives as servants, distant kin as friends.[16] Naomi Tadmor's work on the literary and historical concepts of household and family reveals the nexus of interests and expectations that contemporary terms conveyed: authority, responsibility, possession, household management.[17] Demographic historians studied 'households' and 'families' on the assumption that those structures were the central building blocks of communities. In cities in particular, households and families have turned out to be more complicated than anticipated: servants, lodgers, business partners all lived together. Bray's work suggests a further departure from established practice. Both conceptually and in practice, the erotic, the marital, and the domestic might be disjoined. The places of intimacy are not necessarily those of heterosexual relations or those of marital domesticity.

To think about friends also means thinking about love, our first theme. The history of marriage and the family has often come up against the difficulty of historicising affectional relations. Early attempts to do so – by, for example, Lawrence Stone and Philippe Ariès – confined themselves to suggesting that love between husbands and wives was necessarily experienced differently (or not at all) when marriage was primarily an economic contract. The ways in which love and interest were interconnected in early modern relations remain hard to disentangle. But another way into the question of historicising emotion is to reconsider its direction. Pre-modern north-western Europe had two characteristic marriage patterns: the early, often arranged marriages of the elites, where couples might live apart or with relatives until they reached their twenties; and the late marriages of the majority of the population, chosen and arranged by the couple themselves in their mid- to late twenties. Both might be seen to encourage the formation of affectional bonds outside the heterosexual couple through the years of adolescence, where intimacies were likely to be homosocial. Nor was marriage the only destination: in England by the mid-seventeenth century, up to three-quarters of the population was still unmarried at the age of 45.[18] So the ways in which early modern people used the word 'love' – to their friends, to their kin, to those they worked, ate and drank with – bear a good deal more examination than those which focus on marriage.

That love bound a community together was attested in the performance of communion. For both Protestant and Catholic Europeans, communion demonstrated the unity of neighbourhood; to refuse it, to disrupt it, or to be excluded from it marked a disordered community. Faith, our final theme, carried immense social power. This power not only bound people to each other, but also marked those who were outside the circle of amity. While medieval Europe created and sustained ideas about Jews and heretics, Turks and pagans, those beyond the circle of amity in early modern Europe experienced another powerful phase of such distancing. Foes were now most often other Christians, but Christians whose perverse rituals marked them apart, as Jews were since medieval times. Rituals of birth and marriage, of commensality and death, were markers of difference as well as of sameness. In this riven world, fields for intimacy were reinforced by religious choice. Religion also meant that certain friendships were no longer possible. Whole fields of intimacy between men and between women – in monasteries and guilds – were destroyed, diminished or displaced as a result of the Reformation. As faith and family came together within the Holy Household the public sphere lost some of its capacities as a field for making friends.

*   *   *   *   *

If historians in general have been slow to engage with the conceptual and methodological challenges raised by friendship's past, medieval historians have been particularly isolated from the question. While there is an abundant discussion of *amicitia*, the self-reflective articulation of friendship within monastic communities[19] or between partners in epistolary exchanges,[20] the qualities of friendship, support, mutual understanding, reciprocities, have yet to make a mark on our understanding of individual lives and communities during the medieval centuries. As is the case with so many aspects of history between 1400 and 1600, models of 'modernisation' build up strong expectations that the later we look the more refined, individualised, and self-aware should be the life of the actors inhabiting social institutions.[21] Medieval friendship will contribute to the dismantling of such expectations.

Alan Bray always worked with a strong sense of medieval practices, of social life within a religious culture. *The Friend* begins with a monument from fourteenth-century Constantinople, commemorating the friendship of Sir William Neville and Sir John Clanvowe, two English courtiers who perished in 1391 during a crusade against the Turks. The men died within days of each other, and the stone which was placed in the Dominican convent of Galata to commemorate them depicts two helmets facing each other, as if in a kiss.[22] What did this petrified medieval kiss mean? Was it indeed a kiss? Would men have had their friendship represented so publicly and enduringly? Was the intimacy implied metaphorical or a token of their physical bond? In debate with John Bossy and Eamon Duffy, Bray argued that we should take the kissing helmets to mean a great deal; and yet an ambiguity remains even in his discussion: was the Clanvowe/Neville friendship one which could only be acknowledged publicly after death, or was the commemorative stone an act of posthumous defiance?[23]

Bray's interlocutor, Eamon Duffy, preferred to see the kiss as a sign of Christian brotherhood, making one of the most polysemous of symbols – the kiss – into a symbol of religious conformity and social cohesion. The kiss during the mass, a sign of Christian charity, is seen by Duffy as the defining moment of the liturgy, a focus for discovery of social bonds, and an expression of desire for self-improvement. But religious rituals were also markers of difference, hierarchy, and varying degrees of religious commitment. Liturgy and rituals of commemoration also offered opportunities to mark distinction from the parish group, into more select, exclusive and sometimes demanding frames of interaction and amity.[24] In fraternities men gathered, and women related to them, for enhanced experiences of liturgy, conviviality, commemoration, and expected these to continue after death. Fraternities – groups of amity – did what friends and family should do, but were more reliable than kith and kin: fraternities were vigilant in auditing their activities and they never died out (until the Reformation, that is). So those who could spare time and income entered into frames of amity, pooling and sharing, drawing comfort, keeping secrets, all within a carefully scrutinised group. Such friendship groups provided stages for religious observance, but the experience in them differed from that of the parish. Fraternities offered friendships of sameness, which tested people's willingness to share through the communal kiss less acutely than did the parish mass.

Although Alan Bray was extremely interested in female friendship, and wrote movingly about it, only a small part of his work engaged with it.[25] Eighteenth-century historians have looked to letters, diaries, and poetry to reconstruct the affectional bonds between women; for an earlier period, Sara Mendelson and Patricia Crawford have combined the ego-documents of early modern Europe with court records, the basis for so much study of social relations.[26] This offers us a newly nuanced sense of women's amity, through trust, intimacy, erotic proximity, sharing of secrets, the familiarity of smell and touch. No such studies exist as yet for the late Middle Ages; but they could. For there is an abundance of material which might be worked into the frame offered by Laura Gowing for a later period: tracing the circulation of gifts and bequests – jewellery, items of clothing, knick-knacks, all personal and cherished – may reveal important friendships and intimacies; depositions in court records hitherto studied for the making and breaking of marriage may reveal trails of trust and support through hard times, as well as the rhythms of women's work.[27]

Alan Bray was a keen student of iconography, as we have seen in the case of the kissing helmets – and as shown by his more general interest in tombs, evident throughout *The Friend* – and he reflected deeply on representation. An ethnography of female friendship may be found in the very many late medieval representations of the scene of the Visitation: Mary and Elizabeth, distant kinswomen, brought together during their pregnancies.[28] Hundreds, if not thousands, of representations of the Visitation, produced in a wide range of media, aimed to capture the quality of this encounter: female delight, mutual support, bodily empathy alongside the message of the impending incarnation. These offer a rich field for the historical study of female friendship.[29]

* * * * *

This book is intended to forward the debates sparked off by Alan Bray's work. In it, we consider a variety of aspects of the themes that were central to it and suggest an agenda for future study. Most of the essays here were originally given in 2002–3 as papers to the 'Society, Culture and Belief' seminar at the Institute of Historical Research (University of London), of which Alan, with us, had been a convener; or they were delivered at the colloquium to commemorate Alan and to celebrate the publication of *The Friend* held at Birkbeck College on 20 September 2003.

The book opens with Valerie Traub's assessment of Alan Bray and *The Friend*, a revised version of the keynote paper given at the colloquium in 2003. After placing Bray's work in the historiography of homosexuality, she indicates the broader context in which it should properly be seen: the understanding of intimate relationships in the early modern period. Her attention to the 'unacknowledged tension' in Bray's corpus over the relationship between friendship and emotion, between homosociability and homosexual practices, illuminates not just male relationships, but also female ones. The chapter ends with a powerful agenda for future work in this field, based not least on invoking *The Friend*'s challenge to standard periodisations.

In his chapter, Klaus Oschema takes up one of the themes of this Introduction by providing a crucial analysis of the evolution of medieval attitudes towards love and friendship. He shows that there was a tension between models of friendship inherited from classical antiquity and the new constraints imposed by Christianity, which entailed a distinction hitherto lacking between the sacred and the profane. He gives a number of examples of intimate relations between men being used to cement social and political bonds, including a relationship between Philip Augustus and Richard the Lionheart which John Boswell interpreted as homosexual but which instead seems to have been interpreted at the time in quasi-Biblical terms. From the twelfth century, on the other hand, one sees the rise of a more affective attitude, showing a preparedness to transgress divine principles in the name of friendship, and this more secular attitude looks forward to later developments which are epitomised here by reference to the example of Montaigne.

Jonathan Durrant's case-study considers the idioms of friendship in the context of the German prince-bishopric of Eichstatt in the early seventeenth century. The opportunity for this is provided by the witch-hunts which occurred there in this period, which – contrary to prevailing views – Durrant argues were the result of Counter-Reformation zeal on the part of the authorities, rather than of neighbourly tensions or economic hardship. Indeed, so far from showing evidence of deep enmity, he stresses that most of what the confessions of those accused of witchcraft reveal was friendship, and he is able to use the evidence that they give to show the degrees of friendship that existed; the ways in which this was expressed, particularly through communal eating and drinking; and the festive occasions when abnormal degrees of intimacy, not least sexual, occurred.

Alan Stewart's chapter takes the form of a commentary on and critique of one of the preconceptions of Alan Bray's own work. After a survey of Bray's intellectual agenda, he suggests that Bray's Catholicism made him take a less critical view of the common Protestant association of sodomy with Roman Catholicism than he might otherwise have done. Stewart refines Bray's view of the stereotyped nature of accusations of sodomy by showing how, with Catholicism, it achieved its plausibility by being linked with closed institutions which were deemed to encourage such practices. On the other hand, this was reversible, as he illustrates by a rare but telling case where sodomy was associated with Puritans, whose free public association was seen as favouring sodomy in a distinct but revealing variant on the theme which has a paradoxical amount in common with the molly houses of a century later.

Alexandra Shepard looks at a form of male intimacy which stands in contrast to the densely woven ties of friendship between individuals by which Alan Bray was preoccupied in *The Friend*. Instead, she studies the culture of 'comradeship', 'good fellowship' in contemporary parlance, usually associated with excessive drinking and resulting in superficial intimacy in a fleeting, public context as part of a group. This was part of a counter-culture of youth masculinity, much attacked at the time by moralists whose complaints Shepard is able to use to probe the values underlying the behaviour that they deprecated. Indeed, she even finds that there may have been a more overt sexual overtone to such polemic than was usually openly expressed. The paper enriches our view of early modern social relations by further illustrating the range of behaviours in which different kinds of relationships might be expressed.

Laura Gowing reconsiders friendships between women in early modern England, seeing them as having a political dimension, but a different one from that associated with men. In doing so, she draws on some extraordinary correspondence between close female friends to illustrate the degree of intimacy that existed at the time, and the tensions that this engendered, particularly in relation to the state of marriage which it was presumed was a woman's natural duty. In particular, using the case of Frances Apsley and the future Queen Mary, she shows how women could have strong friendships described in quasi-marital terms, which then had to be mediated with the actual marriages that the partners entered into and the childbearing that followed. She also argues that, by the late seventeenth century, this was becoming more problematic than hitherto, reflecting a change in attitudes mirroring but different from that observed by Bray for men.

In her essay, Naomi Tadmor broadens the scope of the book by considering an important semantic shift in the concept of 'friendship' as presented in the Old Testament, a key text for early modern religious and social values. As she shows, whereas 'friend' and 'neighbour' were used in distinct, if sometimes interchangeable, ways in the Hebrew Bible, in English translations from Wyclif onwards a significant change occurred so that 'neighbour' was made the prime term for moral injunctions concerning fellow men, reflecting a telling shift towards the language of manorial and parochial life. It was in this context that mutual 'love' was enjoined, and she indicates how pervasively the concept was deployed in the early modern period, in official injunctions, catechisms, and more popular pronouncements. For Tadmor, in a radically different yet not alien way to Bray, friendship's meaning was shaped by the particular characteristics of early modern social relations.

Tim Hitchcock seeks to explore the way in which class distinctions interrelated with notions of masculinity in eighteenth-century England, looking particularly at beggars and other figures on the margins of society. He considers the extent to which, in circumstances of destitution, it was possible to retain any sense of identity at all, but finds that in practice the poor and dependent adopted a range of personas which interrelated effectively with the expectations and anxieties of men of higher rank. Those down on their luck might attempt to draw on previous friendships and obligations to obtain support. Beggars might appeal to values of religious sincerity, or present themselves as the maimed victims of militaristic nationalism. More common still was the role of trickster, which re-established a sense of independence on the part of the poor man in duping his social superior. Through case studies based on court records and the autobiographical literature of the period, Hitchcock illuminates the possibilities and impossibilities of friendship on the margins of society.

In his chapter, Adam Sutcliffe explores the way in which friendship related to the philosophical universalism of the Enlightenment. Central to his exposition is the figure of Spinoza, seen in the eighteenth century as the archetype of the philosopher – remote and universal – yet also as a friend, indeed a philosopher who uniquely inspired friendship, not least among his followers after his death. Spinoza was also a Jew, and this adds a further dimension to Sutcliffe's exposition, which focuses on the friendship between another Jew, Moses Mendelssohn, and the influential Enlightenment figure, Gotthold Ephraim Lessing. Matters were complicated by the hostility to the intimacy between the two men and the values underlying it on the part of Friedrich Jacobi, which acted as a test of this, with different ethics of friendship emerging: Jacobi saw friendship as inextricably linked to (Christian) faith. Yet, as Sutcliffe indicates, the racial difference between Jews and gentiles could itself interrelate with and to an extent dissipate the effect of gender stereotypes of the day. In all, in Enlightenment discourse, friendship comes across as a transcending influence, humanising philosophy and acting as a bridge between the universal and the particular, and Sutcliffe ends by reflecting on this in the context of the views on friendship of Derrida and of Alan Bray.

*   *   *   *   *

With the publication of *The Friend* and this garland of offerings prompted by its method and its message, friendship has arrived, as a concept around which fruitful historical conversations may evolve. Representation and experience, men and women, the mundane and the poetical, the expressive and the repressive: friendship is in them and of them. For the friend, as early modern readers knew, is a mirror of sorts. Just as identity is an amalgam of what we are, what we hope to be, and what we are told we ought to be, so are our friends. Some are intimates in unbridled self-exploration, others exhortative guides towards self-improvement, and yet others take us as we are. While seeking friends in the past, we may find some unfamiliar configurations, but we will also delight in the discovery of that which transforms our understanding of ourselves.

This realisation may not be the crux of Alan Bray's understanding, but it is one we could not have reached without him. Bray confronts us with a world of friendships lost. *The Friend* unveils friendships past, which few historians had appreciated before him, only to lament their passing, as an old world turned into a new. Yet, as this book's rich contributions show, intimacies were woven in new and unexpected places: at the tables of rich burghers, between the bedclothes of servants, among the down-and-outs on city streets, in the minds of religious polemicists, during bouts of male drinking, in the letters of philosophers, and in the vision of those who gave the Bible to the English-speaking people. There were doubtless others, too, for historians to discover and understand. It is an exciting prospect.

Notes

1. A.L. Rowse, *Homosexuals in History* (London: Weidenfeld & Nicholson, 1977); see Alan Stewart's discussion of the two, 'Homosexuals in History: A.L. Rowse and the Queer Archive', in K. O'Donnell and M. O'Rourke (eds), *Love, Sex, Friendship and Intimacy Between Men, 1550–1800* (Basingstoke: Palgrave, 2002), pp. 51–67.
2. M. Rocke, *Forbidden Friendships: Homosexuality and Male Culture in Renaissance Florence* (Oxford: Oxford University Press, 1998), p. 148.
3. See, for example, B. Smith, *Homosexual Desire in Shakespeare's England* (Chicago: University of Chicago Press, 1991); J. Goldberg, *Sodometries: Renaissance Texts, Modern Sexualities* (Stanford: Stanford University Press, 1992); A. Stewart, *Close Readers: Humanism and Sodomy in Early Modern England* (Princeton: Princeton University Press, 1997); M. DiGangi, *The Homoerotics of Early Modern Drama* (Cambridge: Cambridge University Press, 1997).
4. A. Bray, 'Epilogue' to T. Betteridge (ed.), *Sodomy in Early Modern Europe* (Manchester: Manchester University Press, 2002), pp. 164–8; see also Stewart, 'Homosexuals in History'.
5. J. Goldberg, 'Margaret Cavendish, Scribe', *GLQ*, 10/3 (2004), 433–52, on p. 450 (n. 7).
6. See p. 21 of this book at n. 32.
7. A. Bray, 'Homosexuality and the Signs of Male Friendship in Elizabethan England', *History Workshop Journal*, 29 (1990), 1–19.
8. A. Bray and M. Rey, 'The Body of the Friend: Continuity and Change in Masculine Friendship in the Seventeenth Century', in T. Hitchcock and M. Cohen (eds), *English Masculinities 1660–1800* (Harlow: Longman, 1999), pp. 65–84.

9. P. Carter, *Men and the Emergence of Polite Society, Britain 1660–1800* (Harlow: Longman, 2000).

10. A. Bray, 'To Be a Man in Early Modern Society: The Curious Case of Michael Wigglesworth', *History Workshop Journal*, 41 (1996), 155–65. On the social and economic anxieties of manhood, see A. Shepard, *Meanings of Manhood in Early Modern England* (Oxford: Oxford University Press, 2003).

11. J. Masten, 'Toward a Queer Address: The Taste of Letters and Early Modern Male Friendship', *GLQ*, 10/3 (2004), 367–84.

12. J. Derrida, *The Politics of Friendship* (London: Verso, 1992).

13. F. Harris, *Transformations of Love: The Friendship of John Evelyn and Margaret Godolphin* (Oxford: Oxford University Press, 2002).

14. M. de Montaigne, *The Essays*, trans. John Florio (London; 1603, facsimile; Menston: Scolar Press, 1969), p. 91.

15. See for example D. O'Hara, *Courtship and Constraint: Rethinking the Making of Marriage in Tudor England* (Manchester: Manchester University Press, 2000).

16. L. Stone, *The Family, Sex and Marriage in England, 1500–1800* (London: Weidenfeld & Nicolson, 1977).

17. N. Tadmor, *Family and Friends in Eighteenth-Century England: Household, Kinship and Patronage* (Cambridge: Cambridge University Press, 2001).

18. For details, E.A. Wrigley and R.S. Schofield, *The Population History of England 1541–1871: A Reconstruction* (Cambridge: Cambridge University Press, 1989), p. 260; K. Wrightson, *Earthly Necessities: Economic Lives in Britain* (London: Penguin, 2002), p. 223.

19. B.P. McGuire, *Friendship and Community: The Monastic Experience, 350–1250* (Kalamazoo: Cistercian Publications, 1988); J. Haseldine, 'Friendship and Rivalry: The Role of *amicitia* in Twelfth-Century Monastic Relations', *Journal of Ecclesiastical History*, 44 (1993), 390–414; J. Haseldine, 'Understanding the Language of *amicitia*: The Friendship Circle of Peter of Celle (*c*.1115–1183)', *Journal of Medieval History*, 20 (1994), 237–60.

20. E. Bos, 'The Literature of Spiritual Formation for Women in France and England, 1080–1180', in C. Mews (ed.), *Listen Daughter: The Speculum Virginum and the Formation of Religious Women in the Middle Ages* (Basingstoke: Palgrave, 2001), pp. 201–20.

21. The *longue durée* encourages smoother chronologies: see J.M. Bennett and A.M. Froide (eds), *Singlewomen in the European Past, 1250–1800* (Philadelphia: University of Pennsylvania Press, 1999).

22. *The Friend*, pp. 16–22, 106–8.

23. The monument was discussed by Bray, John Bossy and Eamon Duffy on 'The Kiss of the Crusaders', BBC Radio 4, 12 June 1999, 2:30 p.m.

24. On brotherhoods see M. Rubin, *Corpus Christi: The Eucharist in Late Medieval Culture* (Cambridge: Cambridge University Press, 1991), ch. 4; M. Rubin, *Charity and Community in Medieval Cambridge* (Cambridge: Cambridge University Press, 1987), pp. 250–9; V. Bainbridge, *Gilds in the Medieval Countryside: Religion and Social Change in Cambridgeshire, 1350–1558* (Woodbridge: Boydell and Brewer, 1996); on Italy see J. Henderson, *Piety and Charity in Late Medieval Florence* (Oxford: Oxford University Press, 1994).

25. *The Friend*, pp. 261–7.

26. See for example B. Rizzo, *Companions Without Vows: Relationships among Eighteenth-Century British Women* (Athens: University of Georgia Press, 1994);

S. Mendelson and P. Crawford, *Women in Early Modern England* (Oxford: Oxford University Press, 1998), ch. 4.

27. P. Cullum, '"And hir name was Charite": Charitable Giving by and for Women in Late Medieval Yorkshire', in P.J.P. Goldberg (ed.), *Woman is a Worthy Wight: Women in English Society c.1200–1500* (Stroud: Alan Sutton, 1992), pp. 182–211; K.J. Lewis, 'Women, Testamentary Discourse and Life-Writing in Later Medieval England', in N. Menuge (ed.), *Medieval Women and the Law* (Woodbridge: Boydell and Brewer, 2000), pp. 57–75.

28. See, for example, the Visitation, c.1310 by Meister Heinrich of Constance, at the Metropolitan Museum, New York. Some of these ideas were communicated in a paper delivered by Miri Rubin to the Women's History Seminar at the Institute of Historical Research , University of London, on 12 November 2004.

29. The artist Bill Viola created the video installation 'The Visitation': see the catalogue *Bill Viola: The Passions*, ed. J. Walsh (Los Angeles: J. Paul Getty Museum, 2003).

1
Friendship's Loss: Alan Bray's Making of History

Valerie Traub

In the headnote that precedes his essay, 'The Body of the Friend', Alan Bray describes the painful occasion that gave impetus to his work:

> In 1987 I heard Michel Rey, a student of J.-L. Flandrin in the University of Paris, give a lecture entitled 'The Body of My Friend'. The lecture was only an outline, and his early death left his doctoral thesis uncompleted and his loss keenly felt by many. But in the years that followed that lecture Michel and I often discussed the history of friendship, and I have sought in this paper to complete that paper as he might have done had he lived, as a tribute to his memory. It is a paper about the body of the friend at the onset of the modern world and its loss.[1]

In a position not unlike that of Bray, I – along with you – now confront the loss of a scholar who has done more, perhaps, than any other to return the body of the friend, and with it the complex meanings of intimacy, to historical consciousness. Although it did not fall to me to complete the monumental piece of scholarship that is *The Friend*, the manuscript Alan was finishing at the time of his death, it does fall to me to try to do justice to a scholarly legacy that has had a singular, indispensable, and galvanizing effect on the history of sexuality, and that will, in its now complete form, transform the histories of friendship and the family.[2]

Bray's first book, *Homosexuality in Renaissance England*, forcefully exposed a cultural contradiction: whereas sodomy was associated apocalyptically with debauchery, heresy, foreignness, and sedition, and thus the dissolution of the social order, intimate male friendship enabled all manner of legitimate social ties and mutually beneficial obligations, advancing homosocial relations within the patriarchal social order.[3] There was nonetheless an affinity and a symmetry between representations of universally admired masculine friendship and officially condemned sodomy – as Bray later put it, 'They occupied a similar terrain.'[4] The result of this 'unacknowledged connection between the unmentionable vice of Sodom and the friendship which all accounted commendable' was widespread cognitive dissonance, a reluctance to recognize in idealized friendship the dreaded signs of sodomy.[5] The disparity between the rhetoric of unspeakability which governed public discourses and those social and erotic practices in which many men engaged indicated to Bray a 'quiet, nominal adjustment', perhaps unique to Renaissance England.[6] This accommodation began to show signs of strain by the end of the sixteenth century, when changes in social relations and modes of symbolizing them caused the overlap in legitimate and illegitimate forms of male intimacy to become an identifiable social problem. With the rise of economic individualism and social pluralism – represented most visibly in the advent of London molly houses – male homoeroticism was dissociated from the broad nexus of homosociality. Newly legible as a secular social ill, it increasingly was prosecuted, as raids on molly houses arranged by the Society for the Reformation of Manners from 1699 to 1738 attest.

In advancing this thesis, Bray's book demonstrated that homosexuality is not a stable, unchanging fact of sexual life, but a dynamic field of signification that possesses a history of its own, a history closely tied to other social phenomena: the structure of the household, the growth of cities, the emergence of individualism. To make these connections was to extricate the historiography of homosexuality from its preoccupation with the identification of gay individuals and to refocus it on the analysis of social structures and processes that regulate the intelligibility of same-gender attachments. Thus, despite the proliferation of scholarship on male homoeroticism since the publication of Bray's book in 1982, what Jonathan Goldberg said in his 1994 Introduction to *Queering the Renaissance* is still true today: '*Homosexuality in Renaissance England* remains the groundbreaking and unsurpassed historical investigation for the period.'[7]

As if to make explicit the larger historical narrative of which *Homosexuality in Renaissance England* is a part, *The Friend*, offered as volume two to Bray's history of male bonds, broadens out temporally in both directions. Tracing protocols of masculine friendship from the eleventh to the nineteenth century, Bray constructs an immensely learned archaeology of the 'formal and objective' expressions of intimacy and obligation that are part of a forgotten history of the family, religion, and traditional society.[8] Rather than function as the only basis of social cohesion, the early modern family subsisted within larger structures of relation, including those of Christian ritual, service, and 'voluntary kinship' – the kinship created by ritual or promise, as in the bonds forged by adoption or sworn brotherhood.[9] Insofar as the role of Christianity in traditional society was, according to Bray, to help members of the community to live in peace, its rites recognized several forms of binding connection, including marriage, kinship, and friendship.[10] Focused on the public witnessing of such unions in baptism, the eucharist, the kiss of peace, and burial, as well as the sharing of beds and familiar correspondence, *The Friend* demonstrates friendship's equivocal role not only in giving a social shape to masculine bonds but in threatening them. Friendship, Bray insists, was not an unreserved good; it could be compromised by expectations of material interest, influence, and advancement. Given the precariousness of relations in the public sphere, he argues, even the best of friendships could be shadowed by suspicions of collusion, misuse, and enmity, imparting an ethical uncertainty to friendship even when it was most clearly a matter of love. In a characteristic hermeneutic move, Bray discovers traces of the equivocal nature of friendship not only in the rites of traditional Christianity but in the idealized rhetoric of love and fidelity through which friendship was inscribed in letters, poetry, and burial monuments. Such idealized constructions, which we might assume to be empty conventions, were, in part because of their conventionality, replete with affect; in particular, they negotiated the fear that one's friend might prove to be one's enemy. By excavating the remains of friendship in public sites and rituals heretofore obscured by a historical enterprise intent on recognizing only the kinship created by marriage, by locating the family within an encompassing network of friendship that kinship also created, and by interpreting friendship from the standpoint of the Christian ethics it embodies, Bray's compelling narrative returns to the praxis of friendship a social and historical efficacy that largely has been forgotten. *Why* it was forgotten as the Enlightenment ushered in civil society will be of considerable interest to those who seek to understand how the past paved the way for our present.

The influence of Bray's first book and published essays can be seen in all subsequent treatments of male homoeroticism from 1550 to 1800 in England, in no small part because of his activist commitment to 'play[ing] a part in changing' 'the world around us as history has given us it'.[11] Yet it implies a serious underestimate of the value of *Homosexuality in Renaissance England* that the book most often is cited only for its exposure of cognitive dissonance and its narrative regarding the emergence of a homosexual identity. Because of the stranglehold that questions of identity and the dating of its consolidation have had on the history of homosexuality, and because the critical accent has been on the content of Bray's historical scheme rather than the method by which he composed it, the considerable conceptual advances he made in charting an epistemic shift in the intelligibility of male bonds have not been fully assessed.[12] By highlighting some of his additional contributions to historiographic method, I hope to draw attention to the opportunities and challenges they offer for future engagement and critical dialogue.

It is one of the paradoxes of Bray's scholarly career that the history of sexuality is not the discipline in which he would have located his work. Repeatedly he insists that to begin with the question of sexuality is to misconstrue the issue.[13] The point, articulated throughout his corpus, is to view sexuality in a wider social and interpretive frame, whereas 'the effect of a shaping concern with sexuality is precisely to obscure that wider frame'.[14] This is true because 'What is missing [in Renaissance discourses] is any social expression of homosexuality based on the fact of homosexuality itself.... What we look for in vain are any features peculiar to it alone.'[15] Bray's determined ambivalence regarding the disciplinary field of sexuality studies is, I want to suggest, simultaneously a product of his historical inquiry and the ground out of which his historiography emerged. His insistence that sexuality – by which I mean not only the identity categories of homo and hetero, but the very idea of an autonomous field of erotic relations – was a post-seventeenth-century phenomenon motivates what I believe is his most decisive contribution: the location of male intimacy in a range of early modern social systems. Having described in his first book the forms of social life in which homosexuality was embedded – the village, the household, the educational system, apprenticeship, prostitution, the theatre – in subsequent work he situates male bonds within the symbolic gift systems of patronage, preferment, and service associated with the medieval great house. What he calls 'the gift of the friend's body' – signified by public kisses and embraces, eating at the common table, the sharing of beds, the familiar letter – functioned up through the sixteenth century as a crucial form of 'countenance'.[16] Such public signs of favour and intimacy, Bray argues, were not only normative but instrumentally oiled the wheels of social relations. With the demise of the open-handed household – a change both architectural and social – the public conveyance of countenance through the friend's body ceased to be advantageous; lacking its prior symbolic capital, it became unintelligible.[17] As England was transformed into a modern, civil society, friendship was recast as a non-instrumental affinity: 'rational, objective, universal', and for the most part irrelevant to Christian ethics and public affairs.[18] Situating this change within a new regime of visibility – the disappearance of lower servants from view, of gentlemen from service, of crowds drinking in the great hall – Bray offers a causal explanation for the growth of suspicion regarding behaviours previously deemed unexceptional, as well as for the persecution of mollies. Just as the 'sodomite' took on a 'new actuality', so too a 'radically new meaning to the desire for the body of the friend' took shape.[19] As Bray memorably describes this shift, the public kiss and embrace were replaced by the handshake.[20]

Michel Foucault's corpus is often credited, rightly, with articulating the theoretical import of reading for silences, absences, and exclusions. Bray's corpus, it seems to me, demonstrates the payoff of this approach. Characteristic of Bray's rhetorical stance is the adoption of the persona of the sleuth, embarked on a slow process of detection: painstakingly following a 'forensic trail' of clues, sharing his mind as it works through assumptions and doubts, examining evidence from multiple angles, entertaining objections, and devising alternative methods in light of them.[21] The discovery of clues, of course, often is an effect of what is not said, and Bray's favoured trope for this function in his own work – as well as that of others – was 'the detective story where the clue was that the dog did *not* bark'.[22] With steady tough-mindedness, he draws significance out of what is, and what is not, available in the archive. In so doing, the archive is reconfigured: it is not a storehouse or treasure chest waiting to be opened but a palimpsest of fragments, on the ragged edges of which hang unexpected meanings. Bray's articulation of the difference between Elizabethan and later discourses of male intimacy, for instance, hinges on 'what is left out' in idealized expressions of friendship: the 'tactful omission of those bonds of mutual interest of which the everyday signs were such conventions'.[23] When suspicion *is* generated by accounts of friendship, as it increasingly was, it is because 'some of the conventions of friendship are missing ... and the missing ones are precisely those that ensured that the intimacy of these conventions was read in an acceptable frame of reference'.[24] What could convert signs of male friendship into signs of sodomy, it turns out, was partly the mixing of status or degree – and it was only by looking for 'the silence between the lines' that Bray hit upon the significance of social inequality to the sodomy–friendship interrelation.[25] For a social historian generally committed to traditional protocols of evidence, this emphasis on silence and insignificance, on traces and fragments and the difficulties of intelligibility they pose, was a strikingly unconventional move.[26]

That erotic behaviour might not signify in or by itself implicitly links the problem of representation to the issue of social embeddedness. The combined effect of this connection is to emphasize the uncertainty of sexuality's power of signification. In her recent book, *Sovereign Amity*, Laurie Shannon cogently rearticulates and extends Bray's argument, maintaining that there is nothing fully dispositive about eroticism to convey particular meanings; erotic acts operate only unreliably as a trigger for articulation.[27] Correlating the gift of the friend's body to the changing fate of homosexuality, for instance, Bray argues that the proximity of exalted and excoriated male bonds means that erotic affects and acts *could* be an element of both – it depends on how you look at it. How you look at it is itself influenced by historical factors, including what counts as sex in a given culture. What counts, of course, can be highly contingent, variable, and incoherent, even within a single culture and historical moment – as was brought home to everyone in the United States when President Bill Clinton avowed that whatever he did with Monica Lewinsky, it was not sex.[28]

One effect of showing that sodomy and friendship could be recognized at one moment as utterly distinct and at another moment as close to the same thing was to deconstruct, from a historically specific angle, the boundary between them. The complex elaboration of male intimacy throughout early modern society, coupled with the potential for erotic acts *not* to signify, creates the interpretative field into which *all* erotic behaviours fall: 'Mediated as homosexuality then was by social relationships that did not take their form from homosexuality and were not exclusive to it, the barrier between heterosexual and homosexual behaviour...was in practice vague and imprecise.'[29] One might expect, then, that changes in the social articulation of male bonds might affect the meanings of male intimacy with women – and indeed they did. Just as the sodomite became identifiable as a perversion of normative cross-sex alliance, so these alliances increasingly relied on the sodomite to secure their own status as natural and inevitable. Arguing that the transformation in male intimacy 'placed a burden of social meaning on the heterosexual bond between husband and wife that before it had not been required to carry alone', and that, with the ascendance of civil society, the gift of the body came to be acknowledged 'only as a sexual gift between men and women',[30] Bray brings to the theoretical dictum of the dependence of the hetero on the homo a historical specificity it otherwise often lacks.[31]

Yet, it is important to acknowledge that, despite this deconstructive impulse, Bray never adopted the inversive desideratum of queer theory: that the burden of proof belongs to those who assume the presence of *hetero*sexuality. Committed as he was to the historian's protocols of evidence, and taking seriously sexuality's lack of dispositive power, he was extremely cautious about assigning erotic signification to particular gestures, behaviours, texts, people. He especially discounted the truth value of Renaissance accusations of sodomy, whose evidentiary basis he rightly judged unreliable: 'We will misunderstand these accusations if, beguiled by them, we uncritically assume the existence of the sexual relationship which they appear to point to, for the material from which they could be constructed was rather open and public to all.... Homosexual relationships did indeed occur within social contexts which an Elizabethan would have called friendship.... But accusations [of sodomy] are not evidence of it.'[32]

It is here, perhaps, that we can catch a glimpse of an unacknowledged tension in Bray's corpus: on the one hand, the open and public nature of friendship protected early modern men from suspicion of sodomy; on the other, it also somehow provides an indication in the present that they were not involved in a 'sexual relationship'. In his first book, after noting the difficulties involved in using modern conceptual categories, Bray adopted the solution of using 'the term homosexuality but in as directly physical – and hence culturally neutral – a sense as possible'.[33] How 'culturally neutral' derives from 'directly physical' has long puzzled me, especially since the meaning of 'physical' seems here, by default, to imply anal intercourse – perhaps the least culturally neutral, most overdetermined erotic activity during the Renaissance and today. Throughout the first book, then, homosexuality, implicitly conflated with a single erotic practice, is also functionally equated with sodomy. One result of this series of conflations is that the baseline meaning of homosexuality, its status as an analytical object, is fore-known and foreclosed – even as the locations in which it is expressed and the significations it accrues change over time.[34] Another result is that friendship – for all its structural affinity with and proximity to homosexuality – is definitionally posited as something *other* than homosexuality: not, as it were, 'directly physical'.[35]

This is in fact Mario DiGangi's critique of the way that Bray manages the tension between sodomy, homosexuality, and friendship: 'Bray effectively conflates "homosexuality" with "sodomy", implicitly reduces both to the commission of sexual acts, and then cordons off these proscribed sexual acts from the nonsexual intimacy appropriate for "friends" '.[36] In contrast, Jonathan Goldberg confidently affirms that the combined theses of *Homosexuality in Renaissance England* and the influential essay 'Homosexuality and the Signs of Male Friendship in Elizabethan England' imply that 'much in the ordinary transactions between men in the period . . . took place sexually'.[37] The possibility of two such opposed interpretations of Bray's core argument is symptomatic not of misreading or misappropriation but of a pervasive ambiguity animating his work. The analytic tension between eroticism and friendship became clearer to me while reading the manuscript of *The Friend*, where the embedding of intimacy in a vast range of social relations and the foregrounding of ethical considerations had the subtle but persistent effect of minimizing the possibility that the bonds being described were at all sexual. Throughout Bray's work, there is a recurring expression of concern that the reader might be 'misled' by the appearance of erotic meanings, leading him or her to 'misconstrue' the forces at work in the construction of male intimacy.[38] *The Friend*'s brief for the ethical import of friendship is particularly punctuated by such cautions against misconstruction. Indeed, the ambiguities and tensions present in Bray's earlier work are heightened in his final book.

On the one hand, the intense emotional affects Bray excavates in *The Friend* – affects that give rituals and conventions their experiential salience and contribute to their social efficacy – would seem to belie any strict dichotomy between friendship and eroticism.[39] Early on Bray notes that the ethical praxis he aims to uncover need not have excluded the erotic: 'The ethics of friendship in the world I describe began with the concrete and the actual, and the only way to exclude anything would be by abandoning that starting point. That hard-edged world included the potential for the erotic, as it included much else.'[40] Throughout the book, he acknowledges the erotic *potential* of the physical closeness that, at any given moment, might signify one way or the other: bonds that, because of their association with social excess and disorder, signified sodomy; bonds that, due to their coherence with legitimate forms of social organization, signified friendship, kinship, obligation, love. On the other hand, sometimes Bray dismisses the historian's access to 'the possible motives and nature of [a] physical relationship' by reducing such interpretation to 'no more than specula-tions' – as in his discussion of Amy Poulter's marriage to Arabella Hunt.[41] Sometimes the potential eroticism of friends is specifically, even categorically, denied – most emphatically, perhaps, in the exposition of

John Henry Cardinal Newman's shared grave with Ambrose St John, which forms the coda of Bray's book: 'Their bond was spiritual. . . . Their love was not the less intense for being spiritual. Perhaps, it was more so.'[42] Whereas Bray in his final chapter pointedly asks (in response to the sexual escapades recorded in the diary of Anne Lister), 'Would a sexual *potential* have stood in the way of the confirmation of a sworn friendship in the Eucharist? The answer must be that it would not, in that it evidently did not do so here',[43] at the telos of his argument he resurrects, seemingly without hesitation, a stark division between spiritual and carnal love.[44] This division is apparent as well in Bray's objections to John Boswell's scholarship on same-sex unions; one of Boswell's mistakes was his inability to grasp 'that the expected ideals of the rite would not have comprehended sexual intercourse'.[45] Here, however, the circumspection of the qualifier 'expected' perhaps carries Bray's central point: that is, the ease with which a distinction between love and sodomy was maintained in the official discourse of traditional society, whatever the actual nature of the relation.[46] The analytic ambiguity at the heart of *The Friend*'s emphasis on erotic *potential* thus pulls in two contradictory directions. At times this ambiguity expands the meaning of homoerotic affect, rendering it as something more than 'just sex', a point about which Bray was explicit: 'The inability to conceive of relationships in other than sexual terms says something of contemporary poverty.'[47] But when this ambiguity slides into a categorical denial of eroticism, it risks conceding the defining terms of the argument to those who would protect the study of intimacy from eroticism's embodied materiality.

The risk of dematerializing eroticism was articulated a decade ago when Goldberg warned that sexuality 'can always be explained in other terms, and in ways in which anything like sex disappears'.[48] This caution has been addressed anew by Cynthia Herrup in a short polemical essay, 'Finding the Bodies'.[49] It is worth noting that, despite the symbolic centrality of the gift of the friend's body in Bray's book, bodies themselves play a very small part in his discussion. One is tempted to say that the materiality of the body is displaced onto the memorials – the gravestones and churches – that populate his account.[50] Nonetheless, I wonder what Bray would have made of the triumphant proclamation on the inside dust jacket cover of *The Friend*: 'He debunks the now-familiar readings of friendship by historians of sexuality who project homoerotic desires onto their subjects when there were none.'[51] Certainly, Bray warned repeatedly against anachronism and misconstrual: he considered them bad history. But his own negotiation of this problem was considerably more nuanced than an effort to 'debunk' the assertions of others; nor does the preemptive rejection of the mutual engagement between past and present implied in the term 'projection' accurately convey his own historical method.[52] 'Readers of this book can and will appropriate the past for themselves, if I stick to my job of presenting the past first in its own terms', he declares in the introduction to *The Friend*, and he follows up that remark with a pointed reference to the politics of the present: 'Could it be that that very appropriation might prelude a resolution of the conflict between homosexual people and the Christian church today?'[53] Insofar as Bray stressed repeatedly that his scholarship grew out of an activist engagement with contemporary gay life, I suspect that any denigration of contemporary gay identification with a homoerotic past may have given him pause.[54]

It is not just that levelling a charge of projection in this way is inaccurate and offensive; more important, it circumvents, and thereby obscures, questions tacitly raised by Bray's scholarship but not resolved in it, namely the relations between emotional and bodily intimacy, and what we make of them. Indeed, it is one of the legacies of his work that, although the tension between friendship and eroticism informs it at almost every turn, nowhere is the unstable line separating these forms of intimacy brought into sharp focus and treated as an object of analysis. Bray casts his eye first on the conventions of friendship and then on those of sodomy, but in analyzing their connection, he seems to take his cue from early moderns themselves, who were unwilling 'to take seriously the ambiguous borderland between the "sodomite" and the shared beds and bonding of its male companionship'.[55] For a historian to 'take seriously' this 'ambiguous borderland' would mean to submit to analytic scrutiny the movement across borders, the places where and the moments when (and not simply the processes by which) one thing becomes another. Bray's apparent preference was much like that of the early modern society he describes, which 'knew that the gaps – and the overlaps – between one thing and its other had their utility'.[56] Rather in the manner of the 'accommodating ambiguity' he identifies elsewhere,[57] Bray does not parse his terms too precisely, as evinced by the sleight-of-hand in his remark that 'the word "love" in this society could comprehend as easily the public relation of friends as the more private meaning we give the word today, but wherever on that wide spectrum the gift of a friend's body might lie, it gestured toward a place of comforting safety in an insecure world'.[58] Indeed, if one substitutes the term 'eroticism' for 'friendship' in Bray's statement that 'the indirection of the language of friendship provided a circumspect path around it',[59] one comes close to describing the rhetorical strategy he deployed in regard to the confused relations among the sexual, the physical, the subjective, and the affective.

Examining the ambiguous borderland, the overlap, between one thing and another might particularly have paid off in relation to one of Bray's key terms: voluntary kinship. It is striking that Bray ignores the applicability of voluntary kinship to the social structure of the molly house. Because of the tight link between sodomy and social disorder – a link that for Bray goes to the heart of what sodomy is – he fails to consider whether the vows of mollies, some of which follow the traditional script of marriage, might not also operate as an alternative form of kinship. The analytic division between friendship and sodomy, social disorder and social cohesion enables him to recognize bonds of kinship only within the received structure of traditional society: in the form of male couples whose formal vows are backed by Christian ritual.

It may well be wrong to characterize Bray's circumspection in this regard as reticence or reluctance to confront the radical implications of his own work. As a historian, he appears to have approached the relation between friendship and eroticism primarily from the standpoint of evidence. In his final chapter, for instance, he asks of the body of the friend:

> But did it not also have the body's genitals? Did its symbolic significance stop short there? The laughter that closed an earlier chapter suggested that it did not. Yet the sexual potential in these gestures has repeatedly come into view only to slip away again.... This is not, of course, to say that the erotic has not been part of this history. But sexuality in a more narrow sense has eluded it whenever it has come into view. With the diary of Anne Lister that problem falls away.[60]

Yet even as the evaluation of evidence must be the historian's preoccupation, important questions remain untouched by it from the standpoint of theoretical investigation. Whether Bray's disinclination to probe, rather than work adroitly around, the precise means of the overlap of friendship and eroticism *as a theoretical problem* indicates the historian's discomfort with the deconstructive ramifications of his own radical history, or whether, conversely and paradoxically, it is a further measure of his own deconstructive commitments, is a question about which I remain unsure. Bray delights, for instance, in the enigma of Shakespeare's sonnet 20, which he calls a 'dazzling tour de force' that 'can be read *both* as asserting the chastity of friendship in the most transcendent of terms *and* as rejecting it in the most bawdy and explicit of terms'.[61] In puzzling through this problem, I am reminded that a decade ago Goldberg recognized that Bray's work raises 'formidable questions' of 'ontology and epistemology': 'what sodomy is and how it may be recognized'.[62] In its performance of what appears to be a strategic ambiguity carried out in the name of ethics, Bray's new book invites, if only to defer, questions just as formidable about the ontology and epistemology of friendship, eroticism, and sexuality.

In this regard, it is useful to unpack Bray's concluding comments in a review of books on homosexuality, in which he notes, with what appears to be mixed appreciation and apprehension, that the books

> have succeeded in undermining their very starting point in the questions they have steadily been drawn into asking. What then is the nature of sexual identity, or of any personal identity? What is the difference between the sexual and the nonsexual?...The history of sexuality will not provide answers to these questions, if indeed there are any, but it has disturbingly raised them; and it is there that its importance lies.[63]

It is telling that Bray's scepticism regarding the history of sexuality as a field of knowledge production is articulated in the same breath as his apparent doubt regarding the field's ability to resolve ontological questions about the identity of, and relations between, sexuality and friendship. Both, I believe, are worthy cautions. Nonetheless, as the charge of 'projection' of homoerotic desires that has been levelled in Bray's name vividly suggests, a countervailing epistemological and political danger is that *not* to pursue such ontological questions – what is sexuality? what is friendship? what is the nature of the difference between them? – risks ceding authority for answering them to those who would assert their own tendentious criteria for how sexuality is to be known. Rather than '[debunk] the now-familiar readings of friendship by historians of sexuality', Bray's historical scholarship intersects with the theoretical work of Eve Kosofsky Sedgwick in inviting several queries: How do we *know* when there were no homoerotic desires between historical figures? What is the basis of our knowledge of the eroticism of the past? How *do* we know what (we think) we know?[64]

In response to these questions, the logic of Bray's corpus suggests several propositions: First, if eroticism is always embedded in other forms of social relation, if acts of bodily intimacy are rendered intelligible only from within a precise social location, if the power of eroticism to signify is variable and uncertain, if we cannot always be confident that we have interpreted its presence or absence correctly, then eroticism, like sodomy and friendship, is apprehensible only as a relational structure – not only between people, but between people and history.

Not only will our desires for a usable past necessarily inform the history of sexuality we create, but the epistemological opacity of sexuality will be constitutive of the methods by which we investigate it. This recognition leads me, as it did not, apparently, lead Bray, to a second proposition. If we do not know the extent to which relations may have been erotic, it is as mistaken to assume that they were not as it is to assume that they were. In her afterword to *Queering the Renaissance*, Margaret Hunt urged scholars to 'scramble the definitions and blur the boundaries of the erotic, both so as to forestall the repressive uses to which rigid understandings of it almost inevitably lend themselves, and to gain access to a much larger analytical arena'.[65] In *The Renaissance of Lesbianism in Early Modern England*, I took that invitation as far as seemed historically responsible by adopting, as a heuristic axiom, a studied skepticism about any *a priori* dividing line between female friendship and female homoeroticism.[66] It may be that the difference gender makes in this regard is particularly salient: not only did cultural images of tribades have little of the apocalyptic force conveyed by images of sodomites, but the practices of female friendship may have been more congruent with the expression of female eroticism than masculine friendship was with sodomy.[67] What counts as erotic, in other words, may involve gender differentials of which we are only now becoming sufficiently aware.

Insofar as the precise criteria one might use to sequester friendship from sexuality are nowhere theorized in Bray's work, we might approach the question of their relation as a productive faultline upon which his corpus is built – the 'blindness' that enabled his considerable insight. If, as I have argued, Bray negotiated this faultline by deploying a strategic ambiguity – by seeming at one point to concede or advance an erotic interpretation while at other points explicitly denying that possibility – it may be because of some criteria of evidence known only to him. The fact remains that nowhere does he submit to *systematic* comparison any evidence of erotic affect in order to better delineate the homosocial from the homoerotic. Rather than preclude further investigation, the identification of this problem – and the hijacking of Bray's work to privilege asexual friendship over sexuality – should spur us on.

Indeed, just how far the rhetoric and practice of masculine friendship comprehended the expression of erotic desire and the performance of erotic acts and whether it is possible to construct a legitimate definition of such criteria remain two questions unanswered by Bray's corpus – questions, in other words, for the rest of us.[68]

Additional questions embedded in Bray's work likewise deserve consideration. In the afterword to the 1995 edition of *Homosexuality in Renaissance England*, for instance, Bray boldly asserts that 'attitudes to homosexuality unquestionably have been symptomatic of fundamental changes in European society and in substantial part *constitutive* of them'.[69] Sexual representation is not merely mimetic; it has an efficacy, an agency, of its own. Such an assertion urges a greater appreciation of sexuality's ideological utility – not only its pliability and susceptibility to pressure, but its ability to exert pressure on practices, discourses, and institutions external to it. But from where, one might ask, does this agency derive? Of one thing we can be sure: it is not a function of desire. Strikingly absent from Bray's work is any concept of desire as an internal, generative mechanism or drive. Such a concept is, to his mind, alien to the psychic, emotional, and ideological landscape of early modern culture. In his discussion of the sexual dreams and fantasies expressed in the diary of Michael Wigglesworth, for instance, Bray argues that the sexual impulses over which Wigglesworth agonized (the 'filthy lust . . . flowing from my fond affection to my pupils') were experienced by this colonial subject as unbidden, separate from his will, not a matter of his own *desire* at all.[70] As Bray notes in *The Friend*, the 'desire for the gift of the friend's body . . . does not correspond easily to anything in our culture several centuries on'.[71] Even as Bray may contribute to what David M. Halperin has called 'the possibility of a new queer history of affect', his contribution is not to explain what intimacy tells us about the desires of an individual subject (or, for that matter, to historicize emotion), but to describe the instrumentality of intimacy in creating (or threatening) social cohesion.[72] Sworn brotherhood, for example, is a response to the ethical uncertainty of friendship, and its meaning exists primarily in the wider social responsibility assumed by friends when they formalize their vows. So too, the desire for the friend's body functions, much like the homosocial desire anatomized by Sedgwick, as the glue that holds early modern society together.

Yet, the question remains: What does it mean to assert for representations of sexuality an agency that does not depend on a subject of desire? The answer to this question is everywhere implied by the dense historical interconnections Bray excavates among religion, ethics, the family, and friendship, but the most trenchant indication of it is recorded in a memorial headnote to an essay he published in an anthology that appeared after his death. According to Katherine O'Donnell and Michael O'Rourke, when Bray was asked 'How would [your current work] change the exploratory maps constructed twenty years ago?' he said this: 'it would be a shift from studies of sexuality into ethics and from the politics of identity into the politics of friendship'.[73] There is much for historians of sexuality to ponder in that proposed shift, including the presence or absence of the body and erotic desire in ethics and friendship and the risks involved in leaving their material histories behind.

A further consideration is the relation of Bray's work to the category of gender. On the face of it, Bray's corpus seems to offer little to the history of female friendship or female sexuality. Although I tend to think otherwise, certain problems with his approach to gender deserve acknowledgement. Bray duly noted the restricted scope of *Homosexuality in Renaissance England*: 'Female homosexuality was rarely linked in popular thought with male homosexuality, if indeed it was recognized at all. Its history is, I believe, best to be understood as part of the developing recognition of a specifically female sexuality.'[74] This may have been true when this book was written; whether it remains true today is a question to which I will return. To his credit, Bray recognized then that the dissonance between friendship and sodomy was in part a function of gender: 'So long as homosexual activity did not disturb the peace or the social order, and in particular so long as it was *consistent with patriarchal mores*, it was largely in practice ignored.'[75] Yet, because of the asymmetrical application of the legal and theological category of sodomy to early modern English men and women, Bray's first book does not afford ready analytical purchase to scholars working on women. Perhaps predictably, major studies of female homoeroticism have limited their engagement with his thesis primarily to the perception of parallels between a growing stigma regarding female intimacies and the increasing legibility of sodomy.[76]

Bray's published essays on friendship likewise retain a focus on men, in part because the formal displays of intimacy that characterized male patronage in the sixteenth and seventeenth centuries were, he argues, less relevant to women, who on the whole were denied access to the public sphere. As Bray remarks in 'The Body of the Friend', it was precisely because of the male body's privileged ability to confer cultural capital that the gift of the friend's body was definitively male. In addition, much of Bray's analysis of the symbolic gift exchanges among men hinges on the fact that 'the daily cycle of working, eating and drinking, the bodily functions, and sleeping was carried on outside the marital home'. 'Service in the great houses was men's work', Bray contends, and although women served as washerwomen, herdswomen, and traders, they did so from outside the great house walls.[77] Where, one might ask, did these women live? Given the importance of the patriarchal household, it seems unlikely that they resided in all-female collectives. Does the mere fact that they were not mentioned in household records provide sufficient support for Bray's claim?[78]

A portion of *The Friend*'s long final chapter concerns female relations, mainly by means of the figure of Anne Lister. Prior to this chapter the book treats female friendship as 'the silence between the lines' of male friendship, referring briefly and sporadically to a few female burial monuments.[79] Lister's voluble diary breaks this silence, both because of its erotic explicitness and because Lister was intent on enacting with two of her lovers the kind of formal, public, and binding union that sworn brothers had vowed for centuries. She thus provides Bray with a 'vantage point' for reconsidering the congruity between a relationship that was 'unquestionably sexual' and 'the confirmation of a sworn friendship in the Eucharist', as well as a frame for thinking about the extent to which 'that traditional world of kinship and friendship at the heart of religion's role' survived in the byways of the nineteenth century.[80] Nonetheless, the criteria Bray uses to admit women's entrance into the historical picture imply that there is little evidence with which to track the path of female friendship prior to Lister's relatively late incarnation. Bray admits that the friendship between Ann Chitting and Mary Barber 'had a sufficiently formal and objective character for them to be buried together' in the early seventeenth century, but this does not impact his general view that women's role in the history of friendship is the 'silence between the lines'.[81] One is left to wonder whether Lady Anne Clifford's apology, in a letter to her mother, for her inability to travel 'to Oxford, according to your Ladyship's desire with my Lady Arbella [Stuart], and to have slept in her chamber, which she much desired, for I am the more bound to her than can be', demonstrates something of the public conveyance of countenance that Bray charts in familiar letters between men.[82] In other words, there is the question of how Bray actually reads the lives of the women whom he includes, and what these readings do to broaden the terms of feminist and lesbian histories. Finally, one is left to wonder about the historiographic irony that a woman should have been the means to reinsert sex back into the historical narrative. Early in the historiography of homosexuality, the boys had sodomy and the girls had romantic friendship; in *The Friend*, as in other recent work, the history of male homosexuality is all about male love.

If we shift our focus from what Bray says about women to what his work makes available to those of us working on women, however, a more enabling set of procedures emerges. Adoption of Bray's insights about the unstable nature of erotic signification and consideration of the ontological and epistemological issues raised by his work, for instance, would greatly nuance scholarship in this field, which has tended to presuppose a certain knowingness about what constitutes sexuality. Indeed, insofar as a central question in the history of female homoeroticism has been how to talk about 'lesbianism' before the advent of modern identity categories, we would do well to consider how this question of anachronistic terminology can morph into an ontological question – what *is* lesbianism in any given era? – as well as how these queries might be supplemented with an epistemological question: how do we know it?

Although nothing in Bray's corpus provides clear answers to these questions, in its performance of ambiguity, tension, and irresolution his work urges us to ask them. In the expanse of its historical sweep, *The Friend*, in particular, gestures in a direction that might draw us closer to an answer. Perhaps not since Lillian Faderman's *Surpassing the Love of Men: Romantic Friendship and Love between Women from the Renaissance to the Present* has a responsible scholar of gay/lesbian history approached large-scale historical change and continuity with such confidence and ambition. In part because the postmodern suspicion toward the explanatory power of metanarratives has taken firm hold in those subfields where the history of homosexuality is most often written (social history, women's history, literary studies),[83] the creation of densely local and socially contextualized knowledges has been constitutive of the field. As a result, the history of homosexuality has been constructed in and by means of research segmented along traditional period lines. Even as queer theory has pressured many of the methodological premises of historians, the power of periodization has not been shaken – as such titles as *Queering the Renaissance*, *Queering the Middle Ages*, and *Queering the Moderns* attest.[84] Although it has become a tenet of queer theory to disrupt the 'straight' logic of sequential temporality, to expose periodization as a fetish, and to keep one eye on our contemporary situation, the ensuing conversation between past and present generally has been accomplished by relying on a period-bound concept of the past: one historical moment, situated in proximity to modernity (or postmodernity). To queer the Middle Ages, for instance, is also to historicize the modern – with the injunction to 'get medieval' pursued by considering how medieval concepts inhabit, resonate, or are at odds with contemporary categories and crises: the military policy of don't ask, don't tell; the sexual politics of the Clinton impeachment; the discourse of HIV/AIDS.[85]

Bray's widening of the temporal lens in *The Friend* allows us to consider anew how the retrospective fiction of periodization has functioned as an epistemic force field, permitting certain questions to advance while occluding others.[86] In particular, the common sense of periodization has kept our attention off those problematic areas where period boundaries meet: the ragged edges, margins, and interstices of periodization that frame our narratives. It is here that historical claims, especially about the advent of change, rub up against one another – often leading to charges of scholarly ignorance or worse. As understandable as is the desire to expose other scholars' epistemic privileging of their own turf, a strategy of border surveillance does not help us learn to speak across period divides.

To the extent that the suitability of assuming a longer vantage has been raised within the history of homosexuality, it has been approached primarily via the debate between acts and identities or, in its more historiographical formulation, between the assertion of alterity or continuism. In the context of this debate, responsible reconsideration of taking the long view has gone, precisely, nowhere. Yet, as archival materials come to light that support more nuanced conceptions of identity, orientation, and predisposition than early social constructivist accounts would have allowed, these debates have begun to diminish in importance.[87] Recent attempts to move beyond the impasse produced by these debates have demonstrated that it is the precise nature and interrelations of continuities and discontinuities that are of interest, not the analytical predominance of one over the other.[88]

Bray's final book is perhaps the most subtle mediation between the claims of historical continuity and historical difference in this field to date. In addition, by insisting that friendship can be understood only in terms of the wider context that gives it meaning, it confutes a basic, if undertheorized, premise of the historiography of homosexuality: that we must conceptualize our object of analysis by provisionally isolating its parameters and claiming for it, however tacitly, a relatively independent social status. That is, whether one historicizes the sodomite or the molly, tribadism, sapphism, or queer virginity, in order to gain a foothold for these phenomena in a landscape unmarked by modern identity categories, scholars have tended to approach the phenomena as discrete, internally unified, and relatively bounded. Despite our adoption of Bray's argument that homoeroticism is part of a networked system of social relations, we have failed to recognize the full ramifications of that insight and so have treated homoeroticism much like the historical periods in which we locate it.

Could it be that this bounded conceptualization of our analytical object is related to the problem of period boundaries? I am not sure, but it seems no accident that Bray's final book flouts both at once. There is no question that many of the issues prominent in the history of homosexuality traverse historical domains. I have already mentioned some: the vexed relation of friendship to eroticism, the problem of anachronistic terminology, the relationship between erotic acts and erotic identities, and the differences between concepts of erotic identity, predisposition, and orientation. To this we might add: the dynamic of secrecy and disclosure; the role of gender-segregated spaces; the relevance (or irrelevance) of age, status, and racial hierarchies; the existence (or nonexistence) of communities and subcultures; the relationship of homoeroticism to gender deviance and conformity; the role of medical and legal discourses in the production of knowledge; and the effects of racial or geographical othering. Additional issues are specific to the history of female bodies and experience: the role of female anatomy, especially the clitoris, in cultural representations; the derivative, secondary order of lesbian visibility within patriarchal culture, which underpins conceptual misrecognitions such as lesbian 'impossibility' and 'imitation'; and the constitutive social force of representations of female homoeroticism compared to those of male homoeroticism. Each of these issues assumes different contours, contents, and emphases when examined from historically specific locations. At the same time, their persistence as issues suggests that we might reconsider whether what is sometimes presented as whole-scale diachronic change (before and after sexuality, before and after identity) might rather be a manifestation of ongoing synchronic tensions in conceptualizations about bodies, desires, and their relation to gender as they confront the realities of new social formations.

Given the number of sophisticated period-based studies produced in the past twenty years, are we not now in a position to stage a dialogue among the sets of questions, concepts, and propositions that have emerged from both synchronic and diachronic analyses? I want to propose that we might consider indexing such conceptual coordinates across time so as to devise a genealogy of male and female same-sex intimacies over the *longue durée*. To do so would be to create a temporally capacious, conceptually organized, gender-comparative history of homosexuality. This history would derive precisely out of the questions, issues, and theses of our temporally bounded, fragmented, and discontinuous research. Fitted together in a dialogic rather than a teleological mould, viewed from a wide angle and with all the rough edges showing, this research might find a form that is both conceptually coherent and energizing of new areas of inquiry. (This project is made all the more urgent by the recent proliferation of anthologies of gay and lesbian literature, which tend to recuperate traditional teleological schemas.)[89] But the conversation I now want to hear, frankly, is not principally one between the past and the present – queer theory, influenced by Foucaultian genealogy, has provided an ample set of procedures for that, usable even by as devout a social historian as Bray. What requires new theorizing, I want to suggest, is how to stage a dialogue between *one* past and *another*.

It may seem that I have strayed far from the terrain mapped out by Alan Bray. These were not his questions, to be sure, but they are the questions that arise for me out of the exploratory maps that he so diligently and generously offered. I am not the scholar to do it – and I suspect I am not alone in my feelings of inadequacy – but collectively, and following the signposts he has offered, we are in a position to chart more precisely the overlapping coordinates of love, friendship, eroticism, and sexuality that comprise part of his historiographic vista. Perhaps the most humbling legacy of the friend whom we have lost – and of friendship's loss – is this: just as Alan's first book provided guideposts for much of the historical work that followed, his final gift of friendship beckons us to a new landscape, which is also, as he eloquently testifies, quite old yet, because of his work, quite near.

Notes

This chapter was originally published in the special issue of *GLQ: A Journal of Lesbian and Gay Studies*, edited by Jody Greene, vol. 10, no. 3 (2004), memorializing Alan Bray. I thank George Haggerty for organizing, at a difficult time of personal loss, a special session in honour of Alan Bray at the 2002 Modern Language Association convention; David M. Halperin for asking me to co-teach a course with him on the historiography of homosexuality; Jody Greene for her astute responses to a draft of this essay; and Laura Gowing, Michael Hunter, and Miri Rubin for inviting me to speak at the Birkbeck College Memorial Symposium on Alan Bray in September 2003.

1. A. Bray and M. Rey, 'The Body of the Friend: Continuity and Change in Masculine Friendship in the Seventeenth Century', in T. Hitchcock and M. Cohen (eds), *English Masculinities 1660–1800* (London and New York: Longman, 1999), pp. 65–84, on p. 65.

2. See A. Bray, *The Friend* (Chicago: University of Chicago Press, 2003). I cannot claim for myself the status of Alan's friend; although we had corresponded about each other's work, we did not meet until the year before his death. It was only after we had met, when he revealed to me that he would be reading the manuscript of my book *The Renaissance of Lesbianism in Early Modern England* for Cambridge University Press and suggested that we might dispense with the protocol of confidentiality in order to further our conversation, that we became regular correspondents. Portions of this essay were communicated to him in my response to the book manuscript that he shared with me the summer before his death.

3. A. Bray, *Homosexuality in Renaissance England* (London: Gay Men's Press, 1982); unless otherwise noted, citations taken from this edition.

4. A. Bray, 'Homosexuality and the Signs of Male Friendship in Elizabethan England', *History Workshop Journal*, 29 (1990), 1–19; reprinted in J. Goldberg (ed.), *Queering the Renaissance* (Durham, NC: Duke University Press, 1994), pp. 40–61, on p. 42; and Bray, *The Friend*, p. 186.

5. Bray, 'Homosexuality and the Signs of Male Friendship in Elizabethan England', p. 47; idem, *The Friend*, p. 186.

6. Bray, afterword to *Homosexuality in Renaissance England*, new edition (New York: Columbia University Press, 1995), p. 116.

7. J. Goldberg, 'Introduction', in Goldberg (ed.), *Queering the Renaissance*, pp. 1–14, on pp. 4–5.

8. Bray, *The Friend*, p. 25.

9. Ibid., pp. 104–5.

10. Ibid., p. 125.

11. Bray, *Homosexuality in Renaissance England*, p. 11. Scholars have variously adopted, nuanced, or attempted to refute Bray's constructionist account. As Goldberg notes, almost all the essays in *Queering the Renaissance* are heavily indebted to Bray (p. 4). See, subsequently, J. Goldberg, *Sodometries: Renaissance Texts, Modern Sexualities* (Stanford: Stanford University Press, 1992); G.W. Bredbeck, *Sodomy and Interpretation: Marlowe to Milton* (Ithaca: Cornell University Press, 1991); B.R. Smith, *Homosexual Desire in Shakespeare's England: A Cultural Poetics* (Chicago: University of Chicago Press, 1991); R. Rambuss, *Closet Devotions* (Durham, NC: Duke University Press, 1998); M. DiGangi, *The Homoerotics of Early Modern Drama* (Cambridge: Cambridge University Press, 1997); J. Masten, *Textual Intercourse: Collaboration, Authorship, and Sexualities in Renaissance Drama* (Cambridge: Cambridge University Press, 1997); A. Stewart, *Close Readers: Humanism and Sodomy in Early Modern England* (Princeton: Princeton University Press, 1997); S. Orgel, *Impersonations: The Performance of Gender in Shakespeare's England* (Cambridge: Cambridge University Press, 1996); G.E. Haggerty, *Men in Love: Masculinity and Sexuality in the Eighteenth Century* (New York: Columbia University Press, 1999); R. Trumbach, *Heterosexuality and the Third Gender in Enlightenment London*, vol. 1 of *Sex and the Gender Revolution* (Chicago: University of Chicago Press, 1998); and T. Hitchcock, *English Sexualities, 1700–1800* (New York: St. Martin's Press, 1997).

12. For analysis of the effects of 'The historical search for a Great Paradigm Shift', see Axiom 5 of E. Sedgwick's *Epistemology of the Closet* (Berkeley and Los Angeles: University of California Press, 1990), pp. 44–8. Bray's initial account continues to be nuanced by reflections on the meanings of identity, even as the contours of his chronology have gained general acceptance. See, for instance, D.M. Halperin, *How to Do the History of Homosexuality* (Chicago and London: University of Chicago Press, 2002).

13. For instance, Bray remarks that his study of sodomy 'places it outside a discrete history of sexuality' ('Homosexuality and the Signs of Male Friendship in Elizabethan England', p. 56).

14. Bray, *The Friend*, p. 6.

15. Bray, *Homosexuality in Renaissance England*, pp. 55–6. See also his review, 'Historians and Sexuality', *Journal of British Studies*, 32 (1993), 189–94.

16. Bray, *The Friend*, p. 150.

17. Regarding the temporality of change, Bray notes that, 'As a social form the personal service of early Tudor England was in decay by the end of the sixteenth century, but as a cultural form it was not; here the language of "friendship", as a set of assumptions and expectations, was still very much alive.' Nonetheless, 'the protecting conventions that ensured that [male intimacy] was seen in an acceptable frame of reference were often absent by the end of the sixteenth century' ('Homosexuality and Male Friendship', pp. 53, 56).

18. Bray, *The Friend*, p. 217.

19. Bray, 'The Body of the Friend', p. 80; *The Friend*, p. 218.

20. Bray, *The Friend*, p. 212.

21. Ibid., p. 209.

22. *The Friend*, pp. 6, 272. See also Bray's headnote to my essay, 'The Perversion of "Lesbian" Desire', *History Workshop Journal*, 41 (1996), 19–49.

23. Bray, 'Homosexuality and the Signs of Male Friendship in Elizabethan England', p. 46; slightly altered in *The Friend*, p. 156.

24. Bray, 'Homosexuality and the Signs of Male Friendship in Elizabethan England', p. 50; *The Friend*, p. 190.

25. Bray, *The Friend*, p. 174.

26. Bray's other break with traditional protocols of historical evidence was his frequent use of literary representation as one means of access to the social.

27. L. Shannon, *Sovereign Amity: Figures of Friendship in Shakespearean Contexts* (Chicago and London: University of Chicago Press, 2002), pp. 93–4: 'Eroticism, especially homoeroticism . . . seems not to operate as a device governing meanings in the Renaissance; its presence or absence is not determining in nomenclatures, knowledges, or social practices.' The language used in my text draws on Shannon, 'Queerly Philological Reading' (paper presented at the 'Lesbianism in the Renaissance' seminar, 30th Annual Meeting of the Shakespeare Association of America, Minneapolis, April 2002).

28. As Lauren Berlant and Lisa Duggan point out, the 'Clinton Affair' was 'a moment of stunning confusion in norms of sexuality; of fantasies of national intimacy – what constitutes "ordinary sex" and "ordinary marriage", let alone the relation between law and morality, law and justice' (Introduction to L. Berlant and L. Duggan (eds), *Our Monica, Ourselves: The Clinton Affair and the National Interest* (New York: New York University Press, 2001), p. 4). Several essays in *Our Monica, Ourselves* remark upon, but none actually analyze, this

constitutive confusion. In 'It's Not About Sex' (pp. 73–85), James R. Kincaid remarks of Clinton's infamous denial, 'I did not have sexual relations with that woman, Miss Lewinsky': 'What the "it" is that isn't sex shifts, of course, according to the context: anatomical, moral, legal, or causal. My point is that it always shifts so *as to keep the bodies themselves out of the picture*. The idea that oral sex isn't sex is just one of those refocusings' (emphasis mine, p. 75). In 'The First Penis Impeached' (pp. 116–33), Toby Miller likewise has other fish to fry: 'But Bill's dalliance with desire, his carefully calibrated, Monigated, sense of how far he could go – what constituted sex – was in fact part of the dance of management (not denial) that characterizes high office and its organization of low desires' (p. 118). Eric O. Clarke, in 'Sex and Civility' (pp. 285–90), notes the 'telling incoherence' that 'defined the events surrounding the president's actions, the media coverage of them, and the political response: his alleged crimes and misdemeanors both were and were not about sex'; but for Clarke, this incoherence is less about sex than 'the fraught place of sex in the public sphere' (p. 286). Not incidentally, a survey of Midwestern college students in 1991 revealed that 60 per cent of them did not think that they had 'had sex' if it involved oral contact rather than intercourse.

29. Bray, *Homosexuality in Renaissance England*, p. 69.
30. Bray, 'The Body of the Friend', p. 83, slightly reformulated in *The Friend*, p. 218. *The Friend* foregrounds the importance of the advent of civil society, arguing that it divorced sworn kinship from marriage, and, in doing so, removed 'the family from the traditional setting that this diverse and complex world had created. "Friends" could still negotiate marriage and did, but friendship was no longer to be created in relations that overlapped with it and were akin to it' (p. 217).
31. The dependence of the hetero on the homo has been a tenet of queer theory since Sedgwick's *Epistemology of the Closet* (1990) and Judith Butler's *Gender Trouble: Feminism and the Subversion of Identity* (London: Routledge, 1990).
32. Bray, 'Homosexuality and the Signs of Male Friendship in Elizabethan England', p. 54; see also *The Friend*, p. 193. Also suspicious of the reliability of literary texts as indicators of their author's sexual orientation, Bray assumes an exclusive hetero orientation in some of the subjects he analyzes, a problem that Bredbeck, Goldberg, and Smith attempt to address.
33. Bray, *Homosexuality in Renaissance England*, p. 17.
34. Incisive critiques of *Homosexuality in Renaissance England* along similar lines include that of Eve Kosofsky Sedgwick, who points out Bray's 'inadvertent reification of "the homosexual" as an already-constituted entity', which has a 'disturbing functionalist effect' on his argument (*Between Men: English Literature and Male Homosocial Desire* (New York: Columbia University Press, 1985), p. 86); Goldberg, who questions the anachronistic role of individualism as well as the foreclosure of meaning in Bray's narrative (*Sodometries*, pp. 68–71); DiGangi, who charges that Bray does not consider the homoerotics of Elizabethan male friendship (*The Homoerotics of Early Modern Drama*, p. 10); and Bredbeck, for whom the stigma of sodomy is less perfectly inscriptive or monolithic than Bray would seem to suggest (*Sodomy and Interpretation*, pp. 4–5, 144).
35. 'The image of the masculine friend', Bray writes, 'was an image of intimacy between men in stark contrast to the forbidden intimacy of homosexuality' ('Homosexuality and the Signs of Male Friendship in Elizabethan England', p. 42).

36. DiGangi, *The Homoerotics of Early Modern Drama*, p. 10. See also Orgel, *Impersonations*, p. 42.

37. Goldberg, *Sodometries*, p. 162.

38. More than once, Bray expressed anxiety about the controversy he believed our books would encounter; my *Renaissance of Lesbianism*, he cautioned, required 'armour-plating' from the attacks that he believed would be inevitable from British historians (pers. comm.).

39. The kisses of greeting that we bestow on our sexual partners, for instance, may not always be qualitatively different from those we bestow on our friends, just as the waning of sexual desire between long-term lovers may not turn them, automatically, into 'just friends'.

40. Bray, *The Friend*, p. 7.

41. Ibid., p. 225.

42. Bray cites as evidence a letter Newman wrote following St John's death, in which he articulates St John's 'hope that during his whole priestly life he had not committed one mortal sin', which Bray takes as 'definitive' (Bray, *The Friend*, p. 293).

43. Bray quickly follows with a second question: 'How much does that answer tell one? I have written this book for those interlocutors who are willing to ask that question' (Bray, *The Friend*, p. 269). Bray's point is that the good of these formalized bonds 'lay for them self-evidently beyond the individuals for whom a friendship was being made' (p. 277), and that focusing on sexuality does not get us to that point.

44. One can infer from Bray's reading of Newman's life that the line between the erotic and the spiritual depends in part on a division between the private and the communitarian: spiritual love creates bonds of community, whereas carnal love is more limited in its reach. Because such a division is belied by Bray's argument regarding the wide nexus of elective kinship that friendships created up through the seventeenth century, it may be that this separation is itself a further effect of the social change he charts. Or, this could simply be the place where his own Roman Catholicism, to which Bray converted as an adult, most comes to the fore.

45. Bray, *The Friend*, p. 316.

46. David Halperin incisively articulates the issue: 'if the funerary monuments Bray describes had conveyed even the faintest suggestion that the *connubium* of friends celebrated in them had consisted in a sodomitical union, we would not find those monuments enshrined in Christian churches. I do not infer from this alone that Piper and Wise never had sex (though Bray makes a very strong claim to that effect about John Henry Newman and Ambrose St John); in most cases, I assume, the evidence does not allow us to draw any firm inferences one way or the other. But I do deduce that the *rhetoric* of friendship or love employed in those monuments succeeded in sealing off the relationships represented in them from any suggestion of being sodomitical.' See D.M. Halperin, Introduction to K. O'Donnell and M. O'Rourke (eds), *Love, Sex, Intimacy, and Friendship between Men, 1550–1880* (Basingstoke: Palgrave, 2003), pp. 1–11, on p. 10, n. 9.

47. Bray, *The Friend*, p. 6.

48. Goldberg, 'Introduction', *Queering the Renaissance*, p. 6.

49. C. Herrup, 'Finding the Bodies', *GLQ: A Journal of Lesbian and Gay Studies*, 5 (1999), 255–65.

50. This point was made by David Wootton in his remarks during the Birkbeck College Symposium on Alan Bray in September 2003.

51. A similar incarnation of this problem occurs in a blurb on the cover of a 2002 Routledge anthology, K.M. Phillips and B. Reay (eds), *Sexualities in History: A Reader* (London and New York: Routledge, 2002). 'Sexual behaviours and mentalities are embedded in systems of power', David Levine observes in his puff for the book, but this recognition is preceded with the claim: 'Sex is, perhaps, the *least* interesting aspect of the history of sexuality' (emphasis mine).

52. I have found only two moments in *The Friend* that remotely smack of 'debunking', and in each instance the issue is not eroticism but rather an anachronistic understanding of the role and meaning of homoeroticism in early modern culture. In his discussion of other scholars' assertions of *covert* homosexuality (p. 166), for instance, the issue is not the projection of homoeroticism but the assumption of the need for secrecy.

53. Bray, *The Friend*, p. 6. At the same time, he warns 'that to read this book within the narrow terms of a debate as to whether homosexual friendship constitutes a family would be to misunderstand it, perhaps gravely. The ethics it deals with overflow that question. To widen the terms of this debate ... is to see it within a broader contemporary crisis in the ethics of friendship, the signs of which have been the diverse loyalties of identity, region, culture, or language that have come to mark the pluralism of the late modern world, of which sexuality has been one, but only one, strand' (p. 8).

54. In the Introduction to *The Friend*, for instance, Bray characterizes the motivation of his own historical enterprise as 'seeking among the tombs of the dead those lost friends' who died of HIV/AIDS – 'against all expectations I found such friendship there in these monuments' (p. 5). So too, his coda concludes: 'As in our own time the permafrost of modernity has at last begun to melt ... the world we are seeing is not a strange new world, revealed as the glaciers draw back, but a strange *old* world: kinship, locality, embodiment, domesticity, affect' (p. 306).

55. Bray, *The Friend*, p. 197.

56. Ibid., p. 224.

57. Ibid., p. 134.

58. Ibid., p. 158.

59. Ibid., p. 125.

60. Ibid., p. 268.

61. Ibid., p. 139.

62. Goldberg, *Sodometries*, pp. 19–20.

63. Bray, 'Historians and Sexuality', p. 194.

64. I have taken up these questions in 'The Joys of Martha Joyless: Or, Queer Pedagogy and the (Early Modern) Production of Sexual Knowledge', unpublished manuscript.

65. M. Hunt, Afterword to Goldberg, *Queering the Renaissance*, pp. 359–77, on p. 372.

66. V. Traub, *The Renaissance of Lesbianism in Early Modern England* (Cambridge: Cambridge University Press, 2002).

67. It is worth noting that the relation between eroticism and friendship looks different from the standpoint of the history of lesbianism. Efforts to stake

claims on one side of a rigid divide separating sexuality from asexuality have been constitutive of the field. From Lillian Faderman's implication in *Surpassing the Love of Men: Romantic Friendship and Love between Women from the Renaissance to the Present* (New York: Morrow, 1981), that romantic friends were not sexual to Terry Castle's rejoinder in *The Apparitional Lesbian: Female Homosexuality and Modern Culture* (New York: Columbia University Press, 1993), that sex is the basis of a definition of lesbianism, the question of erotic content has been central to lesbian historiography. With very few exceptions, scholars have tended to reproduce rather than question the applicability of that binary.

68. Bray seemed content that others might push the ramifications of his work in a more explicitly erotic direction. He acknowledges, for instance, those scholars who not only welcomed his work, but critiqued or used it for their own analysis of the historical relation between the homosocial and the homoerotic (afterword to *Homosexuality in Renaissance England*, new edition). Based on the citations of other scholars and personal testimony offered since his death, many have experienced Bray's work and feedback as not only generative, but enabling of their own more explicitly erotic interpretations of the archive.

69. Bray, afterword, p. 118, emphasis mine.

70. A. Bray, 'The Curious Case of Michael Wigglesworth', in M. Duberman (ed.), *A Queer World: The Center for Lesbian and Gay Studies Reader* (New York and London: New York University Press, 1997), pp. 205–15, on p. 206. Given that, from a certain point of view, Wiggleworth's dreams are a perfect illustration of what desire is, Bray's own conception of desire and how it functions in the modern world is worth further investigation.

71. Bray, *The Friend*, p. 172.

72. Halperin, Introduction, *Love, Sex, Intimacy, and Friendship between Men*, p. 5.

73. K. O'Donnell and M. O'Rourke, 'In Memoriam – Alan Bray (1948–2001)', which precedes Bray's 'A Traditional Rite for Blessing Friendship' (pp. 87–98) in *Love, Sex, Intimacy, and Friendship between Men*, pp. 82–6, on p. 85.

74. Bray, *Homosexuality in Renaissance England*, p. 17.

75. Ibid., p. 74, emphasis mine.

76. The question of influence is complex. Bray has obviously influenced Laurie Shannon, whose *Sovereign Amity* (primarily on masculine friendship, but attentive to female friendship as well) seeks at several points to extend Bray's analysis of the dangers of inequality, as well as K. Schwarz, *Tough Love: Amazon Encounters in the English Renaissance* (Durham, NC: Duke University Press, 2000), whose analysis draws heavily on Bray's treatment of cultural intelligibility. Yet, it is notable that neither of these books is primarily about female homoeroticism. Elizabeth Susan Wahl sees in Bray's focus on those who threaten social stability 'a particularly useful approach for analyzing England's apparent cultural indifference to the desire of one woman for another', but she does not develop that observation (*Invisible Relations: Representations of Female Intimacy in the Age of Enlightenment* (Stanford: Stanford University Press, 1999), p. 52). Harriette Andreadis approvingly cites Bray's historical argument about a homosexual subculture in order to speculate about 'an analogous female homosexual subculture' emerging around the same time in London (*Sappho in Early Modern England: Female Same-Sex*

Literary Erotics, 1550–1714 (Chicago: University of Chicago Press, 2001), pp. 52, 95–6). Based on the presence of citations as well as on critical approach, Bray appears to have held little utility for T. Jankowski, *Pure Resistance: Queer Virginity in Early Modern English Drama* (Philadelphia: University of Pennsylvania Press, 2000), E. Donoghue, *Passions between Women: British Lesbian Culture 1668–1801* (New York: HarperCollins, 1993), or the essays on female intimacy in S. Frye and K. Robertson (eds), *Maids and Mistresses, Cousins and Queens: Women's Alliances in Early Modern England* (New York: Oxford University Press, 1999).

77. Bray, 'The Body of the Friend', p. 75; Bray, *The Friend*, p. 158.
78. I owe this question to Laura Gowing.
79. Bray, *The Friend*, pp. 10, 174–6, 199.
80. Ibid., pp. 268, 269, 244.
81. Ibid., p. 223.
82. G. Williamson, *Lady Anne Clifford: Her Life, Letters, and Work* (Kendal: Titus Wilson & Son, 1922), p. 76. This question is also raised by Laura Gowing in her recent book, *Common Bodies: Women, Touch and Power in Seventeenth-Century England* (New Haven and London: Yale University Press, 2003), pp. 65–8.
83. This critique focuses on such metanarrative's retrospective investment in progress, causality, and supersession; its sequential requirements of the pre- and the post-; its tendency toward false synthesis; and its press-ganging of all prior formations of same-sex desire into modern identities. See, for instance, A. Jagose, *Inconsequence: Lesbian Representation and the Logic of Sexual Sequence* (Ithaca and London: Cornell University Press, 2002); L. Fradenberg and C. Freccero (eds), *Premodern Sexualities* (London and New York: Routledge, 1996); and G. Burger and S.F. Kruger (eds), *Queering the Middle Ages* (Minneapolis and London: University of Minnesota Press, 2001).
84. In addition to Goldberg (ed.), *Queering the Renaissance*, and Burger and Kruger (eds), *Queering the Middle Ages*, see A. Herrmann, *Queering the Moderns: Poses/Portraits/Performances* (London and New York: Palgrave, 2000).
85. See C. Dinshaw, *Getting Medieval: Sexualities and Communities, Pre- and Postmodern* (Durham, NC: Duke University Press, 1999); K. Lochrie, 'Don't Ask, Don't Tell: Murderous Plots and Medieval Secrets', *GLQ*, 1 (1995), 405–17; Lochrie, 'Presidential Improprieties and Medieval Categories: The Absurdity of Heterosexuality', in Burger and Kruger (eds), *Queering the Middle Ages*, pp. 87–96; and S.F. Kruger, 'Medieval/Postmodern: HIV/AIDS and the Temporality of Crisis', in Burger and Kruger (eds), *Queering the Middle Ages*, pp. 252–83.
86. The major studies of lesbianism, for instance, are generally respectful of traditional period boundaries. In addition to those listed above, see B. Brooten, *Love between Women: Early Christian Responses to Female Homoeroticism* (Chicago and London: University of Chicago Press, 1996); J. Abraham, *Are Girls Necessary? Lesbian Writing and Modern Histories* (London and New York: Routledge, 1996); L. Moore, *Dangerous Intimacies: Toward a Sapphic History of the British Novel* (Durham, NC: Duke University Press, 1997); J. Halberstam, *Female Masculinity* (Durham, NC: Duke University Press, 1998); V. Rohy, *Impossible Women: Lesbian Figures and American Literature* (Ithaca: Cornell University Press, 2000); and L. Doan, *Fashioning*

Sapphism: The Origins of a Modern English Lesbian Culture (New York: Columbia University Press, 2001).
87. Classical, medieval, and early modern medicine, astrology, and physiognomy, for instance, describe some homoerotic behaviours, especially those associated with gender deviance, as linked to, and sometimes caused by, anatomical aberrations, diseases of the mind, or habituation due to sexual practices. Although this view does not constitute 'homosexual identity' in its post-sexological construction, neither is it the undifferentiated concept of sin to which all were subject.
88. See Dinshaw, *Getting Medieval*, and Halperin, *How to do the History of Homosexuality*. Despite these advances, too often the concept of 'identity' remains undertheorized and hazily defined, associated with such different concepts as sexual inclination, tendency, preference, predisposition, orientation, consciousness, subjectivity, self-perception, and subculture – listed here according to a spectrum from 'soft' to 'hard' identity claims. Several problems and questions arise from this definitional confusion and associational logic. Are identity, orientation, and subjectivity synonymous? If they are, do they mean the same thing as inclination, predisposition, tendency? Does an inclination, even if defined as innate, necessarily signify something causal, or is it merely probabilistic? Does the subcultural grouping of like-minded persons necessarily constitute an identity or subjectivity? Does the *content* of a homoerotic subjectivity alter historically?
89. See, for instance, S. Coote (ed.), *The Penguin Book of Homosexual Verse* (London: Penguin, 1983); E. Donoghue, *Poems Between Women: Four Centuries of Love, Romantic Friendship, and Desire* (New York: Columbia University Press, 1997); and T. Castle (ed.), *The Literature of Lesbianism: A Historical Anthology from Ariosto to Stonewall* (New York: Columbia University Press, 2003).

2
Sacred or Profane? Reflections on Love and Friendship in the Middle Ages

Klaus Oschema

I. Introduction

'The most holy bond of society is friendship', Mary Wollstonecraft declared in 1792, explaining that 'true friendship' existed even less often than 'true love' – thus putting the two emotionally based types of relationship on an equal footing,[1] leaving the reader puzzled with the apparent connection between an individual, personal bond and the sphere of sacrality. The concept of friendship that Wollstonecraft develops in this brief passage is not easily to be reconciled with modern everyday perceptions of the phenomenon: she forwards its importance as a foundation of female–male relationships and thus seems to perpetuate an idea that reminds the historian of medieval ideas on love and marriage.[2] However she might have imagined the concrete realization of this ideal, she obviously did not draw a rigid line between relationships including sexual activity and non-sexual types.

Even if Wollstonecraft does not address the question of these different characteristics explicitly, she provides some insight into a historical development which lies at the very heart of recent discussions: Common knowledge usually considers that friendship excludes sexual activity. In this respect products of popular culture, like Rob Steiner's movie 'When Harry met Sally', do not differ significantly from the ideas expressed in standard dictionaries.[3] Most of them forward the idea that friends could have an intimate relation, without, however, adding a sexual dimension, which would make them lovers. This culturally formed background helps to explain, to a certain extent, the difficulties of modern historians when dealing with emotion-based concepts and their physical expressions in pre-modern societies. Whereas some authors began very early to reflect on the changes in sensibilities,[4] it was obviously tempting to interpret pre-modern particularities on the basis of modern perceptional concepts. One of the most famous examples for this kind of misreading can be seen in parts of the discussion about Richard the Lionheart's alleged homosexuality, as we will see below. Seen from a medievalist's perspective, Alan Bray's reflections on the practices of friendship are thus particularly instructive where they bring out the slow changes of sensibilities:[5] gestures of physical proximity, which are nowadays considered to be of erotic or even sexual nature, can be interpreted as part of varying systems of sociability and communication.[6] Moreover, their interpretation also depends on the analytical framework which underlies the approach. As a consequence, the undeniable medieval tendency to spiritualize concepts of personal relationships might have influenced their representation as well as their functional purposes in the larger context of communication in the public sphere. In the following pages, we attempt to outline the development of ideas on love and friendship along the dichotomy of the sacred and profane, thus proposing to focus on a hitherto neglected dimension of this particular topic.

Modern sociologists and psychologists tend to analyze friendship either as a functional and institutionalized relationship or as a vessel for self-disclosure in personal contact.[7] Translated into the perceptional mode of a pre-secularized society, both of these approaches seem to imply a certain amount of profanity, since they exclusively concern relationships between human individuals. On the other hand, Mircea Eliade's studies demonstrated that various aspects of life can be connected with the sacred without explicitly being labelled accordingly,[8] their characteristic not being the apparent connection to the divine sphere but rather the acceptance of certain social or individual practices and arguments as being immutable.[9] By means of 'small transcendencies', they are excluded from constant renegotiation by the members of a given culture and form the basis of what Berger and Luckmann chose to call the 'social construction of reality'.[10] According to this criterion, I would like to argue that love and friendship had been the object of sacralization during long periods of the Middle Ages before having been affected by secularizing discursive tendencies at the end of the epoch – just to be elevated to a new kind of transcendency on the eve of modern times, thus reflecting a rupture in sensibilities.[11]

A particular difficulty of the historical analysis of love and friendship consists in their at once evasive and perpetual nature. The written evidence seems to imply that human beings always reflected about the nature of emotion and there is no proof that the affective basis of love would have changed with time.[12] Neither do the difficulties of communicating emotions even among contemporaries. As a consequence it seems to be impossible to detect them in individuals who are long gone by scrutinizing the texts they produced or, even worse, that have been produced about them. Nevertheless, a large number of studies have proven during the last decades that love and friendship can indeed be subjected to historical analysis. This kind of work can (and does) usually not pretend to pin down the emotional disposition of a concrete person at a specific moment,[13] but rather concentrates on the discourse about love and friendship or the social practices which are connected with it.[14] Seen from this perspective, our sources can reveal people's reflections about love and friendship and where they located them in their social world.

II. Philosophical and religious foundations of medieval theories on love and friendship

Medieval concepts of love and friendship heavily rely on older reasonings from ancient philosophy and Christian doctrine. In ancient Greek theory, love occupied an ambivalent status, situated on the level of emotion as well as in the sacral sphere by its being part of the basic cosmological forces. In Plato's *Symposium*[15] and *Phaedrus*,[16] the philosophical discussion embeds love not only in an individual context, but also connects it with a divine force, personified as *Eros*. His influence not only makes people fall in love, but also furnishes the global principle of attraction: it keeps the universe together in the steady tension of love and hate, it makes the human spirit desire knowledge and elevates human beings from their material existence to the level of the divine through the perception of beauty. The concrete outline of *Eros'* shape is of secondary importance:[17] by their connection to him, love, affinity and sexuality refer to something numinous outside the 'profane' frame of human existence.[18]

Similar ideas apply to the Greek friendship (*philia*),[19] discussed systematically by Aristotle in his *Nicomachean Ethics*.[20] The philosopher tried to identify the force that kept human societies together, and in books 8 and 9 of his *Nicomachean Ethics* he attributes this role to friendship – qualified as virtue. For him, it represented 'one of the most indispensable requirements of life',[21] that even 'appears to be the bond of the state'.[22]

This assessment was based on practical observations of political life in the Greek *polis*, which depended heavily on the social networks of free men who ruled communal life.[23] For Aristotle, however, friendship represented more than just a functional structure of social interaction – it was also invested with transcendental forces. Even if he explained some of its basic effects in terms of pragmatic foundations, like the proximity of the partners or their likeness (thus furnishing arguments for the cohesion between members of one family),[24] his differentiation of three kinds of friendship seems partially to invalidate the preceding deliberations. According to Aristotle, three motivations for mutual affection can be distinguished: practical benefit, pleasure inspired by the partner, and the partner's virtuous nature.[25] The varying appraisal of the variants brings us back to the differentiation of sacred and profane. A friendship based on benefit or pleasure relied on a transitory foundation: if one of the partners lost his treasure or his beauty, the bond was likely to end. But true friendship, real *philia* should be endless! This necessitated the foundation on the only potentially unchanging characteristic in a human being, the wise man's virtue – a phenomenon which existed in this world but provided a connection with the transcendental.

Some centuries later, Cicero continued this logic partially in his *Laelius*, where he declared friendship to be a divine gift and a prerequisite to a meaningful human life.[26] He adopted the threefold system of friendships based on benefit, pleasure or wisdom without explicitly citing the Aristotelian model even once – a sign for the widespread acceptance of the Greek philosopher's theories.[27] Through its immense success and large readership, the *Laelius* transmitted the basic traits of the Aristotelian system to posterity, providing for example a model for Ambrosius' discussion of friendship.[28] From the twelfth century on, it became part of the literary canon.[29] When Jean Miélot presented his translation of Ciceronian texts into French in the middle of the fifteenth century, he praised Laurent de Premierfait's translation of the *Laelius*[30] – a work which is preserved in at least fourteen manuscripts dating from the fifteenth century.[31] Alongside the French version, the Latin original was also still eagerly copied.[32]

Why this immense success of a philosophical work dating from the late Roman republic? More than other texts on friendship, Cicero's dialogue lent itself to Christian re-interpretation. By deriving the notion of *amicitia* from *amor*[33] it provided a link between love and friendship. More important, however, was its explicit definition: according to Cicero, friendship was nothing less than 'the agreement' of people 'in all things, human and divine, together with love and benevolence'.[34] This formula had great success amongst Christian authors, from St Augustine to Aelred de Rievaulx' *De spiritali amicitia* in the twelfth century.[35]

This ongoing interest was decisively formed by the Christian tendency to spiritualize the structure of social relations. In the case of love and friendship, this effect can be traced back to Old Testament models. The commandment to love one's neighbour appeared not only in the Gospels,[36] but already in Leviticus (albeit in a slightly modified way), where every Israelite was ordered to love her or his friend like herself (Leviticus 19:18). Divine sanction thus underlined friendship's value as a social institution along with its duties and norms of behaviour.[37] Early Greek *philia* provides a near contemporary analogy: on a functional level, it implied the affiliation to a given community, the latter being defined by a state of inner peace. Strangers were *a priori* excluded from this system and virtually rightless. One means to achieve integration consisted in the creation of a bond of friendship with a group member, resulting in a recognized relationship with the group itself.[38] The divine orders for the Israelites did not allow for this option, since they requested to integrate strangers into the community of love – thereby memorizing the Israelites' sufferings during the Egyptian exile (Leviticus 19:34) – but not to make them friends!

In this context, 'love' hardly refers to an intimate relationship, but rather concerns the harmonious organization of social life on a more general level. Christianity then brought about a rupture, since it not only preferred the paradigm of 'brotherhood', but also introduced some major linguistic shifts: While the Greek language disposed of four different verbs referring to love,[39] used in different contexts, the New Testament writers and the translators of the Old Testament narrowed down this variety to *agapan*, equivalent to the noun *caritas* in Latin.[40] Both words already existed in pre-Christian vocabulary, but now they were re-interpreted according to the ideals of the new religion, designating henceforth an unselfish love, which became one of the key concepts of Christian doctrine.[41] Its structure referred to God's creation, an act accomplished out of sheer superabundance of love. It furnished a model for the appropriate mutual love between human beings, and also identified its ultimate source, God himself. Since all human beings represented God's creation, every member of society was to be equally worthy of loving care.[42] This ideal harmonized neither with classical *amicitia*, which had an exclusive character, nor with ecstatic love between the sexes – especially since the ideal of asceticism and chastity rapidly became the guideline for Christian existence.[43]

Christian authors began to distinguish between a 'pure' and laudable kind of love, and tainted forms of lesser value. On a linguistic level, this led to the repression of the verbal form *amare* and its corresponding substantive *amor* in favour of *diligere*, a verb derived from *dilectio* and virtually unknown beforehand. Like *caritas*, it implied a desireless and pure love, addressed to God and redirected to fellow humans only via his intermediate position, thus making 'love' a tripartite structure instead of the bipolar modern concept.

These modifications collided with a well-established system of social practices: in the Roman republic, *amicitia* was central to the politico-social clientele system. In spite of the existing studies, the extent to which patron–client bonds could have been governed by emotion is still not clear, but it seems that many of them have been surprisingly stable. Moreover, the participants in the system saw an important difference between the denomination as *client* or as *friend*, as is attested by Cicero: '...some Romans would have resented it as bitter as death, had they been forced to accept a patron or to be called a client'.[44] Even political alliances of the Roman state with foreign powers were conceptualized as *amicitiae*, thus concealing factual submission under Roman supremacy by integration into a discourse of equality and divine sanction.

The importance of a pagan ideal of friendship explains the reluctance of Christian authors to refer to *amicitia* during the first centuries of our era. Like certain aspects of pagan literature and knowledge, friendship suffered a period of latency before it reappeared in baptized form, as can be seen in the correspondence of Paulinus of Nola.[45] At the same time, St Ambrose reactivated Ciceronian ideas in his tract on the ministers' duties, not without, however, underlining the 'psychological' importance of personal relationships.

St Augustine finally proposed a unified model of love, combining those aspects which were analytically distinguished in the notions *eran*, *stergein*, *philein* and *agapan*. For him, there was only one love which could be differentiated according to the orientation of the affection and received its respective dignity by the value of the chosen object. As a consequence, he used *amor, caritas* and *dilectio* as synonyms.

It seems, however, that Augustine had difficulties to develop a clear position concerning friendship: he never produced an exhaustive text on the subject, but he discussed it in different tracts.[46] In his *Confessions*, Augustine describes the comforts of intimate relationships with friends.[47] Even in old age they kept a sweet taste – accompanied, however, by the bitterness of regret, since he realized that in his youth he had bound his heart to objects which diverted him from God, the only object really worthy of love. He explicitly states: 'Blessed is he who loves you and his friend in you and his enemy because of you'[48] – a formulation which clearly indicates the tripartite structure of love. This conception might have been ideal for the construction of an undifferentiated, open order of society, since all fellow men could become equally worthy of love.[49] Only it could not serve to describe the real conditions of life, for it provided a systematic location neither for the undeniably existent hierarchical differences nor for individual preferences.

III. Social practices of friendship

Perhaps it was this kind of idealization with its egalitarian side that caused people throughout the Middle Ages to recur to friendship in their descriptions of social and political bonds. When adapted to the needs of everyday life, the different facets that could be separated analytically in theoretic reflections had a strong tendency to blend together. This effect appears more clearly when the authors not only talk about love and friendship but refer to concrete practices in this context.

Gregory of Tours furnishes an example with his famous story about the conflicts and conciliations between the noblemen Sichar and Chramnesind.[50] After a first composition between the protagonists, which included a financial compensation, the renewed conflicts necessitated a second, more promising judgment.[51] To a modern reader, the circumstances of the settlement seem quite unusual, since Sichar and Chramnesind are said to have concluded a friendship (*amicitia*) accompanied by 'mutual love' ('in tantum se caritate mutua diligerent'), in spite of the preceding murders of their respective relatives. According to Gregory, they even started to 'eat together and to sleep in the same bed' ('plerumque simul cibum caperent ac in uno pariter stratu recumberent'). This situation was not to last long: during a feast, Sichar insulted his partner and provoked him so much that Chramnesind felt urged to recover his virile honour and split Sichar's head with his sword.[52]

What clearly represents an overreaction when judged by modern standards becomes understandable in the context of a society that was mainly governed by ideals of honour. More surprising, however, are two curious details in the narration: First, the composition of a conflict which gives place to a loving 'friendship', far beyond the scope of an abstract judicial compensation.[53] It is probably safe to interpret this result as some kind of contractual relationship. But a second, more problematic fact consists in the physical gestures which accompany this development. Gregory does not mention an oath of any kind that would have ended the war (*bellum*) between the families. Instead, he focuses on factual harmony, discernable in the protagonists' love, their eating and sleeping together.

Both gestures or rituals have a long history in pre-modern societies; especially the case of the common meal has already been thoroughly analyzed.[54] Because of its ongoing tradition, its effects seem to be quite easily accessible – two reconciled adversaries can prove and reinforce their newly established harmony to each other and to the larger groups which surround them and witness the effects of the union. Incidents like the Emperor Henry IV's allegedly impolite behaviour during the meal he shared with Pope Gregory VII at Canossa in January 1077 only seem to confirm the general acceptance and intelligibility of the ritual.[55]

Sharing the same bed, on the other hand, seems to be a more engaging and even intimate act; as a consequence, there is ample space for misinterpretation. Like Sichar and Chramnesind in the sixth century, the French King Philip II Augustus and Richard 'the Lionheart' apparently shared bed and table after having concluded a peace treaty in 1187. But this was by no means all: the contemporary chronicler Roger of Howden underlined the fervent love (*vehemens amor*) between them, which would have caused young Richard's father, King Henry II, to wonder about its meaning.[56] John Boswell inferred the princes' probable homosexuality and concluded that 'in the twelfth century the future King of England could fall head over heels in love with another ruler without losing the support of either his people or the church'.[57]

This interpretation forwards a 'profane' idea of love (*amor*), referring mainly to an emotional or sexual component – according to Dinzelbacher, *amor* rather signified 'desire' than 'love' until the twelfth century.[58] It was only at this time, that the oft-disputed changes in the perception of the individual was accompanied by important modifications of the discourse about love.[59] As Dinzelbacher argues, interpersonal relationships now came to be perceived through the grid of emotion; a new perceptional mode was added to the accustomed tension between spiritualization and desire. So what about the two men at Gisors? Roger of Howden offers the key to interpretation in an earlier version of the events, where he speaks of the 'vehemens dilectio', 'strong love', after having declared that 'the French king had loved Richard like his own soul'.[60] Klaus van Eickels recently demonstrated that this formula constitutes a modified citation from the Biblical narration about David and Jonathan (I Samuel 18:1). Apparently Roger wanted to present the friendship between the two protagonists as being comparable with the Biblical model.[61] Like the latter, the relationship between the two princes could be regarded as of divine origin.

On a functional level, what resulted was a political contract: Richard concluded a treaty with his father's enemy in order to keep his claims to the throne. Conceptionalizing it as a bond of love and friendship presented two decisive advantages in comparison with the sober designation as a *foedus*: the reference to a divine authority could serve to symbolically secure and reinforce the relationship between the partners (a contravention against the agreement would have been equivalent with trespassing against a relationship sanctioned by God) – the bond gained a transcendent quality. Secondly, the concept might have helped to defend the union on a more practical level: who was to criticize divinely inspired love as a contravention against a son's duties?

IV. The twelfth-century change

Roger of Howden's narration is situated in an era of change. Never before the twelfth century had love and friendship been represented in literature in such a dense succession and discussed so intensely. The literary success of the ideal friends *Ami et Amile* is just one example: According to the story, both friends resembled each other so much that they could easily be confounded.[62] When they met for the first time, they swore immutable friendship, before entering into Charlemagne's service. While Ami marries, his friend Amile seduces the Emperor's daughter, Belissant. This illicit relationship being uncovered by an envious rival, Amile is challenged to a judicial duel. Being guilty of what he is accused of, he has no hope to win and asks his friend to replace him in the dangerous situation, while he himself takes care of the latter's wife. Ami, who can rightfully claim his innocence, wins the duel and is subsequently married to Belissant, still playing the role of his friend. By helping his partner, he is thus forced to enter a bigamous relationship and God's revenge does not take long to happen: Ami suffers from leprosy and only the blood of Amile's children, born in the meanwhile, can offer him healing and salvation.

The story can be interpreted in various ways – it offers rich material for the comparison of male–male friendship with male–female love, a topic that has been tackled in several texts of the epoch.[63] The interesting detail concerning the question of the profane, however, is the partners' decision to contravene God-given moral principles in the name of friendship.[64] Since the transgressive acts are immediately followed by punishment, the narration as a whole reinforces the significance of divine orders. Nevertheless, it contains the discursive expression of a conflict between two different normative systems. In antiquity, philosophers had discussed the question whether the obligations towards friends could be more important and more binding than the civic duties towards the *res publica*.[65] In the early Middle Ages, this kind of reasoning was virtually unknown until the twelfth century – a time when John of Salisbury discussed the legitimacy of tyrannicide and Abelard underlined the importance of the individual's conscience.

No treatise actually legitimized revolutionary acts in the name of friendship, but the fact that philosophers and theologians started to ask the question anew is significant. Analogous discursive shifts occurred in the context of love between the sexes. In the early Middle Ages, an author like Venantius Fortunatus used virtually the same vocabulary when referring to male friendship or to women's love.[66] The first traces of a secular variety of male–female love in literature occurred in the fairly explicit poems of William IX of Aquitaine, the famous 'Duke of the Troubadours'.[67] Texts like his formed a developing discursive layer outside spiritualized Christian theory. It questioned neither God's existence nor his relevance, but developed love and its sexual component as a secular phenomenon in its own right.

How far individual authors could go with their literary experiments may be seen in the anonymous *chantefable* 'Aucassin et Nicolette' (c.1200).[68] The protagonists of this parody on courtly love deeply enamour themselves with each other, but circumstances keep them apart. When Aucassin's father explains to his son how he could win paradise by marrying another woman who would better befit his rank, the latter prefers to renounce the promise of eternal paradise: as long as he can be together with his Nicolette, he would rather 'prefer to go to hell'.[69]

Those parodistic deliberations are not to be taken at face value. Nevertheless, they provide an insight into the discursive options which were at the disposition of the authors. Rüdiger Schnell recently showed how the perception of male–female relationships changed from the twelfth century onwards, beginning to include emotional concepts to a higher degree in the complex of love, sexuality and marriage.[70] The idea of friendship played a crucial role for this development, since Thomas Aquinas himself claimed that *amicitia* was the best foundation of marriage[71] – thus making the the ideal of marriage more 'human' by investing it with a higher degree of emotionality.

The theories of friendship express a parallel tendency: at the end of the twelfth century, Aelred of Rievaulx systematized a spiritual *amicitia*, transcending the Ciceronian model by transferring the concept into a Christian context. For Aelred, the spiritual bond represented the highest aim of friendship, but he also acknowledged the existence of an *amicitia carnalis*, which could furnish the basis for an accession to the higher forms of friendship: 'This is a friendship in the flesh [...] which is to be tolerated in the hope of richer grace, since it might be the basis of a more holy friendship.'[72] The gradual, ascending organization of his concept becomes clearer in his passages on gestures of friendship, where the kiss receives a threefold interpretation according to its physical, spiritual and intellectual dimension.[73] This analysis does not exclude a certain esteem for the physical act – thus marking an intrusion of material and corporeal aspects into the spiritually oriented concepts of Christianity.[74]

V. A new transcendency of the emotional?

The conceptual intrusion becomes more manifest in late medieval texts on friendship, where the authors increasingly mixed up the previously more or less well differentiated phenomena of friendship and love,[75] sometimes shifting from one notion to the other without any explanation. Thus a *Définition d'amour*[76] as well as an *Ars d'amour*[77] from the fourteenth century are not collections of Ovidian advice in matters of love, but rather descriptions of the duties connected with friendship. A thirteenth-century *Art d'aimer* starts in perfect harmony with contemporary ideas about courteous love by enumerating the seven degrees of love from 'sight' (*resgars*) to 'consent' (*volentés*). But in their following discussion, the author rapidly moves from love to friendship.[78] The same technique appears in the *Définition d'amour*, which initially focuses on a kind of romantic love, characterized by *Longinge, Lykinge, Murninge, Meninge, Sorwinge, Sighinge*.[79] In a sudden shift the author then talks about friends and friendship, elaborating a description of what he calls 'love between faithful lovers' which coincides with the classical duties of friendship, namely mutual benevolence, counsel, loyalty, praise and fidelity.[80]

These texts are thus less concerned with spiritual aspects of interpersonal relations. They rather add a new discursive layer by concentrating on practical aspects of social relationships as well as on their individual implications. Especially the complex *Ars d'amour*, attributed to the Liège author Jean le Bel,[81] witnesses the importance of the community of friends, which implies a certain devalorization of the spiritual dimension, without however eliminating it entirely. The author recognizes the friends' desire to share their lives and legitimizes their wish to spend time together.[82] Moreover, he innovates by focusing on the intimate gestures of love and friendship. Avoiding the usual dichotomy between allegoric interpretation and practical pleasure, the *Ars d'amour* discusses the gestures' physiological effects. In this perspective, the kiss becomes not only a sign, but an act of fusion, since it permits to exchange the most subtle medium of the human organism, the breath – just like the embrace through the proximity of the hearts, albeit to a lesser degree:

> in the kiss the two most combinable things combine and become one, by mixing the one with the other: this is the breath of the kissers... This is the reason why the kissers, because of the intensity of the joining and the unity of the hearts, which is like the most desired thing, are very affected while they kiss and ravished and out of themselves... Common usage also shows us that the kiss is a sign of contact and unity of the inner self; because we see that, when there has been a conflict in the form of a war or a feud for a long time between people, and when peace is made, we make them kiss each other in order to signify that now their spiritual breath has been united and – in good faith – their will also... The embrace is also used for this, like the kiss, in this way; because in the embrace we voluntarily join our breasts together and hold each other mutually and close in order to signify the joining and the unity of hearts which are close inside the breast.[83]

If the kiss is used in rituals of peace, in which it also functions as a sign of the newly achieved harmony,[84] the gesture is thus executed because of its practical effectiveness and not only because of its public or allegoric nature. According to this interpretation, the act is mainly performed because of its material and profane effects on the protagonists!

This information helps to better understand why fifteenth-century rulers valued seemingly archaic rites of physical contact when concluding political treaties, in spite of their epoch's status as the cradle of modern state organization.[85] In 1405, when the rival dukes Louis of Orléans and John the Fearless of Burgundy were reconciled by the mediation of the French Queen Isabeau, they kissed each other, ate together and shared one bed.[86] The peace did not last long, however, and on 23 November 1407, Louis was assassinated on his 'friend's' order. Nevertheless, it would not do justice to the peace ritual to interpret it as merely a means of publication or stage play of reconciliation: if we follow le Bel, contemporaries might have seen it as an effective attempt to create real harmony.

The same applies to those meetings between kings or noblemen which happened in an atmosphere of general mistrust.[87] Often enough, their protagonists were protected from each other by special installations whose existence could only pervert the intended symbolic message. According to the chronicler Philippe de Commynes, when Louis XI met Edward IV in 1475 near Picquigny, a wooden bridge was built with a massive barrier to separate the two kings. In spite of these security measures, the construction was equipped with holes to allow the protagonists to stick their arms through to the other side and to touch each other.[88] On other occasions, the barriers allowed more intense contact like an embrace or a kiss. Those gestures evidently had a demonstrative character, expressing the harmony between the protagonists to themselves and to the bystanders. At the same time, and a text like the *Ars d'amours* makes this clear, they were believed to have a real effect on the emotional disposition of the protagonists.

God's participation in these events seems rather discrete. The chroniclers rarely mentioned his influence in these instances, but rather referred to emotions, as they did so often in their descriptions of human activities.[89] Does the end of the Middle Ages thus represent the breakthrough of profanity? Only to a certain extent, since a new kind of sacrality was on its way, this time arising out of humanity itself. A fifteenth-century treatise on friendship exemplifies this development.[90] Starting out with a series of definitions, including St Augustine's adaptation of Cicero, it goes on with the duties of friendship, the distinction between friends and flatterers and so on, declaring virtue to be the foundation of true friendship and reproducing the system of Aristotelian theory. What makes this text valuable, however, is its attempt to vulgarize existing theories about friendship, making them accessible to a broader public of noblemen for didactic purposes.[91] It is thus interesting to note that the presentation also contains surprising innovations. One of the most extraordinary appears in the justification of individual preferences in the choice of partners: asking why he prefers one individual to another, he explicitly denies the usual reasonings about the partner's virtue or the like, just to acknowledge that there was no other valid answer than 'because he pleases me':

> for anything he does, we might ask the reason why man might be moved to do it, except for matters of friendship. If one asks me why I love one man more than another, even if I could answer that it was

for his virtues or for another reason, the principal answer would still
be nothing else than to say that he pleases me, mainly because the
beginning and the reason which moves me is my will, because I want
to love him.[92]

Such an emphatic exclamation is ambiguous. Seen from the twelfth
century's perspective, it certainly represents a climax in the evolution
towards the profane. The reason of attraction is located inside the
partner's person and no longer depends on divine influence. At the
same time, a new kind of sacrality emerges, which perceives the human
being as the ultimate enigma and justification, creating a tension
between emotion and the ideal consecration to God.[93] In spite of
all counter-currents of tradition, does the confession of our anonymous
author constitute anything else than a step towards the monument
which Michel de Montaigne erected for his friendship to Étienne de
la Boëtie at the end of the sixteenth century? Montaigne stylized this
relationship as something extraordinary, extremely rare, and beyond
any rational explanation or exterior reason:

> But in the friendship I speak of, they mix and work themselves
> into one piece, with so universal a mixture that there is no more sign
> of the seam by which they were first conjoined. If a man should
> importune me to give a reason why I loved him, I find it could not
> otherwise be expressed than by making answer: because it was he,
> because it was I.[94]

It seems that he invested with a new kind of sacrality the tradition of
friendship which had for a long time oscillated between a spiritual orientation and human needs, thereby illustrating how it became possible in
the sixteenth century to develop a concept of friendship that was at
once based in this world and transcended it. The mystery was no longer
God's presence in human relations but the irrational parts of the latter.

Due to the 'profane' elements that remain, we may conclude that
Montaigne's theories represented (paradoxically enough) an important
step towards our modern and at least superficially rationalized perception.
He elevated his relationship with de la Boëtie to the rank of something
extraordinary by declaring it to be the result of a most rare coincidence,
something that occurred every three hundred years at best.[95] All that
could thus have been left to the intermediary centuries would be only
common or vulgar friendships that hardly earned the name – but
formed the largest part of human society.

This brief overview has only given some examples for what might constitute a general trend. Even if authors before the twelfth century recognized the importance of human emotionality and the profane aspects of interpersonal relations, they did not accord them a systematic place in their discursive universe. In a paradoxical development, profane aspects were increasingly expressed from the twelfth century onwards. Yet they did not replace the older and more intensively spiritualized concepts, but rather created a sphere where alternative options could take shape, by adding a new layer to an established discourse. In the end, 'profane' elements formed the basis for a new kind of spiritualization that went hand in hand with the emancipation of man in an increasingly secularized world. Bray's work convincingly showed how the role of friendship underwent major changes in the seventeenth century, implicating at the same time long-lasting stability in the premodern epoch. It is tempting to think that the phenomenon he described in such an inspiring manner was itself the product of the slow process of formation we have tried to outline.

Notes

The present contribution is an abridged version of a lecture given at the University of Bern (Switzerland), based on parts of my doctoral dissertation 'Freundschaft und Nähe im spätmittelalterlichen Burgund. Studien zum Spannungsfeld von Emotion und Institution' (Dresden/Paris PhD dissertation, 2004), in which I analysed in more detail the history of the philosophical and literary discourse about friendship in the late Middle Ages.

I wish to thank Paul A. Nielson (University of Berne) for his comments and corrections of the English text.

1. M. Wollstonecraft, *A Vindication of the Rights of Woman* [1792], ed. C.H. Poston (New York/London: W.W. Norton, 1988), p. 30.
2. Thomas Aquinas readily uses the concept of friendship (*amicitia*) in his discussion of marriage, see idem, *Summa contra gentiles*, ed. K. Allgaier, 4 vols (Darmstadt: WBG, 2001), book 3, questions 123–5 – only one of many examples for the far-reaching interchangeability of the concepts *amor, caritas, dilectio* and *amicitia*; see K. van Eickels, 'Kuss und Kinngriff, Umarmung und verschränkte Hände. Zeichen personaler Bindung und ihre Funktion in der symbolischen Kommunikation des Mittelalters', in J. Martschukat and S. Patzold (eds), *Geschichtswissenschaft und »performative turn«. Ritual, Inszenierung und Performanz vom Mittelalter bis zur Neuzeit* (Cologne/Vienna/Weimar: Böhlau, 2003), pp. 133–59, on pp. 135f.
3. *When Harry met Sally*, director R. Reiner, MGM 1989; cf. G. Meilaender, 'When Harry and Sally read the *Nicomachean Ethics*: Friendship between Men and Women', in L.S. Rouner (ed.), *The Changing Face of Friendship* (Notre Dame: University Press of Notre Dame, 1994), pp. 183–96; *Der grosse Brockhaus*,

12 vols (Wiesbaden: Brockhaus, 1954), 4: 290; *Duden. Das grosse Wörterbuch der deutschen Sprache*, ed. Dudenredation, 9 vols (Mannheim, Vienna and Zürich: Bibliographisches Institut, 1976), 2: 900f. On French 'amitié', see H. Legros, 'Amitié, féodalité, liens de parenté dans les chansons de geste d'oc et d'oil au XIIe siècle', 3 vols (Aix-en-Provence, PhD dissertation, 1993), 1: 15–24; in spite of certain exceptions, the OED explains that *friend* was 'not ordinarily applied to lovers or relatives' (s.v. *friend*, n., 1.a.).

4. Cf. C.S. Lewis, 'The Four Loves' [1960], in P. Blosser and M.C. Bradley (eds), *Friendship. Philosophic Reflections on a Perennial Concern* (Landham, NY, and Oxford: University Press of America, 1997), pp. 289–304.

5. A. Bray, *The Friend* (Chicago/London: Chicago University Press, 2003).

6. Ibid., pp. 140–76; A. Bray and M. Rey, 'The Body of the Friend: Continuity and Change in Masculine Friendship in the Seventeenth Century', in T. Hitchcock and M. Cohen (eds), *English Masculinities 1660–1800* (London and New York: Longman, 1999), pp. 65–84. On gestures in the Middle Ages see J.-Cl. Schmitt, *La raison des gestes dans l'occident médiéval* (Paris: Gallimard, 1990), and J.A. Burrow, *Gestures and Looks in Medieval Narrative* (Cambridge: Cambridge University Press, 2002).

7. For an overview on recent developments and further reading see *Placing Friendship in Context*, ed. R.G. Adams and G. Allan (Cambridge: Cambridge University Press, 1998); F.R. Santos, *Amigos y redes socials. Elementos para una sociologia de la amistad* (Madrid: Siglo Veintiuno, 1994); cf. the critical assessment by M. Eve, 'Is Friendship a Sociological Topic?', *Archives Européennes de Sociologie*, 43 (2002), 386–409.

8. M. Eliade, *The Sacred and the Profane. The Nature of Religion*, trans. W.R. Trask (New York: Harcourt Brace, 1959); cf. D.J. Farace, 'The Sacred-profane Dichotomy. A Comparative Analysis of its Use in the Work of Emile Durkheim and Mircea Eliade, as far as Published in English' (Utrecht PhD dissertation, 1982), esp. pp. 2–10; W. Gantke, *Der umstrittene Begriff des Heiligen. Eine problemorientierte religionswissenschaftliche Untersuchung* (Marburg: Diagonal, 1998).

9. W. Gantke, 'Profan', *Lexikon für Theologie und Kirche* (3rd edn), 8: 613.

10. Cf. P. Berger and T. Luckmann, *The Social Construction of Reality* (New York: Doubleday, 1966); see also Gantke, *Der umstrittene Begriff* (n. 8), pp. 229–31.

11. Cf. Bray and Rey, 'The Body' (n. 6), pp. 79–83.

12. See, however, A. Hochschild, *The Managed Heart* (Berkeley and Los Angeles: California University Press, 1983), and her concept of 'emotional work', which unfortunately does not provide a basis for an essential comparison across cultural or historical ruptures; cf. B.H. Rosenwein (ed.), 'Controlling Paradigms', *Anger's Past. The Social Uses of an Emotion in the Middle Ages* (Ithaca and London: Cornell University Press, 1998), pp. 233–47.

13. The psychoanalytical approach is largely discredited nowadays, in spite of the attraction exerted by pioneering articles of Lucien Febvre ('La sensibilité et l'histoire. Comment reconstituer la vie affective d'autrefois?', *Annales d'Histoire Sociale*, 3 (1941), 5–20) and Jean Leclercq ('Modern Psychology and the Understanding of Medieval People', *Cistercian Studies*, 11 (1976), 269–89).

14. Cf. J. Haseldine (ed.), *Friendship in Medieval Europe* (Stroud: Sutton, 1999) (with supplementary bibliography: pp. 275–7). Current interest in friendship is also reflected by recent anthologies, e.g. K.-D. Eichler (ed.), *Philosophie der*

Freundschaft (Leipzig: Reclam, 1999); J. Follon and J. McEvoy (eds), *Sagesses de l'amitié*, 2 vols (Fribourg and Paris: Ed. du Cerf, 1997–2003); Bloser and Bradley (eds), *Friendship* (n. 4).

15. Plato, 'Symposium', *Lysis. Symposium. Gorgias*, ed. and trans. W.R.M. Lamb (Cambridge, Mass., and London: Loeb, 1925), pp. 73–245.

16. Plato, 'Phaedrus', *Eutyphro. Apology. Crito. Phaedo. Phaedrus*, ed. and trans. H.N. Fowler (Cambridge, Mass., and London: Loeb, 1914), pp. 405–579.

17. Plato, 'Symposium' (n. 15), pp. 133–47; cf. also his *Lysis* on friendship, see Plato, *Lysis*, trans. and comm. M. Bordt (Göttingen: Vandenhoeck und Ruprecht, 1998).

18. Cf. for a brief summary A.W. Price, *Love and Friendship in Plato and Aristotle* (Oxford: Clarendon Press, 1989).

19. Cf. J. McEvoy, 'Philia and Amicitia: The Philosophy of Friendship from Plato to Aquinas', *Sewanee Mediaeval Colloquium Occasional Papers*, 2 (1985), 1–23, on p. 3.

20. Aristotle, *The Nicomachean Ethics* (*NE*), ed. and trans. H. Rackham (Cambridge, Mass., and London: Loeb, 1926); see J.-Cl. Fraisse, *Philia. La notion de l'amitié dans la philosophie antique* (Paris: Vrin, 1974), pp. 189–286 (for a concordance with the relevant passages in the *Eudemian Ethics* see pp. 280f.); F.M. Schroeder, 'Friendship in Aristotle and Some Peripatetic Philosophers', in J.T. Fitzgerald (ed.), *Greco-Roman Perspectives on Friendship* (Atlanta: Scholars Press, 1997), pp. 35–58; S. Stern-Gillet, *Aristotle's Philosophy of Friendship* (Albany: State University of New York, 1995); S. Tegos, 'L'amitié politique chez Aristote: un tournant anthropologique', in G. Samama (ed.), *Analyses & réflexions sur ... Aristote. Éthique à Nicomaque. Livres VIII et IX* (Paris: Ellipses, 2001), pp. 63–9.

21. Aristotle, *NE* VIII 1, 1 (1155a, 2–4).

22. Aristotle, *NE* VIII 1, 4 (1155a, 24–6).

23. Stern-Gillet, *Aristotle's Philosophy* (n. 20), pp. 148–61; G. Herman, *Ritualised Friendship and the Greek City* (Cambridge: Cambridge University Press, 1987), pp. 142–56.

24. Aristotle, *NE* VIII 12, 2–3 (1161b, 16–27).

25. Aristotle, *NE* VIII 3.

26. Cicero, *Laelius de amicitia*, ed. and trans. Robert Combès (Paris: Belles Lettres, 1983), cc. 20 and 47; cf. R. Sansen, 'Doctrine de l'amitié chez Cicéron. Exposé – Source – Critique – Influence' (Lille PhD dissertation, 1975); W. Suerbaum, 'Cicero (und Epikur) über die Freundschaft und ihre Probleme', in L. Cotteri (ed.), *Der Begriff Freundschaft in der Geschichte der europäischen Kultur* (Meran: Accademia di studi italo-tedeschi, 1995), pp. 136–67.

27. Sansen, 'Doctrine' (n. 26), pp. 446–51; D. Konstan, *Friendship in the Classical World* (Cambridge: Cambridge University Press, 1997), pp. 131–3.

28. See Ambrosius Mediolanensis, *Les devoirs*, ed. Maurice Testard, 2 vols (Paris: Belles Lettres, 1984–92), 1: 167 and 3: 132.

29. G. Glauche, *Schullektüre im Mittelalter. Entstehung und Wandlung des Lektürekanons bis 1200 nach den Quellen dargestellt* (Munich: Arbeo, 1970), pp. 102, 112.

30. R. Boussuat, 'Jean Miélot, traducteur de Cicéron', *Bibliothèque de l'École des Chartes*, 99 (1938), 82–124, on p. 97.

31. P.M. Gathercole, 'The Manuscripts of Laurent de Premierfait's Works', *Modern Language Quarterly*, 19 (1958), 262–70, on p. 270. The translation by Premierfait is still unedited; for an English translation of the prologue see R. Hyatte, *The Arts of Friendship. The Idealization of Friendship in Medieval and Early Renaissance Literature* (Leiden, etc.: Brill, 1994), pp. 209–26.

32. L. Laurand, 'Les manuscrits de Cicéron', *Revue des études latines*, 11 (1933), 92–128, on pp. 108 and 113–15.

33. Cicero, *Laelius* (n. 26), c. 27.

34. Cicero, *Laelius* (n. 26), c. 20: 'Est enim amicitia nihil aliud, nisi omnium diuinarum humanarumque rerum cum beneuolentia et caritate consensio'.

35. Augustine, ep. 258, 1 in J.-P. Migne (ed.), *Patrologia cursus completus, series Latina*, 218 vols (Paris, 1844–1905), 33; id., 'Contra Academicos', III 6,13, in *Patrologia Latina*, 32, col. 941; Aelred of Rievaulx, 'De spiritali amicitia', in id., *Opera omnia*, ed. Anselm Hoste and C.H. Talbot (Turnhout: Brepols, 1971) (=Corpus Christianorum. Continuatio Medievalis, 1), pp. 279–350, at I 11.

36. Matthew 22:39: 'Diliges proximum tuum sicut te ipsum'.

37. The Hebrew version is problematic, since the language has no precise notion to designate the friend, see K. Treu, 'Freundschaft', *Reallexikon für Antike und Christentum*, 19 vols (Stuttgart: Anton Hiersemann, 1970–), 8: cols 418–34, at col. 424; H.-H. Schrey, 'Freundschaft', *Theologische Realenzyklopädie*, 36 vols (Berlin: De Gruyter, 1976–), 11: 590–9, on p. 592. See further below, chapter 7.

38. Herman, *Ritualised Friendship* (n. 23), esp. pp. 130–42; idem, 'friendship, ritualised', in S. Hornblower *et al.* (eds), *The Oxford Classical Dictionary* (Oxford: Oxford University Press, 1996), pp. 611–13.

39. *Eran, stergein, philein* and *agapan*, their implications ranging from 'desire' to a vaguely defined 'affection'.

40. McEvoy, 'Philia and Amicitia' (n. 19), pp. 12–13.

41. H. Pétré, *Caritas. Etude sur le vocabulaire latin de la charité chrétienne* (Louvain: Université Catholique de Louvain, 1948); Reinhard Schneider, *Brüdergemeine und Schwurfreundschaft. Der Auflösungsprozess des Karolingerreiches im Spiegel der caritas-Terminologie in den Verträgen der karlingischen Teilkönige des 9. Jahrhunderts* (Lübeck and Hamburg: Matthiesen, 1964), pp. 54–75.

42. This reasoning was at the centre of St Thomas Aquinas' analysis in his *De caritate*, cf. C. Baladier, *Érôs au moyen âge: amour, désir et delectation morose* (Paris: Ed. du Cerf, 1999), p. 34.

43. Cf. Peter Brown, *The Body and Society. Men, Women and Sexual Renunciation in Early Christianity* (New York: Columbia University Press, 1988).

44. Cicero, *De officiis*, ed. and trans. M. Testard, 2 vols (Paris: Belles Lettres, 1965–70), 2: 69. Cf. S.N. Eisenstadt and L. Roniger, *Patrons, Clients and Friends. Interpersonal Relations and the Structure of Trust in Society* (Cambridge: Cambridge University Press, 1984), pp. 52–64; R. Saller, 'Patronage and Friendship in Early Imperial Rome: Drawing the Distinction', in A. Wallace-Hadrill (ed.), *Patronage in Ancient Society* (London and New York: Routledge, 1989), pp. 49–62; M. Peachin (ed.), *Aspects of Friendship in the Graeco-Roman World* (Portsmouth: Journal of Roman Archaeology, 2001).

45. S. Mratschek, *Der Briefwechsel des Paulinus von Nola. Kommunikation und zoziale Kontakte zwischen christlichen Intellektuellen* (Göttingen: Vandenhoeck und Ruprecht, 2000), pp. 293f.; cf. P. Fabre, *Saint Paulin de Nole et l'amitié chrétienne* (Paris: Boccard, 1949). On the minor role of 'Christian friendship'

during the fourth century see C. White, *Christian Friendship in the Fourth Century* (Cambridge: Cambridge University Press, 1992). Fraisse, *Philia* (n. 20), pp. 461–8, argued that Christianity put an end to the cult of friendship that was characteristic for Greco-Roman antiquity – a concept that has recently repeatedly been criticized: cf. V. Epp, *Amicitia. Zur Geschichte personaler, sozialer, politischer und geistlicher Beziehungen im frühen Mittelalter* (Stuttgart: Anton Hiersemann, 1999); Konstan, *Friendship* (n. 27).

46. See M.A. McNamara, *Friendship in Saint Augustine* (Fribourg: Fribourg University, 1958); E. Cassidy, 'Le rôle de l'amitié dans la quête du bonheur chez s. Augustin', in J. Follon and J. McEvoy (eds), *Actualité de la pensée médiévale* (Louvain and Paris: Ed. Peeters, 1994), pp. 171–201.

47. Aurelius Augustinus, *Confessiones*, ed. L. Verheijen (Turnhout: Brepols, 1981) (=Corpus Christianorum. Series Latina, 27), IV 8 (13).

48. 'Beatus qui amat te et amicum in te et inimicum propter te': idem, IV 9 (14); cf. McNamara, *Friendship* (n. 46), pp. 204–6.

49. Cf. Thomas Aquinas, *Summa theologiae*, II^a II^{ae}, question 26, art. 8, resp., using the notion of *amicitia caritatis*; see also n. 42. On the tension between universal love and specific friendships cf. Hyatte, *Arts* (n. 31), pp. 43–7, and B.P. McGuire, *Friendship and Community. The Monastic Experience (350–1250)* (Kalamazoo: Cistercian Pub., 1988), pp. xl–xliii.

50. On the author's life and work see M. Heinzelmann, *Gregory of Tours. History and Society in the Sixth Century* (Cambridge: Cambridge University Press, 2001). The text is edited with a German translation in Gregory of Tours, *Zehn Bücher Geschichten*, 2 vols, ed. Rudolf Buchner (Darmstadt: WBG, 1964) (=Freiherr-Vom-Stein-Gedächtnisausgabe, 3).

51. Gregory of Tours, *Zehn Bücher* (n. 50), VII 47 (=2: 152–7).

52. Ibid., IX 19 (=2: 256f.).

53. Cf. for later, analogous examples F.L. Cheyette, 'Suum cuique tribuere', *French Historical Studies*, 6 (1970), 287–99, and M. Clanchy, 'Law and Love in the Middle Ages', in J. Bossy (ed.), *Disputes and Settlements. Law and Human Relations in the West* (Cambridge: Cambridge University Press, 1983), pp. 47–67.

54. Cf. Bray and Rey, 'The Body', pp. 69f.; M. Aurell *et al.* (eds), *La sociabilité à table. Commensalité et convivialité à travers les âges* (Rouen: Publications de l'Univisité de Rouen, 1992); M. Aymard, 'Amitié et convivialité', in P. Ariès and G. Duby (eds), *Histoire de la vie privée*, vol. 3 (Paris: Seuil, 1986), pp. 455–99; G. Althoff, 'Der frieden-, bündnis- und gemeinschaftsstiftende Charakter des Mahles im früheren Mittelalter', in T. Ehlert *et al.* (eds), *Essen und Trinken in Mittelalter und Neuzeit* (Sigmaringen: Jan Thorbecke, 1990), pp. 12–25.

55. See Althoff, 'Charakter' (n. 54), p. 13; *Vita metrica S. Anselmi Lucensis episcopi auctore Rangerio Lucensi*, ed. E. Sackur, *Monumenta Germaniae Historica*, Scriptores 30: 2, pp. 1152–307, on p. 1224.

56. Roger of Howden, *Chronica*, ed. W. Stubbs, 4 vols (London: Longmans, 1868–71) (=Rolls Series, 51), 2: 318.

57. J. Boswell, *Christianity, Social Tolerance, and Homosexuality. Gay People in Western Europe from the Beginning of the Christian Era to the Fourteenth Century* (Chicago: Chicago University Press, 1980), p. 29; see also J.A. Brundage, *Richard Lion Heart: A Biography* (New York: Scribner, 1974), pp. 46, 256; for a critical assessment see K. van Eickels, *Vom inszenierten Konsens zum systematisierten Konflikt* (Stuttgart: Jan Thorbecke, 2002), p. 389.

58. P. Dinzelbacher, 'Pour une histoire de l'amour au Moyen Age', *Le Moyen Age*, 93 (1987), 223–40, on p. 227. On the other hand, the distinction between a pure *amor amicitiae* and a selfish *amor concupiscentiae* seems to have been established at approx. the time of the indicated changes, see R. Schnell, *Causa amoris. Liebeskonzeption und Liebesdarstellung in der mittelalterlichen Literatur* (Bern/Munich: Francke, 1985), p. 57, n. 220.

59. C. Morris, *The Discovery of the Individual, 1050–1200* (London: SPCK, 1972), pp. 96–120; cf. the critical reevaluation by C. Walker Bynum, 'Did the Twelfth Century Discover the Individual?', *Journal of Ecclesiastical History*, 31 (1980), 1–17.

60. [Roger of Howden] Benedict of Peterborough, *Gesta Regis Henrici Secundi*, ed. W. Stubbs, 2 vols (London; Longmans, 1867) (=Rolls Series, 49), 2: 7. On the author's identity, see D. Corner, 'The "Gesta Regis Henrici Secundi" and "Chronica" of Roger, Parson of Howden', *Bulletin of the Institute of Historical Research*, 56 (1983), 126–44; A. Gransden, *Historical Writing in England c. 550–c. 1307*, 2 vols (London and New York: Routledge, 1996 [orig. 1974]), 1: 222f. and 228f.

61. Van Eickels, *Vom inszenierten Konsens* (n. 57), pp. 410–12; on Aelred's predilection for David and Jonathan, see McGuire, *Friendship* (n. 49), pp. 321f.

62. See G. Hasenohr and M. Zink (eds), *Dictionnaire des lettres françaises. Le Moyen Age* (Paris: Fayard, 1992), pp. 56–7. The French version from ca.1200 is edited in *Ami et Amile: chanson de geste*, ed. P. Dembowski (Paris: Champion, 1969).

63. See esp. Hyatte, *Arts* (n. 31), pp. 122–33; another example is the triangular relationship between Lancelot, Galehoud, and Guinevra in the *Lancelot en Prose*, dating from around 1220.

64. Ibid., p. 124: 'In response to what God has willed from the beginning – nothing less than their indissoluble oneness – Ami and Amile place their friendship above human and even divine laws, which each disobeys for the sake of his friend's good.'

65. See e.g. Cicero, *Laelius* (n. 26), pp. 36–7; Valerius Maximus, *Facta et dicta memorabilia*, ed. J. Briscoe, 2 vols (Stuttgart: Teubner, 1998), IV 7, 1–2.

66. Cf. C.S. Jaeger, *Ennobling Love* (Philadelphia: Pennsylvania University Press, 1999), pp. 34f.

67. Cf. *Les chansons de Guillaume IX duc d'Aquitaine (1071–1127)*, ed. A. Jeanroy (Paris: Champion, 1972), pp. 25f. (Ab la dolchor del temps novel): 'Enquer me lais Dieus viure tan/C'aja mas manz soz so mantel!'; on the author, see the brief summary in *Dictionnaire des lettres françaises* (n. 62), pp. 592–5.

68. *Aucassin et Nicolette. Chantefable du XIIIᵉ siècle*, ed. M. Roques (Paris: Champion, 1977); cf. *Dictionnaire des lettres françaises* (n. 62), pp. 111–13.

69. 'Mais en infer voil jou aller, [...] mais que j'aie Nicolette ma tresdouce amie aveuc mi': *Aucassin* (n. 68), p. 6.

70. R. Schnell, *Sexualität und Emotionalität in der vormodernen Ehe* (Cologne, Vienna and Weimar: Böhlau, 2002), esp. p. 471; see also L. Otis-Cour, *Lust und Liebe. Geschichte der Paarbeziehungen im Mittelalter* (Frankfurt am Main: Fischer TB, 2000).

71. See n. 2; for a broader presentation see Schnell, *Sexualität* (n. 70), pp. 158–200; cf. van Eickels, 'Kuss' (n. 2), pp. 133–5, on Hugo of St Victor's theory of marriage.

72. 'Amicitia haec carnalium est [...] spe uberioris gratiae toleranda est, quasi quaedam amicitiae sanctioris principia': Aelred of Rievaulx, 'De spiritali' (n. 35), III 87. On Aelred see McGuire, *Friendship* (n. 61), pp. 296–338; idem, *Brother and Lover*. *Aelred of Rievaulx* (New York: Crossroad, 1994). Cf. Thomas Aquinas' distinction between *amor amicitiae* and *amor concupiscentiae* (idem, *ST* I^a II^{ae}, question 26, art. 4).

73. Aelred of Rievaulx, 'De spiritali' (n. 35), II 24: 'Est igitur osculum corporale, osculum spiritale, osculum intellectuale'. On gestures cf. n. 6.

74. This is typical of the twelfth and thirteenth centuries' revalorization of the physical dimension of existence, cf. K. Ueltschi, 'La chair et le corps: de la morale à la science', in B. Ribémont (ed.), *Le corps et ses énigmes au Moyen âge* (Caen: Paradigme, 1993), pp. 221–32. Cf. the perception of the relation between body and soul as 'friendship', see C. Walker Bynum, *The Resurrection of the Body in Western Christianity (200–1336)* (New York: Columbia University Press, 1995), pp. 329–34, and J. Baschet, 'Âme et corps dans l'occident médiéval: une dualité dynamique, entre pluralité et dualisme', *Archives de Sciences sociales des Religions*, 112 (2000), 5–30.

75. In a critical review, Schnell recently criticized Jaeger's analyses of 'ennobling love' (see n. 66) by referring to its mixing up of both concepts (cf. R. Schnell, 'Genealogie der höfischen Liebe. Ein kulturwissenschaftlicher Entwurf in kritischer Sicht', *Zeitschrift für deutsche Philologie*, 122 (2003), 101–17). Even if this is justified for the early or high Middle Ages, later centuries are definitively characterized by the blending which is outlined in the following passages.

76. P. Studer, 'Une définition d'amour en prose anglo-normande', *Mélanges de philologie et d'histoire offerts à M. Antoine Thomas par ses élèves et ses amis* (Paris: Champion, 1927 [repr. Geneva, 1973]), pp. 433–6.

77. Jehan le Bel, *Li ars d'amour, de vertu et de boneurté*, ed. J. Petit, 2 vols (Brussels: Devaux, 1867–9).

78. J. Thomas, 'Un art d'aimer du XIIIe siècle: [L'amistiés de vraie amour]', *Revue Belge de philologie et d'histoire*, 36 (1958), 786–811, on p. 799: '...amour est engenree par resgart, et resgars est li premiers degrés pour monter a le perfection d'amistié...' The text dates from c.1191/1200, on its authorship see ibid., p. 789.

79. Studer, 'Une définition' (n. 76), p. 435.

80. Ibid., p. 436; on the classical ideal of friendship see e.g. Epp, *Amicitia* (n. 45), pp. 7–16, 299f.; McGuire, *Friendship* (n. 61), pp. xxix–xl; J. Haseldine, 'Love, Separation and Male Friendship: Words and Actions in Saint Anselm's Letters to his Friends', in D.M. Hadley (ed.), *Masculinity in Medieval Europe* (London and New York: Longman, 1999), pp. 238–55, on pp. 240–6.

81. There is no real consensus about authorship; C. Potvin, 'Une énigme littéraire. Quel est l'auteur de Li ars d'amour, de vertu et de boneurté?', *Bulletin de l'Académie royale de Belgique*, II 47 (1879), 455–74, proposed to identify him with the Bishop of Utrecht, Jean d'Arckel.

82. Le Bel, *Li ars d'amour* (n. 77), 1: 33f.: 'Et quant li ami par nature li désirent à vivre ensemble et demorer, li vivres et li demorers ensemble samblent estre nécessaire al amisté. [...] Et encore il covient conpaignie et privance et vivre ensanle et demorer; car puiske li amis se doit pener de faire le plaisir son ami

et ce ke boin li est à son pooir, s'il n'est privés de celui par coi il sache son plaisir, sovent pora fere/chose ki li desplaira'.

83. '...ou baisier les deux choses plus jointables se joignent et un devienent, en mellant l'un avec l'autre: ce sunt les alaines des baisans [...] Dont il avient as baisans pour le perchevance de la jointure et del unité des cuers, laquele est ensi con sovrainement désirée, k'il ont en baisant si très-grand déduit, k'il sunt aussi come ravi et hors d'eaus meismes, [...] Li usages aussi communs nous moustre ke baisiers est signes de conjunction et d'unité de corages; car nous véons s'entre aucuns a eüt lontans rihote par guerre u par rancune, ke à le pais faite, on les fait entrebaisier, en signe de ce, k'ensi con lor alaines aspirituées se sunt entremellées, et lor corage par bone loïauté le soient. [...] Li acolers aussi est pour ce meisme quis, pour quoi li baisiers, selonc se manière; car al acoler joint-on volentiers le pis [=la poitrine] ensanle et s'estraint-on ensanle et près, por le conjunction et pour l'unité des cuers ki sunt desous le pis estraint segnefiier': ibid., vol. 1, pp. 164ff. On the symbolic and ritual dimension of the kiss see K. Petkov, *The Kiss of Peace. Ritual, Self, and Society in the High and Late Medieval West* (Leiden, etc.: Brill, 2003); W. Frijhoff, 'The Kiss Sacred and Profane: Reflections on a Cross-cultural Confrontation', in J. Bremmer and H. Roodenburg (eds), *A Cultural History of Gesture* (Ithaca and New York: Cornell University Press, 1992), pp. 201–36.

84. Cf. Bray, *The Friend*, pp. 146–50.

85. A systematic monograph on princes' meetings in the late Middle Ages is still a desideratum, W. Kolb, *Herrscherbegegnungen im Mittelalter* (Bern, etc.: Peter Lang, 1988), being far from satisfactory. For the French realm see P. Contamine, 'Les rencontres au sommet dans la France du XVe siècle', in H. Duchhardt and G. Melville (eds), *Im Spannungsfeld von Recht und Ritual. Soziale Kommunikation in Mittelalter und Früher Neuzeit* (Cologne, etc.: Böhlau, 1997), pp. 273–89; G.P. Marchal, 'Fehltritt und Ritual. Die Königskrönung Friedrichs III. und Herrscherbegegnungen in Frankreich: Eine Recherche', in P. von Moos (ed.), *Der Fehltritt. Vergehen und Versehen in der Vormoderne* (Cologne, etc.: Böhlau, 2001), pp. 103–38.

86. 'Fragments de la Geste des nobles françois', in A. Vallet de Viriville (ed.), *Chronique de la Pucelle* (Paris: Delahays, 1859 [repr. Geneva, 1976]), pp. 105–204, on pp. 111ff.: '...pour seurté de ferme paix, jurèrent les ducs d'Orléans et de Bougoingne fraternité et compaignie d'armes prindrent; et portèrent les ordres et les devises l'un de l'autre, et après leurs seremens faiz ès/mains de Monsieur Jehan de Montagu adonq évesque de Chartres sur les saints canons et la croiz par eulx touchez, usèrent le corps de Nostre Seigneur parti en deux; souvent, d'illec en avant, burent, mangèrent et couchèrent ensemble tenans toutes manières d'amour et bienveillance'. See van Eickels, *Vom inszenierten Konsens* (n. 57), p. 374; B. Guenée, *Un meurtre, une société. L'assassinat du duc d'Orléans, 23 novembre 1407* (Paris: Gallimard, 1992), p. 167; cf. M. Keen, 'Brotherhood in Arms', *History*, 47 (1962), 1–17.

87. The murder of John the Fearless in the presence of the dauphin at Montereau (1419) provided an extremely notorious case that was still referred to in the Treaty of Arras (1435) between Philipp the Good of Burgundy and Charles VII, cf. Enguerrand de Monstrelet, *Chronique*, ed. L. Douët-d'Arcq, 6 vols (Paris: Renouard, 1858–62), 5: 155–60. In his sceptical

reflections about personal meetings, Commynes cites Montereau as one of the most obviously disastrous examples, see Philippe de Commynes, *Mémoires*, ed. J. Calmette and G. Durville, 3 vols (Paris: Champion, 1924–5), 2: 60; cf. also Jacques du Clercq, 'Mémoires', in J.A.C. Buchon (ed.), *Choix de Chroniques et Mémoires sur l'histoire de France* (Paris: Desrez, 1838), pp. 1–318, on p. 174.

88. Commynes, *Mémoires* (n. 87), 2: 60. Commynes goes on with general reflections on direct encounters of princes and their potential dangers, thereby illuminating the conscience of these negative aspects.

89. See now Oschema, 'Freundschaft'.

90. Bibliothèque Nationale de France, Paris, ms. fr. 19128. For a critical edition see Oschema, 'Freundschaft', pp. 1*–82*; I am currently preparing the text of the treatise for a separate publication.

91. Ibid., fol. 32^r: 'Pour ce icelles exemples ay voulu inserer, car aucungs nobles se delictent a les lyre, affin que en les lisant il les entendent sainement en laissant la paille et prenant le grain'.

92. '... de toutes matieres on peut demander raison, pour laquelle l'omme peut estre meü a ce faire, fors en ceste matiere d'amitié. Se on me demande pourquoy j'ayme ung plus que aultre, combien que je puisse respondre que c'est pour ses vertus ou pour aultre cause, touteffois et principale responce qui y chest n'est aultre, fors dire qu'il me plaist, pour ce principalement que le commancement et la cause qui me meüt est mon vouloir, car je le veul aymer': ibid., fol. 19^v.

93. See B.P. McGuire, 'Jean Gerson and the End of Spiritual Friendship: Dilemmas of Conscience', in Haseldine (ed.), *Friendship* (n. 14), pp. 229–50.

94. *The Essays of Michel Eyquem de Montaigne*, trans. C. Cotton, ed. W.C. Hazlitt (Chicago: William Benton, 1952), p. 85; cf. J.-F. Chappuit, 'Cruauté et amitié d'après Montaigne et Shakespeare. Renaissance d'une théologie laïque' (Paris PhD dissertation, 1999), pp. 245–311; U. Langer, *Perfect Friendship. Studies in Literature and Moral Philosophy from Boccaccio to Corneille* (Geneva: Droz, 1994), pp. 164–76; M. Rey, 'Communauté et individu: l'amitié comme lien social à la Renaissance', *Revue d'histoire moderne et contemporaine*, 38 (1991), 617–25.

95. See n. 94; cf. D.E. Pozen, 'Friendship Without the Friend: The Many Meanings of La Boétie for Montaigne', *Comitatus*, 34 (2003), 135–49.

3
Friendship in Catholic Reformation Eichstätt

Jonathan Durrant

Introduction

The context for this chapter on friendship in the small Franconian prince-bishopric of Eichstätt is perhaps the least likely. It is the brutal imposition of Catholic reform at a time of demographic pressure and acute agrarian crisis with all the attendant consequences of those phenomena: high inflation, epidemic disease, vagrancy and increased criminal activity. These problems characterised late sixteenth- and early seventeenth-century Europe generally, but were compounded in the Holy Roman Empire by the very real threat of a war which was finally to engulf Germany in 1618 and much of the rest of the Continent over the next thirty years. Religious reform, agrarian crisis and warfare have all been cited by historians as contributing to an increase in social tension around 1600 which led ultimately to the destruction of inherently unstable communities which were unable to share declining resources among increasing populations. The rise of individualism has been regarded as both a product of this tension and an accelerant of the processes of social transformation, and the attempts to regulate welfare provision and scapegoat witches are frequently given as the symptoms of this decline in medieval communal life.[1] In this programmatic history, accounts of witchcraft can only be interpreted negatively and a great deal that these witchcraft narratives might otherwise tell us about the communities which suffered persecutions is lost, just as that same programmatic history has obscured from view the ritualised kinships that Alan Bray sought to recover in *The Friend*.[2]

In this chapter, I will argue that the witch-trial documentation from Eichstätt shows that there is little evidence that crisis did always lead to the abandonment of communal values. Rather, neighbours remained relatively solid in their adherence to one another, and this is demonstrated, in part, by their representations of their relationships with each other. The crises and reforms of the period failed to destabilise these local communities not because their inhabitants shared some vague common *mentalité*, but because they had been bound, often over several generations, by a series of overlapping ritualised kinships of the kind that – as Bray has argued – created friendship.[3] Rather than take apparently exceptional instances of these kinships as Bray did in *The Friend*, I want to highlight their existence among ordinary folk.

Catholic reform in Eichstätt

As witchcraft prosecutions have frequently been interpreted as the products of social dysfunction, it is important to place the Eichstätt persecutions in their local context. The death of Prince-Bishop Martin von Schaumberg (r. 1560–90) precipitated a period of political and doctrinal uncertainty in the principality which was only resolved at the election of the reformist bishop Johann Christoph von Westerstetten (r. 1612–37).[4] The new bishop acted quickly to assert his authority and reform the see, but two of his actions had a profound negative impact on his relationship with his subjects, especially those of the town of Eichstätt. Before Westerstetten had arrived to take up his post as bishop in the spring of 1613, his government published a decree banning the celebration of carnival.[5] Unfortunately, carnival was also the day on which the clothworkers in Eichstätt celebrated their crafts by processing around the streets during the day and drinking heavily into the night with their neighbours. They petitioned the chancellor who, in the absence of the bishop, backed down and allowed them to hold their procession, but they were not to carry weapons and a curfew was imposed from nine o'clock in the evening.[6] The right to process around the town at carnival was not, however, successfully reasserted by the clothworkers after Westerstetten's investiture.

The second event which set the reforming clergy against the citizens of Eichstätt was the renewal of witch persecution in 1617. Westerstetten had established a witch commission in the early years of his reign along the lines of the one which he had previously introduced into Ellwangen in 1611 when he was prince-provost there.[7] The prosecution of witches in Eichstätt was therefore taken out of the hands of the *Hofrat* (court council) which had been trying witch-suspects as felons, and placed in the hands of university-trained jurists who prosecuted witchcraft as a heresy. About 275 individuals were condemned to death on the authority of the new witch commissioners between 1617 and 1631.[8] On the face of it, this episode of witch-hunting would seem to fit Wolfgang Behringer's explanation of southern German witch persecution as the product of abnormal climatic conditions, hunger and fear.[9] The persecutions in Eichstätt seem to have taken place during an agrarian crisis which resulted in the death of perhaps a quarter or more of the regional population. Conventionally, modern historians of the persecutions, like Behringer, have assumed that in such circumstances ordinary people found themselves unable to assimilate extreme catastrophe within the wider context of their normal experiences and sought to resolve the material crises of these years through the mechanism of witch persecution. In Eichstätt, as elsewhere, they would appear to have been aided by authorities who saw the eradication of the witch sect as a means of reform. The situation seems to have been compounded by the news of war which had broken out in earnest in 1618.

This analysis is very neat, but does not stand up to close examination. Agrarian crisis, scapegoating and the impact of war had little bearing on Westerstetten's persecution of witches. The population of Eichstätt did not engage in the processes of persecution; they did not need such an extreme mechanism to deal with material crises, much less a metaphor, as Behringer argues, for the ills which beset them.[10] The conjunction of factors which allowed persecution is simply a chimera. The worst years of agrarian crisis, the late 1620s, coincided with a decline in persecution in Eichstätt.[11] What is more, the witch-suspects there did not project their fears of agrarian crisis in their confessions; not one defendant produced a convincing tale of weather magic, for example. More significantly, the disturbing atmosphere of suspicion and conflict which has been identified as a precipitatory factor in other witch persecutions does not appear, as we shall see, to be replicated in the Eichstätt case.

If witch persecution failed to set neighbour against neighbour in Eichstätt, one has to consider why. Catholic reform there (including witch-hunting) was driven by a desire to regain some of the territorial and spiritual losses of the Reformation. At that time the prince-bishop lost two-thirds of his territory to other rulers. By the late sixteenth century, 16 rulers, several of them Protestant, held territory within the diocese of Eichstätt, a largely rural area of just 6,000 km². The area ruled by the bishop as prince was dispersed across his see, and borders were fluid and constantly disputed. The situation was made more complex by the dispersal of fiefs within villages. The prince-bishop of Eichstätt was the principal ruler of Bergrheinfeld, for example, but several other Catholic institutions and Lutheran noble families also held fiefs in the village.[12] In the face of aggressive competing authorities, highly localised identities founded on extended ritualised kinships were more likely than religious, regional or corporate ones to bind the inhabitants of the fragmented communities in Eichstätt together against unwelcome migrants, ill-disciplined soldiers and disruptive priests of one confession or another. The social, cultural and political disruption caused by Catholic reform, rather than social dysfunction, is therefore the context for the following discussion of friendship in the prince-bishopric.

Stories of friendship

From 1617, the witch-suspects in Eichstätt were arrested solely on the basis of denunciations made by other witch-defendants which had accumulated against them during the course of the witch commissioners' investigations. They did not find themselves in custody because of an accusation made by a supposed victim of their malevolence. Likewise, under persistent questioning, threats and torture, the defendants in the principality did not usually denounce as their accomplices those with whom they had unresolved quarrels. Witnesses, too, failed to cite witchcraft, occasioned by social conflict, as the cause of the misfortune which overtook them or the alleged victims on whose behalf they were called to testify. The reason for this failure to engage in the processes of persecution lies in the actual quality of the relationships exposed in a distorted fashion in the witch-suspects' confession narratives. In the identification of accomplices, the suspects simply inverted their own essentially harmonious relations with their neighbours and kin.

In a few of the Eichstätt interrogations the witch-suspect was given the opportunity to comment on her relationships with her denouncers as their names were read out to her. An analysis of these suspects' reported commentaries has led me to challenge the commonly held assumption that witch-trials were symptomatic of social breakdown. Here I want to give my reading of the reactions of just one of the witch-suspects to the list of those who had denounced him.

On his first day before the witch commissioners (14 March 1628), after the customary questions about his personal life, Michael Hochenschildt was asked why he thought that he had been brought to the town hall. Like almost every other witch-suspect, he replied that he did not know, whereupon his interrogators read out to him the list of convicted witches who had testified against him. He claimed the following about his denouncers: that he had no 'knowledge' of Schweizer Casparin, Candler Bartlin or the Große Beckin; that he had always held Hans Baur for his good neighbour with whom he ate and drank; that he knew the Schöttnerin, the Amerserin and the Mosin, but nothing evil about them; that there was no reason why he should be angry with Thoma Trometerin, Anna Theirmayr and Anna Erb; that one time he had not been at peace with the Gelbschusterin, 'but it was no mortal enmity'; that he had caroused with the Langschneider several times, but did not otherwise keep company with him; that Haimen Enderlin was his neighbour; that Michael Rottinger was well known to him, but they did nothing together; that he could not report anything about Michael Girtenstihl; and that he could not say anything about the imprisoned Schmidt Appel because they also did not do anything together.[13]

Hochenschildt was quite clear about where he felt he stood socially with his denouncers. He made an important distinction, for example, between his relationship with Hans Baur and that with the Langschneider, Lorenz Brandt. His cordial relations with the latter stopped after a few drinks, perhaps in the tavern owned by Hochenschildt, and constituted what Alexandra Shepard has termed 'comradeship' in her chapter in this book. Those with the former extended further. Hochenschildt had apparently long held a good opinion of Baur, his 'good neighbour', and he attempted to show this by stating that they ate and drank together.

In Hochenschildt's deposition, therefore, eating and drinking assume importance as the defining activities of a close relationship which one might call friendship. He did not choose to illustrate the relationship with Baur by another activity, like the carousing which characterised his acquaintanceship with Brandt, or by citing, for example, mutual membership of one of the new lay confraternities. Eating and drinking were significant social activities by which neighbourhood, friendship and other associations were confirmed and maintained, but as they were used by Hochenschildt they should be regarded as relational idioms, part of the local restricted language code, and therefore a means by which the quality of the relationship in question, as it was perceived by one person at least, was expressed clearly to others.[14] It is difficult now to produce other evidence to confirm the relationship between Hochenschildt and Baur. Baur had been executed as a witch almost eight years before Hochenschildt's arrest and the trial transcript is no longer extant.[15] Hochenschildt did assert, however, that he had been seduced into the sect by Baur's late wife 15 years previously, which would suggest a long-term association with the couple.[16] Yet, the available parish registers show that neither man was strongly integrated into the community by the bonds of ritualised kinship.[17]

Baur and Hochenschildt were not the only men named as accomplices by witch-suspects under interrogation in Eichstätt. Several other men were named many more times, but escaped arrest. It appears that it was their relatively weak integration into the artificial male kinship networks which made Baur and Hochenschildt easy targets for the witch commissioners. Paul Gabler was, as we shall see, also accused many times of being a witch in these circumstances, but seems to have escaped prosecution because he sought out useful alliances through marriage and godparentage and rose to become secretary to the *Hofrat*.[18] Why were Baur and Hochenschildt unable then to embed themselves and their families deep within a wider, overlapping network of friendship?

Hochenschildt was a recent immigrant and the owner of a tavern, both of which may have contributed to a degree of marginalisation in the town, but his personality or reputation may have limited his fortunes, too. As both Alan Bray and Helmut Puff have observed, for example, contemporaries tended to conflate the sodomite with the heretic, and in the light of their observations one might reasonably ask if it is possible that these men were perhaps sodomites punished as heretic-witches instead.[19] It is certainly conceivable that one narrative obscured another to serve the same end: the elimination of traitors to the Catholic Church and the body politic joined together in the person of the prince-bishop. If this was the case, the authorities did not take the opportunity to resurrect the implied accusation at other points in Hochenschildt's interrogation. Sodomy did not provide the context of his seduction into the witch sect nor was he buggered by the Devil. One should note, too, that the eating and drinking described by Hochenschildt formed part of the symbolism of the gift of the body upon which Bray argues that friendship was created, embracing as it did here the sharing of a common table.[20] Whether or not Hochenschildt had a reputation for sodomy or being a bad neighbour, and despite his limited success in forming kinships in Eichstätt, he presented himself entirely in normative heterosexual terms.

I will return to eating and drinking below. Here, however, I want to discuss the term 'good neighbour'. The phrase occurs on one other occasion in the Eichstätt witchcraft material. On 30 August 1593, the Eichstätt council deliberated upon a report from the administrator of Hirschberg. In it he recounted that the wife of Jesse Vockher, a citizen of Berching, had borne a child which had subsequently died; she herself had gone mad. Suspicious of their neighbour, Vockher and his mother-in-law had sought the advice of a wisewoman, Magdalena Pößl, who inevitably confirmed that Georg Claßner's wife was indeed the perpetrator of the child's murder and the wife's illness. The authorities to whom this case was reported had just emerged from a period of witch persecution, but their decision did not reflect this experience. They observed that Claßner's wife was innocent and that there was 'good reason' to punish Vockher and his mother-in-law for this 'forbidden thing', that is consulting Pößl. The councillors chose, however, merely to admonish the parties from Berching 'to speak again as good friends and neighbours'.[21] To be a good friend and neighbour, therefore, was to live peaceably with one's fellow citizens. In stating that he had always regarded Baur as his good neighbour, therefore, Hochenschildt was trying to convey an image of social harmony.

The circumstances of Hochenschildt's response to the fact that Baur had denounced him also require analysis. Without the transcription of this response, Baur would have gone down in history merely as a witch, perhaps a little unusual because he was male. The record of Baur's execution alone might then have been used to shore up the façade of general witch panic assumed by many historians to prevail among local populations in episodes of witch persecution. As such a foundation, however, it proves flimsy. Baur's friend Hochenschildt retained an image of him as a 'good neighbour' and he had 'always' done so, even in the eight years since his death. He continued to do so even though he had discovered that Baur had been among the 15 witches by whom he had been denounced. The other denouncers fared equally well in Hochenschildt's analysis of his relationships with them; there is no sense in which he perceived them as witches, despite the confessions which had been extracted from them. I do not think that Hochenschildt was alone in this perception. One has always to bear in mind that not one of the Eichstätt witch-suspects for whom transcripts exist had been denounced to the witch commission by a supposed victim of her witchcraft. But the very fact that Hochenschildt could maintain that one of his denouncers was innocent of the crime of witchcraft in these circumstances, and that he could not say that the others were not (implicitly undermining the legitimacy of the commission's convictions), supports the interpretation of his relationship with Baur as being close.

Evidence from England further supports this interpretation. John Bossy has observed that 'good neighbourhood' had a long history of use in England, up until at least the late sixteenth century, to express 'the virtues of peacefulness'.[22] This seems to be precisely the meaning given to the similar expression 'good friends and neighbours' as it was employed by the Eichstätt councillors adjudicating the conflict between the Vockhers and the Claßners. Their conflict was not to be resolved through trial and punishment, but by returning to a state of peacefulness among themselves. Both the alleged victims and the defendants were made responsible for re-establishing the social equilibrium of their community and banishing the disruption to it which they were deemed, implicitly, to have caused. 'Good neighbourhood' was therefore the opposite state of social disorder, the world-turned-upside-down, heresy, witchcraft and sodomy. It was a corollary of the gift of the body of the friend and, like that gift, could be affirmed in the kiss of peace received at the Eucharist.[23]

Hochenschildt's relationships with his denouncers were therefore presented as either cordial or uneventful. It is against his evaluations of these relationships that one should appraise his confession that he had been in dispute with the Gelbschusterin. The quarrel occurred over a pair of shoes, perhaps repaired or made for Hochenschildt by the Gelbschusterin or her husband, and had apparently been resolved. Hochenschildt stated that he had *once* been in conflict with her; but he also judged that it was not a case of mortal enmity.[24] The Gelbschusterin seems not to have referred to any conflict with him in her own deposition.[25] In fact, this falling out apparently over someone's handiwork is an example of the kind of petty disagreement one should expect to find between neighbours in any community. It does not fit the pattern of conflicts which have been identified as producing accusations of witchcraft elsewhere in the early modern world. It did not turn on a refusal of charity, it did not arise at one of the important emotional events in life, such as childbirth, and it did not form part of some local factionalism.[26] The episode had not, therefore, become a source of deep and continuous disruption in relations between the two alleged witches.

By examining the responses to the denunciations laid before the witch-suspects, one can suggest that the population of Eichstätt was bound by a variety of generally cordial relationships. Occasionally individuals might come into conflict, sometimes irreconcilably, but together the defendants' statements about their relationships with their denouncers do not give the impression that this was a territory experiencing deep social crisis. If commentaries like those given by Hochenschildt offered the only accounts of personal relationships to be found in the Eichstätt material, then my discussion would be confined to the rhetoric of innocence. Statements like Hochenschildt's appraisal of his good neighbour Baur were made towards the beginning of each interrogation before torture had been threatened and as the suspect was trying to present herself as honourable and pious. Highlighting good relations with one's neighbours, alongside claims to piety, was part of a strategy to insist on one's virtue as a proof of innocence. Throughout their confession narratives, however, the suspects gave other indicators of the good quality of their relationships with their alleged accomplices.

Sharing food and drink

The idiom of shared meals recurs throughout the Eichstätt transcripts in narratives of communal or social activity which evoke the same intimacy that one encounters in Hochenschildt's description of his relationship with Baur. The suspects whose narratives will be the subject of this section were not, however, attempting to emphasise their innocence and piety. Rather, they were constructing the diabolical stories sought by their interrogators, and they were doing so after they had confessed to being witches. The social content of these narratives was therefore incidental to the diabolical content of the confessions as a whole; it was supplied to ground the fantastic stories of witchcraft activity in reality. The narratives were given substance by the local knowledge and gossip from which they were constructed, and show that the suspects retained a sense of inclusion in existing artificial kinship networks, rather than perceiving themselves as marginalised and alienated from them.

On the second day of her interrogation, 16 October 1626, after she had been tortured, Margretha Bittelmayr began an account of how she was seduced into the witch sect. About 15 years previously she had travelled from the town of Eichstätt to the neighbouring village of Weißenkirch for a wedding. She had journeyed with four companions, all of whom had, by 1626, been executed for witchcraft; they were merry and entered the village carousing because of the wine they had drunk.[27] The scribe did not record the reason why Bittelmayr then refused to continue the story, but the witch commissioners had her tortured again, after which she told a different story of seduction. Twenty-seven years before her arrest, Bittelmayr had sex with a servant, Anna, with whom she shared a bed at their employer's house. This experience, she claimed, helped her win the love of her husband Jacob, the town scribe, with whom she had lived for 26 years. It was in his form that the Devil came to fornicate with her, a deception that led to her joining the witch sect.[28] This alternative narrative conforms more to the conventional tale of diabolical seduction and the interrogators were evidently satisfied with it.

Bittelmayr's first attempt to tell how she was seduced into the witch sect is interesting because it is unconventional. Bittelmayr and her gossips were travelling together to an important communal event. They were enjoying the trip and their pleasure was enhanced by the consumption of wine. Although Bittelmayr could have developed this scene into a narrative of diabolical seduction, she would have had a problem in changing the mood of the story and separating herself from the crowd in order to create a situation in which she had become, quite abruptly, susceptible to the enticements and persuasions of the Devil. In conventional diabolical transactions, the Devil's power derived from his perceived ability to alleviate the disadvantageous financial or emotional situation in which the potential witch found herself. If a person was happy, slightly drunk and in a convivial crowd, the Devil had nothing to exchange for the individual's soul, happiness and fellowship here standing for a general contentment with life, just as being alone at the point of seduction stood for financial, emotional or moral vulnerability.

Bittelmayr offered the wedding trip as the context for her seduction because it had happened at the same time as she had already claimed that she had 'come into this vice'.[29] But why did Bittelmayr select particular individuals as her companions? By late 1626, almost a decade into this wave of persecution, she could have peopled her story with up to 127 other convicted witches.[30] In the context of the journey she described, however, Bittelmayr had to imagine, or remember, accompanying them, carousing with them and celebrating a wedding with them. It is more than likely that these women had participated in these activities together. The biographical information available for them would seem to confirm that Bittelmayr knew them intimately. The five women had all lived in the town of Eichstätt for most of their lives, even if they had not been born there, and they were members of the same class: Bittelmayr's husband was the town scribe; the Bonschabin married into an extensive, politically active family;[31] the Richelin was the wife of the former chancellor and a daughter of the councillor Leonhard Bonschab, and consequently related by marriage to the Bonschabin;[32] the Apothekerin would have been the wife of one of the men of this family of butchers, possibly the court butcher;[33] and Walburga Wölch was the wife of another councillor.[34]

Wölch was also associated with the stepdaughter of one of the Apotheker witches, Barbara Rabel, who included Wölch in the descriptions of her smaller gatherings. At one of these, this pair had gathered with three others in a garden where they had a great meal and attempted to use magic to harm their husbands.[35] On a second occasion, Rabel confessed that she, Wölch and two more women had conjured up three demons.[36] All of Rabel's female companions were wives or daughters of local councillors in Eichstätt, and such relationships between them and the other suspects, as well as their victims and the witnesses to their alleged crimes, can be multiplied several times.[37] It is also possible that in 1626 Bittelmayr and her fellow wedding guests would all have been in their early fifties.[38] Although the relevant records are missing or only fragmentary, I would not be surprised if the four companions named by Bittelmayr numbered among her denouncers too. Sex, residence, class, and possibly age linked these women. Given that the population of the town of Eichstätt was at most only 4500 at this time, and that between 1589 and 1616 there were about 45 marriages a year in the larger of the two town parishes, Unsere Liebe Frau, it is inconceivable that these women would not have celebrated such events together.[39] The journey to Weißenkirch may have been a partly fictional reconstruction of a real event designed to coincide with the date which Bittelmayr had given on the previous afternoon of her interrogation. The mood of the narrative, the camaraderie, had its origins in fact. And the intimate relations drawn on by Bittelmayr were expressed through the same idiom in which Hochenschildt had defined his close relationship with Baur, the sharing of food and drink, in this case the wine consumed on the journey and the anticipated wedding breakfast.

Bittelmayr's second attempt to tell of her seduction is equally interesting because of the description of tribadism: Anna had 'handled her and rolled around with her like a male person'.[40] The interrogators seem not to have known how to deal with this type of sexual act and did not pursue it.[41] But what should we make of it? It clearly sets the scene for the diabolical seduction which follows. Bittelmayr may, therefore, have been aware of its supposed sinful nature and its utility as a narrative device. She may also have deliberately cast herself in the 'correct' passive female role and reconstructed the sex act as an initiatory experience which allowed her to 'win' her husband in order to present herself in heterosexual terms.[42] What is more interesting, however, is the fluidity between same-sex and cross-sex experiences. Bittelmayr presented youthful sexual exploration as the precursor to a mature patriarchal lifestyle, but she did not do so because her sexuality had brought her to the attention of the courts.[43] She was trying to convey a terrible, almost unimaginable seduction and in working up to this told of other real seductions. Bittelmayr, it seems, was not culturally constrained by one sexual identity, at least at an early point in her life.

It may be the case therefore that the sharing of the genitals in Bittelmayr's narrative was part of the gift of the body of one friend to another (either the servant Anna or the husband Jacob), although the text is too brief to argue this conclusively. Likewise, we cannot know whether she shared her body with her later gossips in this way. Bittelmayr did, however, inhabit the world Alan Bray tried to uncover in *The Friend* in which same-sex relationships contained erotic and sexual possibilities whose realisation was neither sodomitical nor confined exclusively to homosexual desire.

Whatever the political possibilities opened up by the recognition of this space in the past in which sexual identity was less constrained by labels and normative practice, its implications for historians are profound. At the very least, the authenticity of normative patriarchal and heterosexual discourses becomes doubtful. The patriarchal world of early modern Europe forced ordinary men and women into institutions which were meant to guarantee survival and identity. When challenged to defend that identity or construct a new one (in Bittelmayr's case, as a witch), they usually resorted to the prevailing heterosexual discourse of their interrogators. That discourse could not, however, circumscribe the objects of erotic desire or its fulfilment. As Bray observed, the conventions of early modern friendship allowed friends to negotiate the difficult terrain between sharing bodies and kisses as acts of friendship and representing those acts in ways which might leave one open to the charge of sodomy.[44]

Of a less extraordinary nature than sex between women, the wedding feast (to which I will return) and the morally ambiguous drunkenness of one group of women were the meals and drinks which friends shared in their own houses. Valtin Lanng confessed to poisoning the beer and wine of up to six companions whom he had entertained in his house. His narrative contains two versions of the first case of such poisoning. Dr Hebich and the Hausmeister had been drinking with Lanng and become ill. As Lanng observed initially, this was because they had been drinking until two o'clock in the morning and when they left it was cold; it was a combination of drunkenness and the weather which had made the two men ill.[45] In the second version of this story retold under duress, Lanng confessed that he had tried to kill Dr Hebich by poisoning his drink, but had only succeeded in making him ill. The Hausmeister who shared the drink was not similarly affected. Whilst this story is about harm between neighbours, neither enmity nor witchcraft were mentioned in its telling (or in Lanng's other tales of poisoning). The first version of the story seems the most likely and here one is confronted with associations between men like that which Hochenschildt was later to describe between himself and both Hans Baur and Lorenz Brandt. One of Lanng's other drinking partners was the court saddler whom the Spitalmeister Hans Stigeliz stated, a decade later, drank with Georg Silbereis.[46] One might also note that Hans Baur was named early in Lanng's long list of fellow witches.[47] A feature of male friendship in Eichstätt was, therefore, the sharing of drink on many occasions in one's own home. Lanng simply took these real occasions and reconstructed them as attempted poisonings. In doing so he revealed his personal close associations with six other men from the same political and craft milieu.

Unlike Hochenschildt, Lanng was never given the opportunity to state that these men were his good neighbours, but in the context of early modern social behaviour this was unnecessary. As a series of recent studies have demonstrated, drinking bonded people and especially specific groups of men together. Alexandra Shepard's chapter on drink culture and male bonding in this book is the latest in this field. B. Ann Tlusty has argued that drinking traditions, especially as they centred on urban tavern, shaped and maintained social identity and personal honour.[48] Drinking rituals, their symbolic significance and the violence which might be associated with them have been analysed by Lyndal Roper.[49] And Alan Bray and Michel Rey have observed that sharing meals was a public display of friendship.[50] In each of these studies, drinking and eating symbolised the unity of the guild or the journeymen's association, or the sealing of business and marriage deals, as well as comradeship or friendship. These shared occasions were public and functional: they gave witnesses a visual referent, for example, in future disputes between craftsmen or families; and a public refusal to share meals or drink could mark a person out as irredeemably dishonourable.[51] One might, however, extend these analyses beyond the obvious public symbolism.

The drinking and eating described by Hochenschildt and Lanng were done in private. They had symbolic meanings only for the participants because there were no witnesses other than them. As Bray and Rey have noted of the great hall table rituals, whether in colleges or in great houses, 'Gestures of this kind did more than indicate bonds of friendship, as a signpost might indicate a town: they created them.'[52] The eating and drinking described by Hochenschildt and Lanng, and one might add Margretha Bittelmayr, were extensions of this public display. The individuals they ate and drank with in these private circumstances were people with whom they would normally have eaten and drunk in public. If public occasions created friendship in the rather formal terms defined by Bray and Rey and others, the private instances of drinking surely sustained and deepened that friendship. In this context, the stories of poisoning by Lanng seem all the more false and unlikely.

Witches' sabbaths

In Eichstätt, neither the witch commissioners nor the suspects referred to the witches' meetings as sabbaths. However the interrogators qualified the event, with the adjectives 'nocturnal' or 'diabolical', the witches of Eichstätt always attended a gathering, meal or dance. Whilst sabbath raises expectations of rites and ceremonies, a gathering is more ambiguous. All sorts of groups could gather together, witches in the case of the Eichstätt trials, the community on occasions like carnival, weddings or spinning bees, or men in the tavern or an individual's house. During an interrogation, this ambiguity left the term 'gathering' open to deliberate or genuine misunderstanding as the suspects sought to describe an event which they had never experienced.

If they said anything at all about when these witches' gatherings occurred, the suspects tended to place them at Easter, Christmas and Pentecost, the major festivals of the Catholic year when communal celebrations would complement the religious activities. Feasting, rather than liturgy, was the central feature of these occasions for the laity. It required organisation and co-operation to prepare venues, food and the activities associated with each feast. For a community, therefore, the preparations as much as the feasting helped to reaffirm the social integration of its members. It is important to bear this integrative function in mind when reading the testimonies of the witch-suspects. At the nocturnal gatherings the feast also assumes a greater importance for the defendants than the inverted liturgy of the Devil's heretical sect. There are very few references, for example, to kissing the Devil on the anus; and fornication with demons was only rarely mentioned. On the other hand, the participants usually claimed to have eaten good food, often fish (in central Europe, a staple food of festivities), and drunk good wine.

It is also possible that the issue of feasting and communal gathering was on the minds of the citizens of Eichstätt at this time. I have already outlined the confrontation between the clothworkers and the chancellor over the ban on the celebration of carnival and consequently of their crafts. One could, however, go further and argue that the prohibition on carrying weapons and the curfew of nine o'clock imposed as part of the compromise to allow the clothworkers to process in 1613 rendered these men politically impotent and effectively emasculated them. To carry a weapon was a symbol of citizenship and access to political power. In the context of the procession, it symbolised inclusion in the corporate body of the town. Without their weapons, the clothworkers, among the poorest of the male citizens of Eichstätt, were just a bunch of clothworkers, nothing more, meandering about the streets. Depriving them of the opportunity to seal the bonds of corporation (and perhaps friendship) by sharing drinks and liberality among themselves and with other men meant that the sorry display of solidarity may well have fizzled out as the marchers were forced to drift homewards.

It seems likely therefore that the families of the secular councillors had been thinking about feasting, gathering and its moral consequences in the period immediately prior to the witch persecution of 1617–31. Their thoughts had probably been sustained by attempts to lecture the citizens on the immorality of carnival and similar occasions from the pulpit as a supplement to Westerstetten's decrees. Clearly the chancellor had been concerned that the exceptional celebration of 1613 should not become violent (hence the ban on weapons) or continue into the night, as seems to have been common for such gatherings throughout Europe, notably in Romans in 1580.[53] These concerns were indirectly reflected in the witch commissioners' conception of the congregations of the witch sect, at once disorderly and nocturnal. The clothworkers and other tradesmen on the other hand were no doubt exercised by the denial of a procession that they had considered a right at a time of year traditionally associated with relaxed moral attitudes. When asked to think about the sabbaths, the Eichstätt witch-suspects, who were mainly drawn from craft and professional households, would have concentrated on those aspects which they missed in the banned communal gatherings: the feasting, dancing, drinking and gossip. It seems unlikely that they would have been concerned about the darkness which was supposed to characterise the witches' convents. At carnival especially the prolonged drinking and dancing would probably have been one of the attractions.

Descriptions of feasting at the nocturnal gatherings were in fact much more orderly than one would expect from contemporary portrayals of them. Margretha Bittelmayr described what each of her 30 accomplices had done at their gatherings. Almost all 'ate and drank' or 'did everything that the others did', but there were some deviations from these accounts.[54] As well as eating and drinking, the Kuchenschreiberin, Grafencker, the cleric Jacob Nick and Peter Porzin all made merry; Michael Girtenstihl, on the other hand, had 'vexed' people at the feast. Only the Old Schleifferin was said to have indulged in fornication. On a practical level, three professional cooks prepared the witches' meals.[55] Although Bittelmayr did not mention it, Peter Porzin was twice referred to in the witch-trial documents as the 'Platzmeister' ('place-master'), once by Egina Penner and once by himself (without having been told of Penner's description).[56] A Platzmeister seems to have had some function ordering the celebration. What is one to make of these details? That three cooks prepared the food and Porzin kept order suggests that the Eichstätt witch-suspects imagined the nocturnal gathering as an organised, orderly communal activity. It was also a convivial occasion, the vexatious Michael Girtenstihl notwithstanding. Not only did Bittelmayr observe who among her accomplices had made merry, recalling her earlier evocation of happiness on the way to a wedding, but a previous witch-suspect Walburga Knab claimed that the gatherings were 'as if at a wedding'.[57] Margretha Hackspacher, too, stated that the witches sat at their usual places 'as at a wedding'.[58] It was, I think, a wedding or similar celebration that every Eichstätt suspect described to their interrogators in place of a gathering of the witch sect which they could not conceive of imaginatively. The diabolical elements of their confession found at this point were superficial and originated in the commissioners' questions.

If these narrative details were likely to be based on fact, what then should one make of more salacious excerpts from the suspects' confessions? For the most part they described paramours which took on forms appropriate to the class or profession of the alleged accomplice, but occasionally they adopted more curious shapes. Of the 22 suspects who named Paul Gabler among their accomplices, seven described his relations with real women in terms which were inappropriate for the married secretary of the *Hofrat*: he had danced with Anna Schrad who, as she confessed, had kissed him on the foot, revered him and fornicated with him; Waldburg Hörmann and Sabina Walch both said that he had danced or made merry with the executed Hofwachtmeisterin; Anna Maria Böhm confessed that she had sat next to him, chatted with him and then fornicated with him, whilst Veronica Brändl had only kissed him when she had sat by him; and he had sat next to the Biebl Lenzin, heads together, after which they had danced.[59] Among the accomplices named by Bittelmayr, the Oblaierin's paramour appeared in the form of Herr von Seckendorf; Barthlme Ging and his cook Ursl accompanied each other; and Jacob Nick 'gave his whole attention to Endres Halbmayr's wife'.[60]

One might dismiss the appearance of Ging with his cook as a normal event. It would not have been uncommon for employers and their servants to be seen discussing household management together, or even getting along socially. It is also possible, of course, that the cook was the clergyman's concubine. The other pairings cited above are more problematic. Seckendorf was a member of a Franconian noble family with well-established ties to all local cathedral chapters. The canons drawn from this family were too grand to have been mere parish priests or confessors, minor clerics with whom one would have expected the Oblaierin to have met frequently. In coupling the Oblaierin and Seckendorf, Bittelmayr was, perhaps, drawing on gossip, or her own suspicions, about the nature of this relationship.

This interpretation is given substance by the last inference of adultery. Elisabeth Halbmayr had been executed as a witch four years previously on 23 April 1622. Nick, the object of Bittelmayr's denunciation, escaped prosecution for witchcraft. There is no traceable close relationship between Halbmayr and Nick. They were not mother and son, for example, or master and servant. There was no good reason why Nick should have given his whole attention to her. Why then did Bittelmayr add this detail to her denunciation of Jacob Nick, a detail which, if true, was so strongly embedded in her memory of Elisabeth Halbmayr that it had not faded in the four years since her execution? The most likely explanation would seem to be that Nick and Halbmayr were associated together either in fact or in gossip. Whatever the true nature of their association, the language of Bittelmayr's observation suggests that she and perhaps her circle of gossips did not think that the relationship was entirely innocent. The same may also be said of the several sightings of Paul Gabler with other women.

Descriptions of accomplices at the diabolical gathering as wedding feast expose cracks in the image of social cohesion found in other contexts in which the witch-suspects spoke about the sharing of food and drink with their neighbours and kin. These cracks in local neighbourly relations did not, however, reflect a social crisis within the community itself. The strained relationships were not those which cut across the class or gender divisions separating the witch from her victim, and which were perhaps becoming untenable in the context of an emerging individualistic psyche. Rather, the relationships which were threatened were those between spouses, the Halbmayrs, the Gablers and the Schrads, and it was the adultery, real or merely supposed, of a husband or wife with someone of approximately equal social status which made those couples vulnerable to gossip. Whilst the potential political and economic consequences for the parties and households in these adulterous liaisons should not be underestimated, such impropriety is not indicative of a fundamental breakdown of local kinship networks.

Like the disagreement between Hochenschildt and the Gelbschusterin over a pair of shoes, adultery is a feature of social relations which one should expect to find in any early modern community. The few suggestions of adultery do not appear in the denunciations of the witches' accomplices because mention of this sin reinforced the accusation – in the case of adultery, predisposing the sinner to seduction by the Devil (which involved fornicating with him). They appear because larger communal gatherings allowed amorous couples to get together. In normal circumstances men like Michael Hochenschildt or Valtin Lanng drank with other men; women like Margretha Bittelmayr drank with their gossips. The wedding feast, however, allowed men and women to mix together, and their conversations and flirting were aided by the festive atmosphere. For some couples, whether they were courting or adulterous, communal gatherings afforded the opportunity to get to know each other better than they could in everyday situations where the routines of the household and the constant proximity of other household members might inhibit the development of intimate relationships. But by taking their relationships further at a celebration, couples risked exposing their feelings and becoming the subject of gossip. When the witch-suspects were listing their accomplices, they named those whom they would normally have expected to see at a wedding or similar communal event, and in this context the gossip which had attached itself to certain individuals found its way into the descriptions of others incidentally rather than consciously.

Conclusion

In *The Friend*, Alan Bray argues that there existed before about 1650 diverse forms of kinship originating in blood-ties, promises, oaths, rituals, nature and love. The effect of this diversity 'was to embed the family, in the more narrow sense of a group of parents and their children, within a wider and overlapping network of friendship. That', he stated, 'has been my argument.'[61] There is a danger that in viewing Bray's work solely through the prism of his sexual politics, this argument will be lost. It is important to acknowledge this political aspect of his work, but for me the utility of *The Friend* lies in the discussion of kinships and the networks of friendship they could create. Beyond the sharing of food, drink and beds and the formal rituals which marked incorporation into all early modern institutions from the household to the church, the people discussed in this chapter probably gave little thought to the expression of their intimate friendships. Yet the kinships and friendships which they did develop found expression in the witch-suspects' confession narratives.

They did so because they were integral to the survival of a community facing agrarian crisis, a witch persecution imposed by an aggressively reformist clergy and, soon after, in 1634, the total destruction of their homes by the Swedes. These same kinships and friendships helped individuals to ground the fantastic stories of diabolical seductions and sabbaths they were forced to tell their interrogators in the reality of ordinary sexual activities and ordinary communal gatherings. They also helped them to retain a sense of identity in the face of denunciations which they knew had been extracted from their neighbours by torture.

Notes

1. The classic accounts of scapegoated witches are A. Macfarlane, *Witchcraft in Tudor and Stuart England: A Regional and Comparative Study*, 2nd edn (London: Routledge, 1999), and K. Thomas, *Religion and the Decline of Magic* (1971; repr. Harmondsworth: Penguin, 1991).
2. A. Bray, *The Friend* (Chicago: Chicago University Press, 2003), pp. 307–23.
3. Ibid., p. 214.
4. Jonathan Durrant, 'Witchcraft, Gender and Society in the Early Modern Prince-bishopric of Eichstätt' (PhD thesis, University of London, 2002), pp. 13–20.
5. Staatsarchiv Nürnberg (hereafter StAN), *Hochstift Eichstätt Literalien* 59, 'Kopialbuch, die unter Bischof Martin und seinen Nachfolgen erlassenen Generalbefehle und Ausschreibungen enthaltend. 1457–1626', fol. 349ᵛ, 'Verbott der Fastnacht alhie zu Eÿstett...1613'.
6. Ibid., fol. 350ʳ, 'Erlaubtnuß der Fastnacht alhie zu Eÿstett Anno 1613'.
7. On Ellwangen, see H.C.E. Midelfort, *Witch Hunting in Southwestern Germany 1562–1684: The Social and Intellectual Foundations* (Stanford, Ca.: Stanford University Press, 1972), pp. 98–115, 212–14. This witch commission had more than 350 witch-suspects executed, 260 of them while Westerstetten was still provost.
8. Durrant, 'Witchcraft, Gender and Society', pp. 62–7.
9. W. Behringer, 'Weather, Hunger and Fear: Origins of the European Witch Hunts in Climate, Society and Mentality', *German History*, 13 (1995), 1–27.
10. Durrant, 'Witchcraft, Gender and Society', pp. 69–86.
11. Ibid., pp. 298–303.
12. L. Weiss, 'Reformation und Gegenreformation in Bergrheinfeld', *Würzburger Diözesangeschichtsblätter*, 43 (1981), 283–341.

13. StAN, *Hexenakten* 45 (M. Hochenschildt), 14 March 1628.

14. On relational idioms, see H. Medick and D. Sabean (eds), *Interest and Emotion: Essays on the Study of Family and Kinship* (Cambridge: Cambridge University Press, 1984), pp. 1–8.

15. Baur was executed on 22 August 1620, Diözesanarchiv Eichstätt (hereafter DiöAE), 'Urfehdebuch 1603–20. August 1627', fols 187r–v.

16. StAN, *Hexenakten* 45 (M. Hochenschildt), 15 March 1628.

17. Franz Xaver Buchner's research shows that Hochenschildt and his wife Eva had migrated into Eichstätt in about 1611, 'Eichstätter Familienbuch 1589–1618', p. 176. No children were born to them after that date. Before 1618, Michael became a godfather of one child (ibid., p. 85) and witnessed one marriage (ibid., p. 374); Eva was twice appointed a godmother over the same period (ibid., pp. 172, 258).

18. Gabler migrated to Eichstätt in January 1594 at the earliest. He and his wife Anna Maria were godparents to over a dozen children (ibid., pp. 127, 343, 404). Anna Maria was the daughter of a town provost, and the witnesses to her marriage to Gabler and the godparents to their 14 children were drawn from the most important families and religious institutions in the town (ibid., p. 127).

19. A. Bray, *Homosexuality in Renaissance England*, 2nd edn (New York: Columbia University Press, 1995), p. 19, and H. Puff, *Sodomy in Reformation Germany and Switzerland 1400–1600* (Chicago: Chicago University Press, 2003), pp. 22–5.

20. Bray, *The Friend*, p. 268.

21. StAN, *Hochstift Eichstätt Literalien* 298, fol. 131r.

22. J. Bossy, 'Blood and Baptism: Kinship, Community and Christianity in Western Europe from the Fourteenth to the Seventeenth Centuries', in D. Baker (ed.), *Sanctity and Secularity: The Church and the World* (Oxford: Blackwell, 1973), pp. 129–43, on pp. 142–3.

23. Bray, *The Friend*, p. 90.

24. StAN, *Hexenakten* 45 (M. Hochenschildt), 14 March 1628.

25. At least, Hochenschildt's interrogators did not make reference back to the Gelbschusterin's testimony which, unfortunately, no longer exists.

26. On the refusal of charity or other social obligation, see, for example, Macfarlane, *Witchcraft in Tudor and Stuart England*; on conflict around childbirth, see L. Roper (ed.), 'Witchcraft and Fantasy in Early Modern Germany', *Oedipus and the Devil: Witchcraft, Sexuality and Religion in Early Modern Europe* (London: Routledge, 1994), pp. 199–225; and on local factionalism and witchcraft, see A. Gregory, 'Witchcraft, Politics and "Good Neighbourhood" in Early Modern Rye', *Past and Present*, 133 (1991), 31–66.

27. StAN, *Hexenakten* 45 (M. Bittelmayr), 16 October 1626.

28. Ibid.

29. Ibid., 15 October 1626.

30. Durrant, 'Witchcraft, Gender and Society', p. 299.

31. Three female Bonschabs were executed before 1626: Anna on 20 December 1617; Kunigunda on 16 February 1618; and Barbara on 10 April 1620 (DiöAE, 'Urfehdebuch', fols 134^r–135^r, 136^{r-v}, 142^v–143^v, 145^v–146^r, 182^v–183^r). Barbara Rom (known as the Bonschabin) was executed on 15 May 1620 (ibid., fols 183^{r-v}).

32. Maria Richel was the wife of Bartholomäus Richel, chancellor of Eichstätt until 1623; she was arrested for witchcraft in 1620, BundesA ASt Frankfurt *FSg.2/1-F 13* 669 (Eichstätt L–Z), frames 92–3.

33. Two of the Apothekers caught up in the persecutions had been executed before 1626: Barbara on 21 March 1620; and Eva on 23 March 1624 (DiöAE, 'Urfehdebuch', fols 181^{r-v} and 214^v–215^r). A third, also called Barbara, was executed with Bittelmayr on 20 November 1626, ibid., fol. 229^r. The first Barbara Apotheker had married the court butcher Adam Apotheker, StAN, *Hexenakten* 48 (B. Apotheker), 3 February 1620 (a.m.). Their daughter Eva also married a butcher, Caspar Apotheker, Buchner, 'Eichstätter Familienbuch', p. 42. The later Barbara Apotheker had also married into the same family, ibid., pp. 41–2.

34. Wölch was executed on 27 November 1620, DiöAE, 'Urfehdebuch', fols 191^v–192^r.

35. StAN, *Hexenakten* 48 (B. Rabel), 5 October 1618 (a.m.).

36. Ibid., 11 October 1618 (a.m.).

37. Durrant, 'Witchcraft, Gender and Society', pp. 180–1.

38. This would depend on which of the Bonschabs was the woman named by Bittelmayr. Not enough is known about Richel or Wölch at this stage to estimate their ages. Barbara Apotheker was about 45 in 1620, StAN, *Hexenakten* 48 (B. Apotheker), 3 February 1620 (a.m.).

39. Buchner, 'Eichstätter Familienbuch', p. 6.

40. StAN, *Hexenakten* 45 (M. Bittelmayr), 16 October 1626.

41. In a similar situation in Basel in 1647, the authorities argued against pursuing the 'sodomitical sin' between the alleged witch Elisabeth Hertner and a female cousin, Puff, *Sodomy*, p. 100.

42. Michael Rocke has argued that sexual roles in male same-sex relations in Florence and Venice were gendered and the punishment of sodomites depended on their age and role in the sex act, M. Rocke, 'Gender and Sexual Culture in Renaissance Italy', in J.C. Brown and R.C. Davis (eds), *Gender and Society in Renaissance Italy* (London: Longman, 1998), pp. 150–70, on pp. 167–70. This may also be the case in female same-sex relations.

43. For prosecutions of female sodomites, see Puff, *Sodomy*, pp. 31–4.

44. Bray, *The Friend*, p. 223.

45. StAN, *Hexenakten* 48 (V. Lanng), 11 May 1618 (a.m.).

46. Ibid.; and StAN, *Hexenakten* 45 (H. Stigeliz), 25 May 1628.

47. StAN, *Hexenakten* 48 (V. Lanng), 11 May 1618 (a.m.).

48. B.A. Tlusty, *Bacchus and the Civic Order: The Culture of Drink in Early Modern Germany* (Charlottesville, VA: University of Virgina Press, 2001).

49. L. Roper (ed.), 'Blood and Codpieces: Masculinity in the Early Modern Town', and 'Drinking, Whoring and Gorging: Brutish Indiscipline and the Formation of Protestant Identity', *Oedipus and the Devil*, pp. 107–24 and 145–67 respectively.

50. A. Bray and M. Rey, 'The Body of the Friend: Continuity and Change in Masculine Friendship in the Seventeenth Century', in T. Hitchcock and M. Cohen (eds), *English Masculinities 1660–1800* (London and New York: Longman, 1999), pp. 65–84, on pp. 69–70.

51. See, for example, the case of the Württemberg pastor Georg Gottfrid Bregenzer, D. Sabean, 'Blasphemy, Adultery and Persecution: Paranoia in the

Pulpit (1696–1710)', in idem, *Power in the Blood: Popular Culture and Village Discourse in Early Modern Germany* (Cambridge: Cambridge University Press, 1984), pp. 113–43.

52. Bray and Rey, 'The Body of the Friend', p. 70.
53. E. Le Roy Ladurie, *Carnival in Romans: A People's Uprising at Romans 1579–1580*, trans. Mary Feeney (Harmondsworth: Penguin, 1981).
54. Egina Penner, for example, 'ate, drank and joined in everything', StAN, *Hexenakten* 45 (M. Bittelmayr), 29 October 1626.
55. Ibid., 29 and 31 October and 5–7 November 1626.
56. StAN, *Hexenakten* 45 (P. Porzin – denunciations), Item 13, and (P. Porzin), 18 September 1627.
57. StAN, *Hexenakten* 45 (W. Knab), 7 August 1621.
58. StAN, *Hexenakten* 49 (N.N. – denunciations), Denunciation 12.
59. StAN, *Hexenakten* 43 (P. Gabler – denunciations), Denunciations 11–13, 16, 18 and 20.
60. StAN, *Hexenakten* 45 (M. Bittelmayr), 31 October and 5 November 1626.
61. Bray, *The Friend*, p. 214.

4

A Society of Sodomites: Religion and Homosexuality in Renaissance England

Alan Stewart

> In the yeare 1632, there was discouered in *London* a Society of certaine *Sodomites*, to the number of fourty, or fifty; all of them being earnest and hoat *Puritans*, who had their common appointed Meeting-place, for their abominable Impiety: Of which number diuers of them (and such as were of good temporall estates and meanes) were apprehended, and the rest instantly fled.[1]

This remarkable paragraph opens a 1633 tract entitled *Pvritanisme the mother, Sinne the davghter*, attributed on its titlepage to one 'B.C.'[2] It is remarkable on at least two counts. First, it strikingly provides perhaps the only English allegation of the existence of a 'Society of . . . *Sodomites*' before the so-called 'molly-houses', flamboyant, often transvestite and sexual gatherings of men brought to light by the raids orchestrated by the Society for the Reformation of Manners at the turn of the eighteenth century.[3] For many scholars working in the early modern period it has now become axiomatic that sodomy was, in Michel Foucault's words, both 'a category of forbidden acts' and 'an utterly confused category';[4] and, following Alan Bray, that even individuals involved in acts legally defined as sodomy may not have associated themselves with the concept of sodomy.[5] Therefore, as Goran Stanivukovic has noted, this passage is 'curious' not only for the way in which it implies that the Society's members as early as 1632 'might identify themselves according to the sexual act they practice' but also for 'the concrete manner in which this early version of a space designated for urban sodomites and an early modern raid on them is imagined'.[6]

Second, and perhaps less obviously, the passage represents one of the few instances in early modern English in which the charge of sodomy is directed against a Protestant sect – since virtually all the religiously aligned accusations of sodomy in post-Reformation England are against Roman Catholics. As its title leaves little doubt, *Pvritanisme the mother, Sinne the davghter* is a virulently anti-Puritan text, published at a time when the fights between English Protestant sects were becoming ever more vicious. Its opening page provides 'The Occasions (lately occurring) of writing this Treatise': first, the apprehension of the puritan 'Society of Sodomites'; second, the scandal of Shropshire man Enoch ap Evan (here, 'Henoch A peuen'), a 'most fiery *Puritan*' who murdered his brother and mother with an axe, 'because both of them (being temperate Protestants) did some few dayes before, receaue the Communion kneeling' – the incident at the heart of Peter Lake and Michael Questier's book *The Antichrist's Lewd Hat*;[7] and third, the case of a minister named Cade, who announced to a vintner that 'he belieued there was *no Christ, no Trinity, no God*, besides other most blasphemous speeches' and that he practised his ministry simply to make a living; although the vintner reported Cade to the authorities, a Justice of the Peace, 'being a *Puritan*', set him free, claiming 'That what he spake, was spoken only by way of dispute and arguing', and not in order to persuade.[8] All three of these 'Occasions', then, are included because of the root of their evil is hinted to be Puritanism: the bulk of the tract (which may date from earlier) provides a genealogy of Calvinist evil as context for these recent events.

A great deal of work on sodomy in early modern England has commented on the association of sodomy with other illicit activities, such as treason, witchcraft, conjuring, adultery, rape, and heresy, and it follows that the supreme heresy of the period is Roman Catholicism. B.C.'s charge against a group of Puritans is therefore notable, but it could be argued, as Stanivukovic does, that 'the scenario only reverses the strategy often employed by the Puritans in associating Catholicism with sodomy'.[9] In this chapter, I aim to modify that assessment by proposing that the ways in which Puritanism and Catholicism were identified with sodomy were importantly distinct, and that it is no coincidence that Puritan sodomites are identified as a 'Society'. In so doing, I also argue that B.C.'s gambit is a useful corrective to the way in which historians and literary critics have accepted and to some degree naturalised the nexus of sodomy and Catholicism in early modern England. This is not, I shall suggest, merely a by-product of the Reformation's grasp on the English imagination; it also derives directly from the agenda of the most influential historian of sodomy in England, Alan Bray.

I. *Homosexuality in Renaissance England*

It is beyond dispute that the most influential study of sodomy in early modern England is Alan Bray's *Homosexuality in Renaissance England*, first published by Gay Men's Press in 1982, a short book of four chapters which did not merely contribute to ongoing debate, but created a new field for historians and perhaps even more strongly, for literary critics and text scholars. Bray's work was quickly taken up by established literary scholars such as Stephen Orgel, Bruce Smith, and Lisa Jardine;[10] through its appropriation by the likes of Jonathan Goldberg and Eve Kosofsky Sedgwick it became a founding text in the emergent field of queer studies;[11] and by the 1990s, Bray's book had sparked the work of such younger scholars as Valerie Traub, Jeffrey Masten, Gregory Bredbeck, and Mario DiGangi.[12]

Bray was an especially reflective historian, who believed in examining the motivations behind his own and others' academic work. The 'Introduction' to *Homosexuality in Renaissance England* made his primary motivation easy to detect:

> The impetus behind [the book] lay in the growth, in the years since the Second World War, of visible homosexual subcultures in the major cities of the western world, which in the last ten or fifteen years [i.e. since the mid to late 1960s] have become increasingly articulate and questioning. And the questions, on the level of the individual or the many, have largely meant asking Who am I? What then are we?[13]

This explicit agenda makes sense of the book's organisation. In the first three chapters of the book, covering chronologically the period from Reformation (or the transfer of sodomy to secular jurisdiction) to Revolution, it trawls the archives of local and state courts to reconstruct sodomy's legal status; it surveys the moralistic and satirical literature of the period to construct the 'sodomite' as a dangerous other, linked with heresy, foreignness, and the devil; and it tracks down numerous traces of sexual experience between men, located most often within patriarchal household relationships (master/servant, master/apprentice, teacher/pupil). Bray explains this apparent contradiction of endemic homosexual activity and endemic condemnation of homosexual activity not as 'tolerance' but as 'rather a reluctance to recognise homosexual behaviour, a sluggishness in accepting that what was being seen was indeed the fearful sin of sodomy'.[14]

By contrast, the final chapter, set in the late seventeenth and early eighteenth centuries, details the persecution of what appears to be a gay male subculture, the 'molly houses' of London. For Bray, the later period is importantly different. He ends his book with an account of a young man named William Brown who was arrested one summer evening in 1726 for committing an act of sodomy on the Moorfields, a popular place of resort near the City, the victim of an entrapment operation involving a known *agent provocateur* named Thomas Newton. When questioned as to why he committed the offence, Brown answered, 'I did it because I thought I knew him, and I think there is no crime in making what use I please of my own body.' For Bray, Brown's response is recognisably post-Renaissance, with its unrepentant assertions of agency, autonomy, selfhood and its physical desire ('my own body'). As he notes, 'It is not that William Brown's claim was any more acceptable in 1726 than it would have been in the England of [a century earlier]; but was not his defiant assertion that his body was his own now more credible, more symptomatic of his time?' To Bray, Brown is part of 'the appearance in England of a separate homosexual culture and a distinctive homosexual identity', which is in turn 'part of that far-reaching transformation which English society underwent in the course of the seventeenth century, a transformation which played its part in making the world in which we now live'.[15] While it is not made explicit in Bray's work what 'that far-reaching transformation' might have been, his model remains hugely influential.[16]

There is, however, another agenda to Bray's work which is less explicitly signposted in his book, and which became most apparent only after his death. Shortly after the publication of *Homosexuality in Renaissance England*, Bray converted to Roman Catholicism. This was not merely a matter of personal conviction, but also of political engagement: later Bray became the principal point of contact between Cardinal Basil Hume and Quest, the support group for homosexual Catholics in England. His academic work increasingly obsessed on the subject. In the late 1980s, while speaking at Cambridge University, he was taken to the chapel of Christ's College to see the monument commemorating Sir John Finch and Thomas Baines, the design of which linked the two men by a knotted cloth symbolising the marriage knot. This inspired Bray to explore the subject of male friendship, first in his seminal *History Workshop* article 'Homosexuality and the Signs of Male Friendship in Elizabethan England', and then in his second book *The Friend*, published posthumously in 2003. *The Friend* explores intense friendships between men in the Middle Ages and the Renaissance, with the explicit agenda of recovering the Catholic Church's previous endorsement of such friendships as quasi-marriages. Bray relished the controversy he knew his book would spark: speaking at a conference at Newman House in Dublin in July 2001, he took advantage of the venue to cause an uproar in the Irish press with his revelation of the joint burial of the Venerable John Henry Cardinal Newman and his friend Rev. Ambrose St John. The working subtitle of the *The Friend* (later dropped) might do service as the title of Bray's intellectual autobiography: *How Friendship, the Family and Religion Fell in Love.*[17]

Although his formal conversion took place after the writing and publication of *Homosexuality in Renaissance England*, there can be no doubt that Bray's growing interest in Roman Catholicism deeply impacted his first book. This can be seen in a short piece entitled 'History, Homosexuality and God' given by Bray in Oxford in 1986 at that year's conference of Friend, 'a national organisation dedicated to the counselling and befriending of homosexuals'. In it, he addresses an audience 'composed of those moral theologians and practical pastors who are troubled by the tension that exists between homosexuals and the Christian Church'. He acknowledges however that what he has to say is 'not equally relevant to all Christian churches', since there are some who are

> ready to construct their moral theology afresh, from the beginning. For good or bad they are free of the past. But for many Christians, in varying degrees, this is not a possible option, and it is fundamentally not a possible option for Catholics, for whom an appeal to scripture and tradition – a willingness to listen to the past – is unavoidable.[18]

The Catholic's 'willingness to listen to the past' had a nasty side-effect, however, since here was something 'somewhat surprising and in several ways disturbing' to be heard about early modern English society: 'for the great majority of men and women in Elizabethan and Jacobean England the sodomite – the word they used – was also very likely a papist'.[19] Bray had made this point before in his book. There he had quoted the jurist Edward Coke, for whom sodomites were 'part of an infernal trio of "sorcerers, sodomites, and heretics", figures which "are not the stuff of daily life but of myth or legend, not of experience but of fear"'. Among these fearful legends the pre-eminent for Bray is the papist:

> Nowhere is this more true than in the figure of the Papist, follower of Antichrist, servant of the terrible King of Spain and, as propagandists

of the Reformation added, sodomite. The Popish sodomite is a familiar figure, which takes us into the heart of the problem, and will be worth looking at at length. Was not the Papacy itself a 'second Sodom', 'new Sodom', 'Sodom Fair', nothing but 'a cistern full of sodomy'.[20]

In Bray's view the Catholic Church was itself horribly vulnerable to such 'wearisomely familiar' propaganda. 'The celibacy of the Roman priests could not have fitted it better', Bray notes; and after the Reformation, '[e]qually amenable to such treatment were the wealthy monastic orders, "on whom the vengeance of God is so manifestly declared for their beastly buggery"'.[21] By the late sixteenth century, the papist had become a useful 'explanation for misfortune' on a grand scale, 'the witchcraft of a malevolent neighbour' became 'a national enemy... at work; and in the Papists one was ready at hand'. These 'Papists', Bray writes,

> were not the remnants of pre-Reformation Catholicism – that had effectively disappeared with the Reformation – but, whether converts or not, they were the adherents of an active mission and – what is more to the point – one directed from abroad... The stories of Papist villany, fanciful though they may seem, were widely believed, and the Papists were variously accused of bringing the plague, burning towns, even of infiltrating Parliament disguised as Puritans and – for their own black-hearted ends – instigating the Civil War.[22]

In other words, what Bray believed was that the Renaissance English vilification of homosexuality was epitomised by the figure of the 'Papist', and thus the Renaissance English vilification of the Roman Catholic Church – and this meant that his reassessment of homosexuality in Renaissance England necessarily entailed a reassessment of homosexuality in relation to the Roman Catholic Church.

In one of his last writings, a short epilogue to Tom Betteridge's 2002 collection on *Sodomy in Early Modern Europe*, Bray returned to his *Homosexuality in Renaissance England*. 'The origin of my book', he wrote, 'was the extent to which, as it seemed to me, the exotic language of "sodomy" could be held suspended from the physical intimacy that pervaded sixteenth- and seventeenth-century culture.'[23] This was the lesson that most readers learned from that book: that there was a radical disjuncture between the various early modern discourses of sodomy – legal, theological – and the lived experience of men in the period. In this chapter, by contrast, I shall endeavour to show how that 'exotic language of "sodomy"' was profoundly implicated in the specific circumstances of that 'physical intimacy' – and in such a way that Bray's argument that a charge of sodomy meant an attack on Catholicism simply does not hold. Instead, I shall argue that the nature of the charges of sodomy is profoundly influenced and differentiated by the doctrinal allegiances of those accusing and those accused.

II. The Reformation of Sodomy

Among the polemicists of the English Reformation, John Bale has an enduring reputation as one of the most prolific and most extreme, the harsh, often obscene tone of his many prose and dramatic works earning him the nickname 'bilious Bale'. His attacks on the institutions of Roman Catholicism obsess on the sexual behaviour of the supposedly celibate English votaries.[24] For Bale, himself an ex-Carmelite friar, the Roman prohibition on sacerdotal marriage has various consequences: he cites numerous instances of fornication by the male inhabitants of the Roman monasteries, often with nuns or with other men's wives, as well as 'nyght pollucyons'. The monks are characterized as 'hote fathers', their religious vocation itself figured as a sexual act, a 'spyrytual occupyenge'. But in particular the votaries' 'chastity' is directly fused with sodomy: Bale recounts the passing of an apocryphal law , 'An Acte for Sodome', that all religious men (and women are significantly not mentioned here) 'shuld eyther lyue chast, that ys to saye, become Sodomytes (for that hath bene their chastyte euer sens) or els be suspended from all spirityuall iursydyccyon'. Central to the institutionalised pedagogy of monasticism is that 'most abhomynable sodometrye, which [a young votary]... lerne[s] in hys youthe of the consecrate chastyte of the holye clergye'.[25] In his myriad polemical publications, Bale rehearses scurrilous antimonastic tales, as of how a Genevan grey friar named Petrus Ryarius procured, through his uncle Pope Sixtus IV, a dispensation 'for the whole howsholde of the cardinall Saynt Lucie to haue the fre occupyenge of buggerye boyes for the .iii. hotter monthes of the yeare';[26] or how Pope Julius II procured 'two young laddes' from the Cardinal of Nantes.[27] The familiar tale of Pope Gregory I's remarks on seeing in the marketplace some beautiful English boys – 'Wele maye they be called *Angli* [English, angels] (sayth he) for they haue verye Angelych visages' – is given a lascivious subtext: 'Se how curyouse these fathers were, in the wele eyenge of their wares. Here was no cyrcumstaunce unloked to, perteynynge to the sale.'[28] The story of John

VIII, the supposedly female pope exposed as she gave birth, is by Bale, ornamented by a gleeful description of how such an embarrassing mistake was avoided in future. Now, according to Bale, at the 'solempne stallynge' of priests, the Cardinal 'doth grope them [the new priests] brechelesse, at an hole made in the seate for that ghostlye purpose, and than cryeth yt out before all the multitude, that he hath ware suffycyent to proue hym no woman', the 'ware' in question being the votaries' 'doutye dymycyeryes'.[29]

In moments of less levity, Bale links monastic celibacy to one of scripture's most notable sanctions against sodomy, Paul's Epistle to the Romans (Romans, 1:24–7):

> For thys presumpcyon God gave them clerelye ouer, and left them to themselues with all their good intents and vowes, whereupon they haue wrought sens that tyme fylthynesse vnspekeable. Their chast women, vestals[,] Monyals, Nonnes, and Begynes, changynge the naturall vse, haue wrought vnnaturallye. Lyke wyse the men in their Prelacyes, presthodes, and innumberable kyndes of Monkerye, for want of women hath brent in their lustes, and done abhomynacyons without nombre, so receyuynge in themselues the iust rewarde of their errour.[30]

Several historians have ignored or felt the need to apologise for Bale's continued fascination with sodomy – a recent editor has even suggested that his virulence must have its roots in personal psychosis: 'Possibly Bale suffered a sexual shock when he entered the order. Though no direct evidence is available, his persistent indignation about the dangers of enforced celibacy seems indicative of long lasting anxiety, or even neurosis.'[31] But, as Allen J. Frantzen has pointed out, Bale was drawing on a tradition of pro-reform literature about the monastic institutions that can be traced at least as far back as the fourteenth-century Lollards.[32] A tract known as the 'Twelve Conclusions of the Lollards' uses much the same language as Bale, making sodomy the key issue in its third conclusion, arguing that '*th*e lawe of continence annexyd to presthod, *th*at in preiudys of wimmen was first ordeynid, inducith sodomie in al holy chirche' and attacks '*th*e suspecte decre *th*at seyth we schulde not nemen it' (sodomy was known as the *crimen non nominandum inter Christianos*).[33]

Indeed, there is compelling evidence to suggest that Bale's yoking of sodomy and clerical celibacy, far from being the result of some personal 'sexual shock', was in fact an integral part of the wider political strategy employed by the architects of the English Reformation. As several historians have noted, sodomy moved from ecclesiastical jurisdiction to become a felony via a parliamentary bill passed in January 1533/34, just before Thomas Cromwell unleashed his campaign to suppress the monasteries.[34] The parliamentary bill was initially a two-pronged attack on sodomy and on the privileges of sanctuary,[35] which Geoffrey Elton describes as 'a curious pair'.[36] The proposed Sanctuary Bill never appeared, but the Sodomy Bill did, and it was at this moment that Cromwell resolved, as an extant memorandum has it, 'Item specyallye to speke of the vtter destrucyon of Sayntuaryes. Item ffor the destrucyon of all franchisys and lybertyes thorowout this Realme. Item the abhomny-acyon of Religyous persons thorowt the Realme.'[37] This memorandum is usually quoted as evidence that Cromwell was planning his suppression of the monasteries; taken in conjunction with the history of the sodomy/sanctuary bill, Cromwell's explicit linking of sanctuary and religious persons in the memorandum suggests that we may be able to review the campaign against the monasteries through that campaign's exploitation of the charge of sodomy.

When the first dissolution act was passed by Parliament in April 1536, its lengthy preamble cited the 'manifest sin, vicious, carnal and abominable living' prevalent in the religious houses,[38] while a later Elizabethan account expanded more pruriently:

[Cromwell] caused visitacions to be made of all the reeligious houses touching their conversations, whereupon was returned the booke called the Blacke Booke, expressing of everie such house the vile lives and abominable factes, in murders of their bretherne, in sodomyes, in whordomes, in destroying of children, in forging of deedes, and other infinite horrors of life, in so muche as deviding of all the religious persons in England into three partes two of theise partes at the least were sodomites: and this appeared in writting, with the names of the parties and their factes. This was shewed in parliament, and the villanies made knowen and abhorred.[39]

The partial records which survive make it clear that in 1535, using the established confessional procedure of the visitation, the male votaries were interviewed according to an explicit brief that prioritised, in the words of the monastic historian G.R.O. Woodward, 'certain offences against the vow of chastity', namely incontinence with women, both single and married, 'voluntary pollution' (masturbation), and 'sodomy'.[40] Only very rarely in the extant records are we given any more than brief descriptions of or possible reasons for the alleged offences of the monks and nuns. The most lengthy comes from West Dereham, where one monk who 'confesseth sod[omy]' as well as incontinence with diverse women, both married and spinsters, asked for the following to be set down in the visitors' records:

> nota. Richard Norwold, *alias*, Marke, says in virtue of his oath and conscience that, if all would so frankly confess their transgressions to my lord King as to speak [out], he would find not even one of the monks or priests who did not come together with women or share a bed with males, or by voluntary pollution or other unmentionable abuses of that kind [vtat*ur* femineo congressu aut masculo co*n*cubitu aut pollucionib*us* voluntarijs vel alijs id genus nephandis abusib*us*].[41]

What this passage gives us is a semantic formulation articulating the ideological difference between the registers' thoroughly divided 'sodomy' and 'incontinence'. The note insists on the spatiality of these encounters: intercourse with women is characterised as a 'congression' ('congressu'), a physical coming together; intercourse with men and boys is depicted purely in terms of sharing a bed ('concubito'). This division is borne out in the formulation of the visitors' questions: the male votaries are asked if they 'keep Chastity, not using the company of any suspect Woman within this Monastery, or without?' and 'Whether Women useth and resorteth much to this Monastry by back-ways, or otherwise' but 'Whether the Master, or any Brother of this House, useth to have any Boys or young Men laying with him', 'Whether ye do sleep altogether in the *Dormitorie*, under one Roof, or not?' and 'Whether ye all have separate Beds, or any one of you doth lay with an other?'[42] Sodomy and incontinence are thus radically distinguished in the rhetoric of the visitations. Incontinence – as the word itself suggests – refers to a lack of respect to being contained by boundaries, in this case the monastery walls. Incontinence is a literal *transgression* of those walls, a going beyond the bounds of the monastic institution. Sodomy, in sharp contrast, is literally *embedded* within the institution, dependent on the organisational requirements whereby men share sleeping quarters and are forced into intimate situations with boys.

III. English Catholicism after the Reformation

One side-effect of the success of the campaign by Reformation polemicists to identify institutionalised Catholicism with sodomy was that, necessarily, the wholesale destruction of the monastic institutions in the 1530s rid England of an easy geographical target for charges of anti-sodomy. It is significant that, once free of the monastery walls, the primary sexual accusation against English Catholic priests was of incontinence, rather than sodomy. As Frances Dolan has argued, from this time on, 'The concern about priests' relations with women that had always been there spread and intensified as priests' locations and relationships changed.' As priests moved into domestic households, '[a]dultery supplants sodomy as priests' particular vice' – 'adultery' becomes the new 'sodomy': 'a clerical transgression that does not require them to breach the walls, since the priests have already been welcomed in as household members'.[43] Dolan collects a set of caricatures that not only clear recusant domestic priests of the charge of sodomy, but actively pits them against others guilty of sodomy. In his attack on Catholic exorcisms, the *Declaration of egregious Popish Impostures*, for example, Samuel Harsnett 'contrasts priests' dalliances with women to actors' dalliances with boys': as 'it is the fashion of vagabond players, that coast from Towne to Towne with a trusse and cast of fiddles, to carry in theyr consort, broken queanes and *Ganimedes*, as well for their night pleasance, as their dayes pastime', so 'every priest' 'departed' from his exorcism 'suted with his wench after the same good custome'.[44]

While the household Catholic priest became an adulterer, however, the all-male setting of the Catholic seminaries at home and abroad meant they remained easy targets for charges of sodomy, as they were often depicted in pornography.[45] Strikingly, by the end of the sixteenth century, these charges were likely to come from other Catholics, mired in internecine factionalism. Working in the Archives of the Archdiocese of Westminster at Westminster Cathedral, Peter Lake and Michael Questier have shown how the community of imprisoned recusants at Wisbech Castle was torn apart by quarrels between the pro-Jesuit priest John Green and his opponent Christopher Bagshaw, who collected testimony concerning Green's behaviour from the adolescent local boys who either worked in the prison or were preparing for the seminary.[46] According to these affidavits, Green's 'familiarities' with the boys included attempting to remove one boy's breeches, and flogging another, then 'kiss[ing his] buttocks a dozen times or more'; when the boy objected, Green proposed that they switch roles. 'These and other like things', the boy allegedly testified, 'which I am almost ashamed to recite . . . were rather a cause of alienating my mind from religion . . . had I not been better instructed' – that final phrase presumably referring to the anti-Jesuit instruction provided by Bagshaw and others.[47]

Similar charges were mobilised against pro-Jesuit priests when the English College at Rome experienced a power struggle between two factions seeking for their candidate to succeed Cardinal Allen: one, a coalition looking to Spain and the Society of Jesus, and the other, a group supporting the Welshman Owen Lewis, a follower of Cardinal Borromeo. Lewis's supporters objected to the 'lewd or at the least suspicious behaviour' of the rector, Girolamo Fioravanti, alleging that 'it was a common bruit in the city that there was an hermaphrodite in the English College', a porter whom Fioravanti had employed to whip the boys.[48] One young English man, Robert Fisher, returned to England and elaborated these rumours about the English Jesuits in Rome:

Firstly, that the Rector of the English College has been accused of causing the death of many scholars; secondly, that he has diverted and alienated the revenues of the College; thirdly, that he has introduced into the house a hermaphrodite, and that this has been found out and exposed by the servant of a druggist when giving him an enema, and that one of the scholars also made investigations with his hand; fourthly, that he was enticing scholars to enter Religion.[49]

Perhaps in retaliation, Fioravanti's vice-rector, Edmund Harwood led a campaign against the students, whom he accused of 'dalliance and acts of incontinency in general'.[50] According to the secular priest Humphrey Ely, in 1594 Harwood, 'finding the youths clapping them selues on the breeches, or rather one for some reveng ierking his fellowe on the buttock with a rodd, before he was out of his bed', suspected 'worser behavior and should (as I haue heard) say, he found the*m* at Buggerie'. When this became known 'it did grieue them full sore, that the fathers (and specially Inglishe fathers) should suspect any of our nation with that abhominablé sinne'. It seems that Harwood had long had his suspicions, causing him to embark on a campaign of surveillance more characteristic of twentieth-century police forces: 'cutting the priuie dores beneath shorter by half a foote, to see if there any more than twoe feet at once at one priuie, and cutting downe a faier groue in the vineyard, because they vsed on their daies of recreation, to walk there two and two'.[51]

But Harwood was vulnerable to the same charges he advanced against his enemies: another student named Henry Bird alleged that Harwood had whipped one Geoffrey Pole 'in a chamber privately at the vineyard house', and refused to stop 'until [Pole] had accused three or four scholars of incontinency...and especially one Fowler...the prettiest youth of many'. Fowler, it seems, had taken to sleeping in a bed with another young student, Francis Isham, 'whether for talk or warmth or pleasure I know not'. Harwood burst into his quarters, 'and found them, after long groping, both lying together, which, they did swear, was [only] the second time that ever they met in one bed'. Harwood, predictably enough beat both the boys; but other students testified that his surveillance was undertaken for base motives, namely 'luxuriously, for the satisfaction of his own lustful desires and sensuality'. Even the rector was suspected of indulging in sexual relations in his lodgings.[52]

What emerges from this tangle of accusations and counter-accusations is not necessarily verifiable facts about life in Catholic seminaries and pseudo-seminaries such as Wisbech Castle. Instead, it points to the extreme ease with which these banal but consistent charges – inappropriate relations involving eroticised beating, sleeping together and genital contact in a limited range of locations – can be levelled at one's opponents. As with the anti-monastic polemic, however, I would argue, these charges could not be levelled in any situation: but rather, they take a very particular form, related specifically to the real living conditions of the institutions that contain them. This can be detected in one of the rare instances of a Catholic attack on a Protestant individual. Michael Questier and Peter Lake tell of a 'renegade seminarist' named Peter Chambers who abandoned his clerical orders in December 1608, and turned to Protestantism. He was employed at Exeter cathedral church 'to teach the singing boys', but was soon 'detected of sodomy with one of the boys', and hanged on 5 October 1609. As he met his death on the scaffold, it was reported by a Jesuit, he 'protested...that he was never infected with that abominable synne until he joyned with them [the Protestants]'. Another version had it that 'in Italy he had practised that sin but, drawn to be a catholic and make his confession, he was by his confessor severely checked and exhorted to vow continency'; but sadly, 'forsaking that profession he fell to his old vomit'.[53] Here, the accusation of sodomy is, apparently against the grain, thrown at the *Protestant* singing master: but significantly, the charge can stick because Chambers is in a choristers' school, one of the few monastic- or seminary-like institutions prone to 'embedded' sodomy left to English Protestantism.

IV. A Society of Sodomites

Is it possible to see B.C.'s depiction of a 'Societie of Sodomites' as the first trace of what by the end of the seventeenth century had become an identifiable subculture? As Goran Stanivukovic argues, 'Discursive as it is, this scenario is founded nevertheless on the idea, even a possibility, that self-identification is a separate and secretive form of masculinist culture in early modern London. Although this urban society does not yet show signs of an organised homoerotic male culture of the kind that, for example, existed in Renaissance Florence, it nevertheless gestures towards imagining what that organisation (and its social policing) might have looked like.'[54] Stanivukovic's point about the 'organisation' is well taken. It is indisputable that B.C.'s depiction of this 'company' calls to mind the descriptions of the molly houses almost a century later: the informant Samuel Stevens claimed in November 1725 that in a house in Field Lane he 'found between 40 and 50 men making love to one another'[55] (interestingly, the same number as the Society of Sodomites); in a house in Beech Lane he discovered 'a company of men fiddling and dancing';[56] another informant referred to 'the company'.[57] By stating that the Puritans were 'in state competent, and some of very good meanes', B.C. might be seen as prefiguring the insistence that the mollies 'cut across social classes',[58] the Puritans have 'their common appointed Meeting-place' as the mollies will have their 'molly-houses'.

Recently, the historian Diarmaid MacCulloch has forwarded explicitly a grand narrative argument that uses Bray's account of the seventeenth century, but to different ends. In his wide-ranging *The Reformation*, MacCulloch writes of the molly houses: 'I suggest that this new phenomenon was a reflection of a decline of the integrated divine view of society, the desacralization of the world, in which ecclesiastical prescriptions and proscriptions were no longer to provide a coherent framework and hold the imagination of everyone in society.'[59] While it is tempting to believe that the emergence of a gay subculture might be an integral part of a progressivist account of secularism, B.C.'s depiction of the 'Societie of Sodomites' must give us pause, and prevent us being swept away by MacCulloch's argument, since it appears to insist not on a secular, but on a particular nonconformist religious allegiance of those 'Sodomites', all of them 'earnest and hoat *Puritans*' of 'good temporall estates and meanes' with 'their common appointed Meeting-place'.[60]

As I have already suggested, *Pvritanisme the mother, Sinne the daughter* is primarily concerned not with sodomy, but with Puritanism. Later in his text, B.C. explains why the discovery of the 'Society of Sodomites' motivated him to write:

> Now, seeing these prodigious Monsters (being so many staines to *Nature*; for *Sodomitæ pessimi erant*, & *peccatores coram Domino nimis* [the men of Sodom were wicked and sinners before the Lord

exceedingly])[61] are *all Puritans* in faith, & hould themselues far more illuminated in the Lord, then the more moderate and learned Protestants; of which number of learned Protestants, most do wholy abandone & disclaime from the others *Puritanicall Doctrines*; And further seeing, that they may make show to warrant that this *their Sodomiticall State* from their owne *Principles*, admitting them for true: Therfore I haue thought good at this present, to set downe all such *Theoricall Positions of Puritanisme*, which do euen iustify *Sin*, and confidently teach its *Proselytes*, that the greatest *Sin* whatsoeuer, cannot become preiudiciall to the saluation of any of the faythfull; of which number, all the foresaid portentuous Wretches (as being *Puritans*) euen by their owne Principles and Doctrines, are taught to be.[62]

In B.C.'s account the *'Sodomiticall State'* of this 'Society' derives directly from the Puritans' *'owne Principles'* (which he is at pains to distinguish from those of 'more moderate and learned Protestants'). These are as follows (as ventriloquised by B.C.): (1) since we lack free will, whatever we have committed 'we could not but commit'; (2) the Ten Commandments 'appertayne not vnto Christians'; (3) what we commit 'is no *Sinne* in vs', since we are of the faithful and therefore good; (4) even if it is a sin, it is 'no *Sinne* in vs, but in *God*' and so we are 'wholly excused'; (5) even if it is a sin, 'yet it is no greater, then any other *Sinne*', even though it be 'tragically amplified by our Enemies'; (6) it is only a venial sin and 'therefore easily pardonable'; (7) even if it is 'a mortall, or grieuous *Sinne* is vs', it is 'in no sort preiudicall to vs', since we are either *'reprobated* to damnation or *predestinated* to saluation'; (8) even if it is a sin in us, that we are 'more to be pittied, then rebuked'; and (9) whatever our sin is, great or small, 'no detriment (touching our saluation) can it bring to vs'.[63] This argument, through a broad parody of doctrine, links sodomy to Puritan beliefs, especially those articulated by Jean Calvin.

But there is something more specific about this 'Society of certaine Sodomites' of 'good temporall estates and meanes' with 'their common appointed Meeting-place'.[64] Just as the Reformation polemicists insist on the embeddedness of Roman Catholic sodomy within the monastery walls, B.C. is very specific in his characterisation of Puritan sodomy:

The first inducement, which importuned my penne to vndergoe this labour, is the late discouery in *London*, of a company of *Sodomiticall Persons* (whereof some are apprehended but diuers fled,) in number about fourty, or more; in state competent, and some of very good meanes; in Religion *all Puritaines*; and in entercourse among themselues (a thing wonderfull to be reported) so linked, as that they made a peculiar *Society* or *Body*, hauing a common designed place for their publike meetings: So iust reason, I haue to say a little before, *Interrogate Gentes, quis audiuit talia horribilia* [Ask ye now among the heathen, who hath heard of such horrible things]?[65]

Most importantly, B.C. insists, the Puritans, 'in entercourse among themselues', have 'linked' into 'a company', 'a peculiar *Society* or *Body*' in 'their common designed place for their publike meetings'. This is not, as with the monks and seminarians, an 'embedded' sodomy, defined by and contained within the monastery and seminary walls. Instead, they meet in 'publike' and in a place that is designated as 'common'. Moreover, and strikingly, all these terms indicate that the Sodomites are making a freely chosen association among individuals. The three terms appropriated, 'Company', 'Society' and 'Body', were all commonly used to describe a very particular form of 'entercourse' in early modern London – that of the mercantile, artisanal, and trades guilds.[66] This gives a different context to the reference of their social and financial 'state competent, and some of very good meanes'.

The charge of sodomy thrown by B.C. at the Puritans is thus clearly not a simple reversal of the commonplace accusation hurled by Protestants at Catholics. Instead, this text reveals how, in its deployment by and against different groups and individuals, the charge of sodomy can and must take a myriad of forms – specific forms that are in themselves at least as important as the 'utterly confused' charge. B.C.'s rhetoric reveals a completely different understanding of the social circumstances of the monastic and seminarian Catholics, and the 'discovered' Puritans of 1632. Whereas the charges against Catholics insist on 'embedded' sodomy, produced by institutional pressures of bedsharing, the charges against Puritans draw out their individual financial independence, and their mutually chosen choice of a 'common appointed Meeting-place' in which their 'company' can meet in public. It might be added that these are importantly *London* Puritans, portrayed in the language of the City guilds, described in terms of individual association in common, public space. By identifying the 'Society of *Sodomites*' in this manner, B.C. may well be intending specifically to tarnish London, often portrayed as a Puritan stronghold, but he also provides a language for the kind of urban subculture that historians have detected a half-century later.

As a result, I believe we need to reconsider the almost kneejerk response to the commonplace association of sodomy and Catholicism in the period. Alan Bray wrote that 'The Popish sodomite is a familiar figure, which takes us into the heart of the problem, and will be worth looking at at length.'[67] The 'Popish sodomite' is certainly 'worth looking at at length' again, but he is by no means 'the heart of the problem'. Instead, I would argue, this stereotype is merely the most prominent of a series of stock individuals and groups produced by early modern charges of sodomy. The fact that he is the most 'familiar' is partly the result of successful Reformation propaganda, but also partly the result of Bray's own critical preoccupations. It is clear, even from this brief survey, that there are other sodomites in the archive, of whom B.C.'s 'Society' is only one example (albeit of forty or fifty) – sodomites that are importantly different enough from the 'familiar' Roman Catholic to suggest that we need to look further to achieve a more nuanced and multivalent understanding of the multiple sodomies of early modern England.

Notes

I am grateful to Will Fisher and Goran Stanivukovic for their comments on an earlier draft of this chapter.

1. 'B.C.', *Pvritanisme the mother, Sinne the davghter* ([Saint Omer], 1633), sig. *2^r.
2. Traditionally, 'B.C.' has been identified as priest and Catholic convert Benjamin Carier (or Carrier), but Carier died in 1614. It is feasible (although unproven) that the main part of the tract was penned by Carier, and the prefatory materials were attached later. For Carier, see M. Questier, 'Crypto-Catholicism, anti-Calvinism and Conversion at the Jacobean court: The Enigma of Benjamin Carier', *Journal of Ecclesiastical History*, 47 (1996), 45–64.
3. On the molly houses, see A. Bray, *Homosexuality in Renaissance England* (London: Gay Men's Press, 1982), ch. 4; R. Norton, *Mother Clap's Molly House: The Gay Subculture in England 1700–1830* (London: Gay Men's Press, 1992); T. Hitchcock, *English Sexualities, 1700–1800* (New York: St Martins Press, 1997), ch. 5; C. McFarlane, *The Sodomite in Fiction and Satire, 1660–1750* (New York: Columbia University Press, 1997); C. Patterson, 'The Rage of Caliban: Eighteenth-Century Molly Houses and the Twentieth-Century Search for Sexual Identity', in T. DiPiero and P. Gill (eds), *Illicit Sex: Identity Politics in Early Modern Culture* (Athens: Georgia University Press, 1997), pp. 256–99; R. Trumbach, *Sex and the Gender Revolution Volume One: Hetero-sexuality and the Third Gender in Enlightenment London* (Chicago: University of Chicago Press, 1998), pp. 55–64; G. Haggerty, *Men in Love: Masculinity and Sexuality in the Eighteenth* Century (New York: Columbia University Press, 1999); D. Higgs (ed.), *Queer Sites: Gay Urban Histories since 1600* (London: Routledge, 1999); S. Shapiro, 'Of Mollies: Class and Same-Sex Sexualities

in the Eighteenth Century', in K. Chedgzoy, E. Francis and M. Pratt (eds), *In a Queer Place: Sexuality and Belonging in British and European Contexts* (Aldershot: Ashgate, 2002), pp. 155–76. For materials relating to the persecution of mollies, see I. McCormick (ed.), *Secret Sexualities: A Sourcebook of Seventeenth and Eighteenth Century Writing* (New York: Routledge, 1997); for the Society for the Reformation of Manners, see R.B. Shoemaker, 'Reforming the City: The Reformation of Manners Campaign in London, 1690–1738', in L. Davison *et al.* (eds), *Stilling the Gambling Hive: The Response to Social and Economic Problems in England, 1689–1750* (New York: St Martin's Press, 1992), pp. 99–120.

4. M. Foucault, *The History of Sexuality: An Introduction*, trans. R. Hurley (London: Allen Lane, 1978), p. 43.

5. See especially Bray's chapter on 'Society and the Individual', *Homosexuality in Renaissance England*, ch. 3.

6. G.V. Stanivukovic, 'Between Men in Early Modern England', in K. O'Donnell and M. O'Rourke (eds), *Siting Queer Masculinities* (Basingstoke: Palgrave Macmillan, 2006), pp. 232–51, on p. 234. I am grateful to Professor Stanivukovic for allowing me to read this chapter in manuscript.

7. B.C., *Pvritanisme the Mother*, sig, *2ʳ. See P. Lake with M. Questier, *The Antichrist's Lewd Hat: Protestants, Papists and Players in Post-Reformation England* (New Haven and London: Yale University Press, 2002).

8. B.C., *Pvritanisme the Mother*, sig. *2ᵛ.

9. Stanivukovic, 'Between Men in Early Modern England', p. 234.

10. S. Orgel, *Impersonations: The Performance of Gender in Shakespeare's England* (Cambridge: Cambridge University Press, 1996); B.R. Smith, *Homosexual Desire in Shakespeare's England: A Cultural Poetics* (Chicago: University of Chicago Press, 1991); L. Jardine, 'Twins and Travesties', in S. Zimmerman (ed.), *Erotic Politics: Desire on the Renaissance Stage* (London: Routledge, 1992), pp. 27–38.

11. J. Goldberg, *Sodometries: Renaissance Texts, Modern Sexualities* (Stanford: Stanford University Press, 1992); his editions, *Queering the Renaissance* (Durham: Duke University Press, 1994), and *Reclaiming Sodom* (New York: Routledge, 1994); and the essays collected in *Shakespeare's Hand* (Minneapolis: University of Minnesota Press, 2003); E.K. Sedgwick, *Between Men: English Literature and Male Homosocial Desire* (New York: Columbia University Press, 1985) and *Epistemology of the Closet* (Berkeley: University of California Press, 1990).

12. See G.W. Bredbeck, *Sodomy and Interpretation: From Marlowe to Milton* (Ithaca, NY: Cornell University Press, 1991); J. Masten, *Textual Intercourse: Collaboration, Authorship, and Sexualities in Early Modern Drama* (Cambridge: Cambridge University Press, 1997); M. diGangi, *The Homoerotics of Early Modern Drama* (Cambridge: Cambridge University Press, 1997); V. Traub, *The Renaissance of Lesbianism in Early Modern England* (Cambridge: Cambridge University Press, 2002).

13. Bray, *Homosexuality in Renaissance England*, pp. 10–11.

14. Ibid., p. 75.

15. Ibid., pp. 113–14. Bray takes the Browne case from *Select Trials for Murders, Robberies, Rapes, Sodomy, Coining, Frauds, and Other Offences at the Sessions-House in the Old Bailey*, 3 vols (London, 1742), 3: 39–40. For a related discussion of periodisation in Bray's work see A. Stewart, 'Queer Renaissance Bodies?

Sex, Violence, and the Constraints of Periodisation', *In a Queer Place*, pp. 137–54.

16. See for example, the introduction of P. Hammond, *Figuring Sex between Men from Shakespeare to Rochester* (Oxford: Clarendon Press, 2002). Hammond shows no interest in challenging Bray's paradigm: 'How and why did the culture change so radically, and so paradoxically, over this century? This is an impossible question to answer . . .' (p. 1).

17. Bray, *The Friend* (Chicago: University of Chicago Press, 2003); see also his 'Epilogue' to T. Betteridge (ed.), *Sodomy in Early Modern Europe* (Manchester: Manchester University Press, 2002), pp. 164–8, on p. 166. The subtitle was used on materials circulated by Bray to a seminar at Birkbeck, University of London, in 2000.

18. A. Bray, 'History, Homosexuality and God', paper given at the annual conference of Friend, October 1986.

19. Ibid.

20. Bray, *Homosexuality in Renaissance England*, p. 19. This propaganda had its roots, of course, in the Roman Catholic Church itself: '[T]he Protestant part was doing no more than adapting to its own use the identification of heresy with sodomy that the Catholic Church had itself constructed during its confrontation with the heresies of the twelfth century, the identification of religious deviation with sexual deviation' (p. 19).

21. Bray, *Homosexuality in Renaissance England*, p. 19. Bray is here citing one of the key early English Reformation texts, Simon Fish's *Supplication of the Poore Commons* in *A Supplicacyon for the Beggers*, ed. J.M. Cowper (London: Early English Text Society, 1871), pp. 63–4.

22. Bray, *Homosexuality in Renaissance England*, p. 27, citing Keith Thomas, *Religion and the Decline of Magic* (Harmondsworth: Penguin, 1973), pp. 647, 667–8.

23. Bray, 'Epilogue', p. 165.

24. For an account of this anticlerical satire that unaccountably avoids its anti-sodomy element, see H. Parish, ' "Beastly is their living and their doctrine": Celibacy and Theological Corruption in English Reformation Polemic', in B. Gordon (ed.), *Protestant History and Identity in Sixteenth-Century Europe*, 2 vols (Aldershot: Scolar Press, 1996), 1: 138–52.

25. J. Bale, *The Actes of Englysh votaryes comprehendynge their vnchast practises and examples by all ages* (Zurich [i.e. Antwerp], 1541), sigs Diiii[v]–Dv[r], D.iiii[v], I[r-v], Cvi[r].

26. Bale, *A mysterye of inyquyte contained within the heretycall Genealogye of Ponce Pantolabus/ . . . here both disclosed & confuted* (Geneva [i.e. Antwerp], 1545), sigs Dv[v]–Dvi[r].

27. Ibid., sig. Cvi[v].

28. Bale, *Actes of Englysh votaryes*, sig. Cvi[v].

29. Ibid., sig. Gii[v].

30. Ibid., sig. Aviii[r-v]. In *Mysterye of inyquyte*, Bale advances a similar argument: 'And thus hath holye wedlock bene vnto them euer sens a most pernycyouse poyson/and stynkynge whoredome with buggerye a most suffren remedye of their naturall dysseease' (sig. Dii[v]).

31. P. Happé, 'Introduction' to his ed., *The Complete Plays of John Bale*, 2 vols (Cambridge: D.S. Brewer, 1985–6), 1: 2–3. For similar pathologizing verdicts, see also J.W. Harris, *John Bale* (Urbana, IL: University of Illinois Press, 1940),

p. 9; T.B. Blatt, *The Plays of John Bale: A Study of Ideas, Technique and Style* (Copenhagen: G.E.C. Gad, 1968), pp. 13–14, 53.

32. A.J. Frantzen, *Before the Closet: Same-Sex Love from 'Beowulf' to 'Angels in America'* (Chicago: University of Chicago Press, 1998), pp. 258–9.

33. 'Twelve Conclusions of the Lollards', in A. Hudson (ed.), *Selections from English Wycliffite Writings* (Cambridge: Cambridge University Press, 1978), pp. 24–9, on p. 25. 'The thirdde conclusiun sorwful to here is that the lawe of continence annexyd to presthod, that in preiudys of wimmen was first ordeynid, inducith sodomie in al holy chirche; but we excusin us be the Bible for the suspecte decre that seyth we schulde not nemen it. Resun and experience prouit this conclusiun. For delicious metis and drinkis of men of holi chirche welen han nedful purgaciun or werse. Experience for the priue asay of syche men is, that the[i] like non wymmen; and whan thu prouist [detect] sich a man make him wel for he is on of tho [them]. The correlary of this conclusiun is that the priuat religions, begynneris of this synne, wer most worthi to ben annullid. But God for his myth of priue synne sende opyn ueniaunce [vengeance].'

34. This account draws on my fuller discussion in *Close Readers: Humanism and Sodomy in Early Modern England* (Princeton: Princeton University Press, 1997), esp. pp. 44–52. See also Smith, *Homosexual Desire*, pp. 43–5; D.N. Mager, 'John Bale and Early Tudor Sodomy Discourse', in *Queering the Renaissance*, pp. 141–61.

35. '*Memorandum*, quod cum diversa scelera detestabilia nuper per eos, qui, ut videntur, morte digni perpetrata fuerunt, quibus ex ordine Juris regni (ut Juris periti aiunt) nulla condigna imponi potest pena; ideo conducibile esse excogitatum est, quod quicunque in Sanctuaria trahens moram, egrediens, et extra, scelus morte dignum perpetrans, ac in Sanctuariam regressus pro suffragio et corporis tuitione, Ecclesiasticum beneficium amittet; ac mittitur duas conficere Billas.' *Journals of the House of Lords*, 152 vols (London: HMSO, 1509–1920), 1: 59b.

36. G.R. Elton, *Reform and Reformation: Thomas Cromwell and the Commonwealth* (Cambridge: Cambridge University Press, 1973), pp. 136–7.

37. London, The National Archives, State Papers [hereafter NA SP] 1/102, fol. 8^v, calendared in J.S. Brewer *et al.* (eds), *Letters and Papers, Foreign and Domestic, of the Reign of Henry VIII*, 21 vols and Addenda (London: HMSO, 1862–1932) [hereafter *LP*], 10: 254 (p. 93).

38. 27 Henry VIII c. 28, cit. G.R. Elton, *The Tudor Constitution: Documents and Commentary*, 2nd edn (Cambridge: Cambridge University Press, 1982), p. 383.

39. T. Wright (ed.), *Three Chapters of Letters Relating to the Suppression of the Monasteries* (London: Camden Society, 1843), p. 114. See also H. Latimer, *The seconde Sermone* (London: John Day, 1549), sig. Diiij^{r-v}: 'when theyr enormities were fyrste read in the parliament house, they were so greate and abhominable that there was nothynge but downe with them'; and G. Burnet, *History of the Reformation of the Church of England*, 3 vols (London, 1679–1715), 1: 190–1: 'for the Lewdness of the Confessors of Nunneries, and the great Corruption of that State, whole Houses being found almost all with Child; for that dissoluteness of Abbots and the other Monks and Friars, not only with whores, but Marryed Women; and for their unnatural Lusts and other brutal practices; these are not fit to be spoken of, much less enlarged

on, in a work of this Nature. The full report of this Visitation is lost, yet I have seen an Extract of a part of it, concerning 144 Houses, that contains Abominations in it, equal to any that were in *Sodom*.' For a more sceptical view of the impact of these reports, see G. Baskerville, *English Monks and the Suppression of the Monasteries* (London: Jonathan Cape, 1937), pp. 141–2.

40.   G.R.O. Woodward, *The Dissolution of the Monasteries* (London: Blandford, 1966), p. 33. For fuller accounts, see G.G. Coulton, *Five Centuries of Religion*, 4 vols (Cambridge: Cambridge University Press, 1923–50), 4: 697; D. Knowles, *The Religious Orders in England*, 3 vols (Cambridge: Cambridge University Press, 1948–59), 3: 297; Stewart, *Close Readers*, pp. 47–8.

41.   NA SP 1/102 fol. 114a; calendared at *LP* 10: 364 (p. 144).

42.   Burnet, *History of the Reformation*, 1.Records. 132–3. See also the questions asked at nunneries (1.Records.136–7) and the General Injunctions read to the houses by the Visitors regarding sleeping arrangements (1.Records.138–9).

43.   F.E. Dolan, *Whores of Babylon: Catholicism, Gender, and Seventeenth-Century Print Culture* (Ithaca, NY: Cornell University Press, 1999), pp. 87, 89.

44.   S. Harsnett, *Declaration of egregious Popish Impostures* (London: James Roberts, 1603), sig, V3ʳ, quoted in Dolan, *Whores of Babylon*, pp. 89–90.

45.   Dolan, *Whores of Babylon*, p. 90, citing R. Thompson, *Unfit for Modest Ears: A Study of Pornographic, Obscene, and Bawdy Works Written or Published in England in the Second Half of the Seventeenth Century* (Towata, NJ: Rowman & Littlefield, 1979), ch. 8.

46.   Lake with Questier, *The Antichrist's Lewd Hat*. Some materials relating to these disputes are collected in P. Renold, *The Wisbech Stirs (1595–1598)* (London: Catholic Record Society [vol. 51], 1958).

47.   Archives of the Archdiocese of Westminster [hereafter AAW] A VI, nos 13, 14, cited and discussed in Lake with Questier, *The Antichrist's Lewd Hat*, pp. 288–9.

48.   AAW A V, pp. 413–14, cited and discussed in Lake and Questier, *Antichrist's Lewd Hat*, pp. 289–90.

49.   'Ea quae nominatim spargit contra Societatis homines qui Romae vivunt, haec sunt. Primo accusatum esse Rectorem Collegii Anglicani quod eius culpa multi scolares mortui sint. 2° quod Collegij reditus averterit et substraxerit. 3° quod Hermaphroditum in domum induxerit, idque cognitum fuisse ac detectum per framocopolae famulum dum clysterium ei subministraret, quendam etiam scolarem illum manu pertractasse. 4° quod scolares ad religionis ingressum alliceret ...' Fr Henry Garnet, Superior to the Fathers of the SJ in England, to Claudius Aquaviva SJ, General of the SJ, 14 May 1597, London. Renold, *Wisbech Stirs*, pp. 212 (Latin) and 214 (English).

50.   AAW A V, p. 414, cit. Lake and Questier, *Antichrist's Lewd Hat*, p. 290.

51.   H. Ely, *Certain Brief Notes upon a Brief Apology* (Paris, 1602), sig. Eviiʳ.

52.   AAW A V, pp. 414–16, cit. Lake and Questier, *Antichrist's Lewd Hat*, p. 291.

53.   AAW A VIII, pp. 657–8, 696; IX, p. 82, discussed by Questier, *Conversion, Politics and Religion in England, 1580–1625* (Cambridge: Cambridge University Press, 1996), p. 72; Lake and Questier, *Antichrist's Lewd Hat*, p. 305.

54.   Stanivukovic, 'Between Men in Early Modern England', p. 234. Stanivukovic is here referring to the Florentine subcultures revealed in Michael J. Rocke's work:

see especially *Forbidden Friendships: Homosexuality and Male Culture in Renaissance Florence* (New York: Oxford University Press, 1996).

55. *Select Trials for Murders, Robberies, Rapes, Sodomy, Coining, Frauds and Other Offences at the Sessions-House in the Old Bailey*, 3 vols (London, 1742), 3: 37.
56. *Select Trials*, 2: 368.
57. *Select Trials*, 2: 257–8.
58. Bray, *Homosexuality in Renaissance England*, p. 86.
59. D. MacCulloch, *The Reformation* (New York: Penguin, 2004), pp. 606–7.
60. B.C., *Pvritanisme the mother*, sig. *2ʳ.
61. The reference is to Genesis 13:13: 'hominess autem Sodomitae pessimi errant et peccatores coram Domino nimis', rendered in the 1611 Authorised Version as 'But the men of Sodom were wicked and sinners before the Lord exceedingly.'
62. B.C., *Pvritanisme the mother*, sigs *4ᵛ–*5ʳ.
63. B.C., *Pvritanisme the mother*, sigs D3ᵛ–D5ʳ.
64. B.C., *Pvritanisme the mother*, sig. *2ʳ.
65. The reference is to Jeremiah 18:13: 'ideo haec dicit Dominus interrogate gentes quis audivit talia horribilia quae fecit nimis virgo Israhel', rendered in the 1611 Authorised Version as 'Therefore thus saith the Lord: Ask ye now among the heathen, who hath heard of such things: the virgin of Israel hath done a very horrible thing.'
66. Although the *Oxford English Dictionary* gives as 1689 the earliest use of 'body' to mean 'A number of persons taken collectively, usually as united and organized in a common cause or for common action' (including business), it also quotes an act from 1 Edward IV (1461) which refers to 'Any Fraternitie, Guild, Companie, or Fellowship, or other bodie corporate'. See *OED*, s.v. body, 15 and 14a.
67. Bray, *Homosexuality in Renaissance England*, p. 19.

5

'Swil-bols and Tos-pots': Drink Culture and Male Bonding in England, c.1560–1640

Alexandra Shepard

When James Hart, a Northamptonshire physician, compiled his regimen *KΛINIKH, or The Diet of the Diseased*, his puritan tendencies came to the fore as he turned his attention to the dangers of excessive drinking, which he chose to treat primarily as a sin rather than a disease. While admitting that his theme was more fitting 'for a divines pulpit than a Physitians penne', he nonetheless begged his readers' patience, 'by reason this vice now so reigneth', while he gave 'this beastly sinne a lash or two'. He proceeded to rehearse arguments against drunkenness that were commonplace in the social and moral commentary of his day, to which men and women in early modern England may well have been exposed almost as frequently as the attractions of wine, beer and ale. It was the drunken man (rather than the drunken woman) that particularly preoccupied Hart. Drunkards, in Hart's view, inverted all that was expected of men, both morally and socially. 'Swil-bols, tos-pots' and their 'pot companions' belched out oaths, were quarrelsome, slanderous, back-biting and even murderous, 'unclean' and adulterous. They loved their ale more than God, cheated their neighbours, wives and children, and ignored the dictates of deference. A drunken man, claimed Hart, 'maketh little difference betwixt superiour, inferiour, equall', and, as well as denying their superiors the 'reverence and respect due unto them', drunkards 'even often mocke[d] and deride[d] them'. In all such ways, swill-bowls and tosspots were represented as severe dangers to the commonwealth.[1]

They were also portrayed as dangers to themselves. While primarily focussing on the sinful behaviour associated with drink, Hart did not neglect its physical effects:

> And as for the diseases of the body procured thereby, they are not a few: as namely, the *Apoplexy*, *Epilepsie*, or falling sicknesse; *Incubus* or

110

nightmare, Palsie, giddinesse, lethargy, and the like soporiferous diseases; besides sudden death, losse of memory and understanding, red and watery eyes, a corny face, all beset with rubies and carbuncles, accompanied with a copper nose.

As if these were not sufficiently deterrent, Hart also associated drunkenness with rotten teeth, a stammering tongue, bad lungs, 'filthy and stinking, belching, *vomitings'*, fevers, inflammations, gout, dropsy and the stone. In addition, the temporary effects of drink were deemed as debilitating as the long-term hazards. The greatest danger was that it robbed a man of his powers of reason, the attribute that justified men's superiority over women and distinguished them from beasts. Drunkards were depicted as no better than brutes: 'these men oftentimes deprive themselves even of the use of their senses, making themselves by this means, as senselesse as blocks'. As Hart concluded, drunkenness 'unmans a man'.[2]

It is not difficult to imagine how a moralist such as Hart might have reacted to the behaviour of two men reported to the Dorchester Justice of the Peace, Sir Francis Ashley, in 1617. A servant, Thomas Ford, a butcher named Patye and one Christopher Edmunds of Dorchester had between them spent nearly eight shillings on beer and tobacco in a single sitting (possibly representing as much as two weeks' income for a wage labourer). Their drinking session had begun on a Sunday before morning prayer and continued well into the evening, when, in the presence of Edmunds (and, presumably, the others also present in the alehouse), Ford and Patye each 'pist both at once into a chamber pott and then one dranke upp the one haulfe and thother the other haulfe, and because one of them should drinke lesse than thother, they measured it out by glasse fulls'.[3] Clearly, to approach this event through the lens of puritan morality would ignore the significance of such ritual intimacies, and of more mundane drinking practices, for the men involved. Yet it is also very difficult to interpret the precise meanings of an incident such as this, particularly as there is no record of the reactions of those who witnessed it since it was documented as part of a series of complaints against the alehouse-keeper rather than against the participants themselves.[4] It is possible the ritual was meant to signal that the men involved had consumed so much beer that they might as well have drunk their own urine. It also seems to have been designed as a public display of prowess, perhaps mimicking the rituals men undertook when drinking each other's health, and it may well have additionally symbolised a form of 'anti-communion' – an inversion of the ritual whereby neighbours would have shared the same cup in the parish church. What it does suggest, however, is that men's drinking culture had the potential to forge a range of intimacies between men, which in this extreme form went as far as sharing bodily fluids. However hard moralists such as Hart laboured to stigmatise the rituals of male drinking culture, they held potent attractions for their participants that were linked with widely endorsed notions of manliness, bravura and strength. Many of its dangers, as couched in the warnings of prescriptive discourse, were in fact its strengths to partakers.

One of the fundamental features of early modern drinking practices was the bonds they facilitated between men – often treated as a threatening form of fraternisation by moralists, while cast in the more positive terms of 'good fellowship' by participants. This chapter will examine the characteristics of male drink culture in early modern England between 1560 and 1640 in order to explore the forms of male bonding that it forged and upon which it was founded, and to discuss why these bonds were deemed so threatening to the social order on the one hand and so attractive to large numbers of men on the other.

The scholarship of Alan Bray is indispensable to making sense of such bonds and intimacies and the functions they performed both in the assertion of individual and collective male identities and more generally in either maintaining or undermining the early modern patriarchal order. Alan Bray was one of the first scholars to connect histories of sexuality with histories of masculinity, by examining the links between concepts of appetite and normative codes of manhood current in early modern England.[5] He was also extremely careful to avoid colluding with such normative codes, by probing their *selective* operation – for example in relation to the signification of sodomy.[6] As Valerie Traub has noted above, this involved the painstaking contextualisation of male intimacy within a range of social systems and an exploration of the instrumentality of affect in either bolstering or undermining social cohesion and networks of power. The rituals of male drink culture were similarly entangled with the tensions between concepts of appetite and manhood, and the male bonds they involved served both to shore up the patriarchal exclusion of women from networks of power, and also to undermine the hierarchical and patrilineal relations between men founded on social status, age and marital status. Like friendship, the bonds linking male drinking companions both oiled *and* threatened the workings of early modern society.

However, it is clear that such bonds were often far removed from the densely woven ties of friendship – ranging from patronage to sworn brotherhood – that Bray's work has done so much to historicise. These bonds, and particularly those underpinning the elaborate rituals of male excess, were often fleeting and transitory rather than deeply rooted in long-term relationships. While highly potent, they were nonetheless unacknowledged and involved very little expectation of on-going obligation or reciprocity. Rather than offering opportunities for self-exploration and self-disclosure, the ties of what might be labelled 'comradeship' in contrast to 'friendship' were instead based on collective activity and the subordination of individual identities to the expectations of the group.[7] The ties of camaraderie, as illustrated by men's group drinking rituals, might therefore usefully be explored in contrast to ties of friendship, in order to shed further light on both. To some extent this goes against the grain of recent trends in the history of sexuality and masculinity that have brought the exploration of deeply felt affect and emotion to the fore – whether in order to acknowledge or deny the erotic potential of friendship.[8] Yet it also involves the exploration of similar issues, and in particular the faultline identified by Valerie Traub above between friendship, or in this case camaraderie, and eroticism.

Men's drinking rituals facilitated a spectrum of fraternal bonds ranging from the routine ties of neighbourhood and community to more intense forms of homosociability and bodily intimacy. What is not clear is whether and/or when such intimacies signified as erotic either in relation to early modern concepts of sodomy or in other senses. Clearly, such gestures – when they can be glimpsed – are illustrative of the greater acceptability of routine intimacies between men in the early modern period.[9] But it is also possible that the fleeting and unacknowledged bonds underpinning the group activities in which men sought to prove themselves to each other created a particular space for bodily intimacy between men and the expression of 'homosocial desire' that escaped categorisation in terms of the friendship/sodomy spectrum analysed by Alan Bray.[10] It may be that it was precisely because such intimacies did not take place within the bonds of friendship (but as part of male camaraderie) that they did not signify as transgressive (at least in a sexual sense), as a result of different conventions governing men's access to each other's bodies in different contexts.[11] This further complicates the relationship between sexual acts and identities that has preoccupied historians of sexuality.[12] The fraternal bonds of camaraderie sometimes enabled the 'safe' (if nonetheless carefully choreographed and contained) expression of male desire, and their analysis affords access to some of its elusive forms that were compatible with, rather than antithetical to, the assertion of manhood and male prowess.[13]

The male bonding facilitated by and expressed through group drinking rituals is therefore approached in this chapter as a form of comradeship, through which fleeting intimacies were enabled between men, without many of the concerns associated with the mutual disclosure and obligation expected of friendship. What follows begins with an exploration of the ways in which men's drinking rituals were represented and condemned in moral, medical and domestic advice literature, which provides indirect evidence of the ties such rituals involved and direct evidence of the ways in which they were deemed threatening to the social order. The second part of the chapter examines disciplinary records in order to glean evidence of some of the actual practices that men's drinking rituals involved. Such bonds are analysed as a form of homosocial cement that could accommodate the expression of same-sex desire, and that, like the bonds of friendship, both upheld male dominance *and* threatened the patriarchal order during an important phase of socio-economic change.

I

Men's drinking habits – when pursued to excess – were represented in contemporary commentary primarily in terms of inversion. According to diatribes against it, drunkenness threatened to invert the social order, the moral order and the gender order. It substituted vice for virtue; effeminacy for manliness; profligacy for thrift; profanity for godliness; antagonism for neighbourliness; marital strife for harmony; and self-interest for friendship. The most lurid representations of men's drinking patterns featured in puritan diatribes against drunkenness and its associated vices, although condemnation of over-indulgence was also common in medical tracts and across a wide range of advice literature as well as in many ballads circulating in the early modern period.

Most moralists dwelt at length on the bodily debilitation associated with drunkenness, which was characterised in terms of deviation from the rational self-control ideally expected of manhood. Drunkards were depicted as descending the gendered chain of being which placed men above women and women above beasts. While the loss of control and excesses associated with drinking were sometimes labelled as effeminate, the imagery most commonly employed was that of beastliness. So, for example, Sir Walter Raleigh advised his son that wine 'transformeth a Man into a Beast', and in his book of characters, Francis Lenton portrayed drunkards as 'more like beasts than men', while Thomas Young's tract on drunkenness categorised nine stages of excess, each of which corresponded to an animal as the drinker progressed from being 'Lyon-drunke' to 'Bat drunke'.[14] The pamphleteer Phillip Stubbes' depiction of the brutish mutation suffered by a drinker is possibly the most vivid: 'doo not his eies begin to stare & to be red, fiery & blered, blubbering foorth a sea of teares? dooth he not frothe & fome at the mouth like a bore? dooth not his tung falter & stammer in his mouth?...Is not his understanding altogher [*sic*] decayed?'[15] Inebriation was also condemned as a form of bodily shipwreck and a temporary state of madness. Thomas Kingsmill's sermon against drunkenness claimed that it was 'the shipwreck of all goodnesse' as the drunkard cast away his 'most precious wares': modesty, sobriety and temperance, whereby 'the shippe of his body is sore shaken, with palsies, and other diseases, that he will have much adoe to patch it up againe'. Such a condition left a man worse than a beast because it deprived him even of the use of his limbs.[16] According to the Elizabethan homily against gluttony and drunkenness, drunkards forfeited their senses and 'playe[d] the madde men openly', which echoed the commonplace that the most important attribute men sacrificed through excessive consumption was reason.[17]

Many moralists attempted to depict drunkenness, therefore, in terms of the loss of. manhood itself. According to Stubbes, drunkenness 'dissolveth the whole man at length' – a process that he associated with the loss of bodily control it engendered. Similarly, the homily against gluttony and drunkenness claimed that drunkards were 'altogether without power of themselves'. The drunkard literally poured himself away, 'some vomiting spewing & disgorging their filthie stomacks, other some...pissing under the boord as they sit', thereby making himself unfit for society. According to Lenton, '[h]e is one that either spues himselfe out, or gives occasion to be spurned out of all civill Company'.[18]

It was the ways in which such 'suckpots', 'swiltubs' and 'filbellies' abnegated their social ties and obligations as a result of their deviation from normative manhood that principally preoccupied their critics, however.[19] According to moral commentary, the practices of excessive drinkers threatened relationships between neighbours, families and friends and were depicted as antisocial in the extreme. A man who could not control himself was not deemed a fit member of the commonwealth. The homily against gluttony and drunkenness discounted drunkards from being profitable members of society, while Thomas Young judged them unfit for 'any honest service' either as a magistrate or even as a subject.[20]

Drinkers were also represented as neglecting their Christian duties towards the poor. In *The Glasse of Mans Folly*, a marginal note cautioned that 'Bibbers are bountifull to abuses, not to good uses', while in the main text excessive drinkers were condemned for their neglect of the needs of others. One of the central concerns driving anti-drinking diatribes, and the tightening of licensing regulations during the early modern period, was that brewing was a waste of malted grain that could be put to better use as bread. It is perhaps unsurprising, therefore, that *The Glasse of Mans Folly*, first published in 1595 during a period of harvest failure and dearth, privileged this theme, condemning drunkards as 'miscreants without comiseration, sympathy, or fellow-feeling of famished folks and children'. Depicting drink as a waste of God's bounty, the anonymous author of this tract exhorted: 'Yee Common-wealth consumers, devote not your selves to the Divell. Your surfetting excesse, so raiseth the price, that the poor cannot maintaine theyr families, but are distressed, some distracted. Yee are the death and undooing of thousands.'[21]

Alehouses, particularly in puritan tracts, were depicted as the cause of many a poor man's undoing not only by diverting resources which could be better used for the relief of the poor, but also by compounding the impoverishment of the poor themselves. Often ignoring the fact that a license to sell ale could provide a means of overcoming poverty for alehouse keepers, campaigns to reform manners emphasised the plight of consumers who were either distracted from their labours or enticed to spend their meagre earnings on ale. According to Keith Wrightson, this was as an attack on the social functions of the alehouse as well an expression of economic concerns.[22] Seventeenth-century legislation banned 'tippling' for more than one hour in attempts to pit labour against leisure, and puritan moralists derided the communal and recreational functions of alehouses as distractions from godliness, especially on the Sabbath. In this way, alehouses were represented as 'anti-churches', associated with sin and the wiles of the devil, and alehouse keepers as 'anti-ministers' competing with divines for the souls of their clientele by offering a satanic form of communion.[23] Thomas Young complained, for example, that the inhabitants of the New Forest and the Forest of Windsor 'goe ten times to an Alehouse, before they goe once to a Church'.[24]

Multiple vices were linked with drinking. Swearing, slander and brawling contravened expectations of neighbourly relations conducive to Christian harmony. Advice to young men frequently warned that the bulk of unwarranted challenges and over-hasty retaliations were fuelled by drink, and it was also a commonplace to link drunkenness to murder.[25] In addition, according to Hart, none were more prone 'to perjury, lying, slandering, back-biting, and taking his neighbours good name from him' than drunkards. In such representations, moralists worked to associate drinking with vexatious rather than convivial exchange. Drinking rituals were sometimes also accorded a dangerously levelling effect, breaking down distinctions of social status. Hart was horrified that 'Gentle-men of faire estates, of antient houses, descended of noble parentage and pedegree' debased themselves by associating with 'any base varlet, swill-bowle, tosse-pot and pot-companion' in taverns and tap houses.[26] While drinking rituals were to be shunned for destroying harmony between neighbours, they were also condemned for encouraging harmony between different social groups at the expense of appropriate status distinctions.

Drinking was also viewed as one of the main causes of domestic strife, primarily between husbands and wives but also between masters and their servants. Representations of thriftless husbands in domestic advice commonly blamed such men's neglect of their wives and children on the rival attractions of alehouse sociability. For example, the puritan divine William Whately warned that one of the 'chief faults' in a husband was 'unthriftyness' which he defined in terms of 'Drunkennesse, gaming, [and] ill company keeping'.[27] Orders against tippling linked it directly to men's neglect of their families, such as that issued by the Leicester authorities in 1563:

> because that many unthriftie persons being poore men & havyng wyfe & children use commonlye to sytt & typple in alehowses & typlynghowses at suche tyme as theye ought both by Godes lawes & by the lawes [of] this realme to be otherwyse occupied, not only to the great displesure of God but also to the impoveryssyng of them that so abuse their tyme, whylst their poor wyfes, chyldren, and famele almost starve at home for lacke of that that the said evyll disposed people superflewusley spend.[28]

The alehouse not only diverted men from their duties of provision, but was also cited as one of the main causes of domestic violence. *The Glass of Mans Folly* rehearsed a stereotypical scene depicting a wife, who 'seeing her goods consuming, and children crying', and begging her husband to be more frugal, met with a violent response: 'The Beere piercing his braine, hee counts her counsell hostilitie: he stamps & staggers, stares, sweares, & blasphemes the Almightie, with hideous othes, wherby Gods wrath is kindled. He gives her blowes, no beefe, whereby love decreaseth, hatred increaseth.'[29] Such scenes, often even more elaborately drawn, were also the stock in trade of ballads depicting ill-fated marriages.[30]

Marital relations were additionally jeopardised by the opportunities for adulterous sex and 'whoring' associated with the alehouse and men's drinking rituals. Excessive drinking was routinely represented as leading to illicit sex, in an extension of the commonplace that drink left men at the mercy of their passions. The seventh category of drunkard condemned by Thomas Young, for example, was the 'Goate drunke, who in his drinke [is] so lecherous, that hee makes no difference of either time, or place, age or youth, but cryes out a Whoore, a Whoore, ten pound for a Whoore.'[31] Occasionally, different concerns surfaced, which suggest that such anxieties extended beyond the desire to keep marital relations (and household economies) intact. *The Glasse of Mans Folly* warned its readers to '[b]ee not a sucking Sodomite', asserting that '[q]uaffing leades to the lake of quaking. Pray and repent' and declaring 'they are worse then Brutes, that are bond-slaves to evill Affections'.[32] Conjuring the image of the sodomite, the author of this tract was unusual in condemning men's drinking bonds with an explicit reference to their erotic potential, any acknowledgement of which more often remained either submerged or absent. Yet given the way in which early modern sexuality was understood, like consumption, in terms of appetite (whether controlled or uncontrolled), it is possible that such links between excessive consumption and the lack of sexual restraint were more generally implicit in complaint literature, if not always explicitly drawn.[33]

More frequently, however, the alehouse was condemned on the grounds that it fostered 'false-friendship' (rather than good fellowship), founded on duplicity and self-interest instead of trust and reciprocity. In the alehouse, principles of merit as well as deference were overturned: '[e]vill people shall be esteemed, and good people contemned'.[34] If not shunned or ridiculed, the 'good' in this moral scheme were likely to be enticed by the flattery and deception of pot companions to follow their evil example. This was a frequently reiterated theme. Printed advice from fathers to sons routinely warned against the dangers of bad company and the so-called 'good fellows' who were likely to lead them astray, offer them false promises, and betray their confidences.[35] The 'swaggering and deboyst companions' excoriated by Thomas Young were purveyors of 'faire words, but faint deeds', since 'for the most part what they promise when they are drunke, they forget when they are sober: or else in their vaine-glorious humour, they promise higher matters than their low estate (consumed with prodigalitie) can performe'. Pot companions were portrayed as fair-weather friends, preying on other men's good will (not to mention their purses), and daring innocents to accompany them in their excesses. So, according to Young,

> Your pot friendship, is no friendship: For as long as thou hast good clothes on thy backe, and money in thy purse, thou shalt have friends plenty, and good fellowes flocke about thee: to give thee drinke, when thou hast too much before, and truely I thinke hereupon comes the name of goodfellow, *quasi* goadfellow, because hee forceth and goads his fellowes forward to be drunke.[36]

Young, and many others, also warned that should a man's money run dry he would find himself deserted by his 'friends', who would not lend him sixpence for food although they would previously have happily spent a crown to get him drunk. Moralists and advice writers also warned men not to disclose any secrets to pot companions, who would inevitably betray the trust expected of true friends, since drink loosened the tongue and forced men to lose control of their speech. Good fellowship, then, was represented as a form of anti-friendship rather than a corruption of true friendship – and, perhaps as a result, as the signs of friendship were absent from such characterisations, this served also to deflect the spectre of sodomy.

Moral commentary therefore portrayed drunkenness and the rituals associated with it in highly condemnatory terms, as both a deviation from manhood and a complete rejection of the conventions expected to govern social relations both between men and women and amongst men themselves. Alehouses were characterised as loci of satanic and seditious fervour, and drink was blamed for inverting norms of charity, neighbourliness, marital harmony and friendship. The intimacies between men afforded by good fellowship were tacitly acknowledged, and condemned on a number of grounds, but only very rarely in explicitly erotic terms. The extent to which such views were more broadly shared is impossible to discern, but, in broad terms, anxieties about drunkenness were certainly not restricted to a minority of puritan clergymen. In a sample of over 300 slander suits begun in Cambridge between 1580 and 1640, just over 5 per cent involved accusations of drunkenness, suggesting that it could be a charge deemed serious enough to warrant legal action.[37] For example, despite widespread expectations that university students routinely indulged in excessive drinking, Richard Hanger of St John's College, Cambridge, sued a fellow of Trinity College for accusing him of being drunk and claimed substantial damages, with one witness supporting his case by declaring that 'if his Sir Hangers father should take any deepe displeasure agaynst him Sir Hanger for the said wordes... Sir Hanger had better lost *Cli'*.[38] Married men also appear to have been rebuked by their neighbours for frequenting the alehouse and neglecting their families, and such charges were sometimes used to discredit witnesses in court.[39]

Yet it is also clear that vast amounts of alcohol were routinely consumed in early modern England. According to Gregory King, towards the end of the seventeenth century around one quart of beer was consumed daily for every man, woman and child, accounting for 28 per cent of annual per capita expenditure.[40] Men are likely to have drunk the bulk of it, both in comparatively moderate ways that were broadly accepted, and in binges of excess, involving rituals which, despite widespread invective against drunkenness, nonetheless held positive meanings and served potent functions for the men involved. Obviously, in some instances, excessive drinking was probably a result of what we would today call alcoholism, and moralists' concerns about the plight of the fortunes and families of the men involved reflected the very dire impact alcohol addiction could have. But in many instances of excess, men enacted complex rituals that were carefully choreographed and not just programmed by the dictates of drink alone. As anthropologists have shown, while alcohol clearly has a physiological impact on the body, there is extensive cultural variation in drinking rituals and drunken comportment, suggesting that drunken behaviour is learned behaviour, and a form of calculated social interaction rather than merely an alcohol-induced physical condition.[41] It is important therefore, to explore the meanings of drinking rituals for the men involved as well as their critics. The fact that moralists worked so hard to characterise them as unmanly and involving false bonds suggests that the opposite may well have been true for participants.

II

There were many early modern drinking rituals that were deemed routinely acceptable to all but the staunchest advocates of temperance. Drink frequently functioned as a mundane marker of accord and good will and, far from undermining neighbourhood ties, served to reinforce them. Wine or beer was often used to seal agreements, with much bargain-making and reckoning performed in alehouses both to ensure it was properly witnessed and to bind the parties in mutual obligation through the symbolic gestures of hospitality. When goodwill foundered, pledging a health was also a common means of patching up quarrels, serving as a sign of restored social harmony.[42] As the sermoniser Thomas Gataker complained, 'every bargaine [is made] over a Winepot'.[43] But it is clear that inns and alehouses were central venues for brokering credit and mediating disputes in early modern England, and may have contributed as much (if not more) to the 'culture of reconciliation' as the law courts.[44]

Drinking was also a common form of leisure in early modern England, especially from the mid-sixteenth century as the alehouse increasingly competed with the churchyard as a forum for communal recreation, much to the chagrin, as we have seen, of puritan objectors.[45] As a recreational pursuit, drinking was more routinely associated with male sociability, although women were by no means absent from alehouses and their festivities. Alehouses and inns functioned as venues for courtship, and women – both married as well as unmarried – often accompanied men to eat and drink there. Women were involved in alehouse culture as purveyors as well as consumers, either as wives, daughters or servants to the host, or as alehouse keepers in their own right – an occupation that appears to have been central to the subsistence of many widows. A few women also drank to excess. Women as well as men sued for defamation in response to accusations of drunkenness, and were sometimes formally disciplined for drunkenness, although far less frequently than men.[46] Punishments meted out to drunken women may, however, have been far harsher than the fines or sessions in the stocks that were the standard penalty for men. Elizabeth Blakey, for example, of Rye (Sussex) was banished from the town, on pain of losing one of her ears, for 'hir incontinent Liff[,] suspected dronkennes and comon Raylinge'. If she dared return she was to 'be sett in the Coller, cucked and a billet to be nailled at her Eare' and once again banished, on penalty of losing *both* her ears.[47] As this last case suggests, women present in or connected to alehouses were particularly vulnerable to accusations of unchastity; the negative association between drunken revelry and illicit sex was certainly not exclusive to men.[48]

Although there was a degree of gender convergence in alehouse conviviality, drinking patterns were nonetheless highly gender related and at times gender specific. The personal honour of both women and men could be at stake in alehouses, but in extremely different ways. Women's status in alehouses was more peripheral than men's, and women were usually denied the unselfconscious enjoyment of drinking that was automatically claimed by men. Besides dominating the routine habits of sociability associated with the alehouse, men also engaged in rituals of excess that were closely tied to assertions of specifically male forms of prowess. Such drinking patterns and the disruptive behaviour associated with them were central to the articulation of counter codes of manhood in early modern England. They replaced the normative virtues of manhood – such as thrift, moderation, sobriety and self-government – with the competing attributes of prodigality, bravado, raucousness and excess. While reinforcing ties between men, and therefore shoring up male dominance (particularly in relation to women), the fraternal ties of comradeship central to such rituals also posed a direct challenge to the dictates of deference and the hierarchies that were expected to govern relations between men.

The deliberately extravagant consumption of large amounts of drink in the context of a group appears to have functioned as a test of manhood not unlike a trial of strength or a feat of bravery. A Cambridge barber-surgeon, for example, complained that his servant was 'in his drinking... most unreasonable & unsatiable' and that 'sometimes *to show his vallor* in that wickednes he hath set a can of thre pints to his head & dr[u]nk it off... & that he drunk indeed a quart or above & many times ordinarily drinketh a pint at a time'.[49] The challenge between Cambridge scholars to 'drinke whole potts', which in turn let to a large-scale brawl, similarly suggested that the ability to both display and withstand profligate consumption was a measure of manhood – to the extent that it also functioned as a form of initiation.[50] Nor were such expectations limited to student culture. A complaint against a Worcestershire alehouse keeper objected not only that he allowed gaming and drinking in his house 'at unseasonable times', but also that he fell out with his neighbours if they did not 'carouse and drink full cups with him calling them cowards with many other base words'.[51] And when the Dorset cowherd James Pierce drove his cattle home on a December evening in 1617 and encountered a group, all of whom, in his opinion, had 'droncke to[o] much', one of them called to him 'come you hither and drincke' and drew his sword on Pierce when he refused, 'saying he would make him drink'.[52] Rather like a challenge to the field, the challenge to drink appears to have invoked a spectrum of values pitting valour against cowardice. The display of appetite in such instances was harnessed to, rather than being seen as inimical to, concepts of manhood.

One of the main characteristics of such consumption – which distinguished it from the habits of the lone tippler – was that it was performed for the group. Participants depended upon their fellow drinkers to provide a platform for, and the endorsement of, such assertions of manhood. This was particularly true of the drinking binges that were a feature of male youth culture. These often involved not only an inversion of the principles of thrift but also direct attacks on the symbols of the established male order in counter codes of misrule. Nightwalkers challenged expectations that men would work by day and sleep by night and, as part of their drunken revelry, young men smashed windows, broke down work stalls, roused neighbours from their beds with charges of cuckoldry, and appropriated forms of regulatory violence in order to assert temporary dominance in defiance of their elders.[53] So, in 1605, the Bishop of Coventry complained of 'certeine lewd youths' who had assaulted the king's watch at around 11 or 12 p.m., and then 'by way of triumphe as yt were for their victorious facte' had set about 'a bibbinge & quaffinge of their ale at the markett Crosse', thereby disturbing many from their sleep.[54] Officials of various kinds were frequently targeted by drunken revellers. Robert and Thomas Talbott, for example, abused the constable of Upway in Dorset on their emergence from an alehouse, calling him 'blacke rogue and blacke knave... and beating their breeches b[a]d him come and kisse their tayles' before going on their way 'holdinge their hatts uppon theire staves whooping and hollowinge'.[55]

In these instances, collective drinking rituals fuelled the expression of antagonisms between men along hierarchies of age and authority. Young men adopted what might be labelled 'anti-patriarchal' stances in direct opposition to normative codes of manhood that required thrift, self-government and deference.[56] It is perhaps unsurprising that in a youth-heavy society, in which the householding status that was the most significant gateway to adulthood was postponed for the majority of men until their late twenties, younger men turned to the rituals of excess as the basis for alternative codes of manhood from which they were not materially barred. This inevitably compounded the tensions between younger men and their house-holding counterparts. However, drinking rituals involving the fraternal ties of the group also served to threaten hierarchies between men by *ignoring* (rather than challenging) the distance that was expected to govern relations between men of different ages and of different rank. The collective drinking binges of youthful misrule, for example, often brought together men of different social groups who would have kept their distance in other circumstances.[57]

Ties of sociability also flouted principles of deference when they bound, rather than divided, younger and older men. A frequent complaint against alehouse keepers was that they led young men astray. The tithingman of Swindon in 1635 informed the Wiltshire magistrates that

Edward Feawtrell had not only allowed gambling in his alehouse on a Sunday night, but also had himself 'played at Shovel board with an apprentice boy for two or three hours' on more than one occasion.[58] The justices of Worcestershire similarly received a complaint against two unlicensed keepers, William Bryan and Thomas Morley, who 'harbour[ed] men's servants and children in the night time' encouraging them and other 'lewd persons' to 'roll men's timber in the night time into the highways and ploughs and harrows out of their places and pull up men's pales and stiles and rails' as part of their drunken revelry.[59] Fraternisation across boundaries of age was also a concern for the Cambridge university authorities, who sometimes had to admonish fellows for leading their charges astray – such as Mr Hakluyt of Trinity College who was punished for 'the misleading [of] a young scholler of the house & often intisuing [*sic*] him unto the taverns'.[60]

There was, therefore, an uneasy tension between the dictates of a hierarchical society that privileged certain men above others and a more broadly shared culture of male prowess involving the selective display as well as restraint of appetite. The rituals of excess were deemed more tolerable when they offset, rather than directly challenged, the hierarchies dividing men, which explains the extent to which youthful excesses in particular could be accommodated within a patriarchal framework as mere 'sport'. Yet the divisions between men were becoming starker over the course of the sixteenth and seventeenth centuries, as increasing numbers were unable to marry (having insufficient resources to set up a new household) and were rendered more permanently subordinate as a consequence of their dependence on wages throughout their adult lives as opposed to during a life-cycle phase of service.[61] This compounded the problems posed by an already youth-heavy society by transposing some of the tensions generated by hierarchies of age to emergent distinctions of class.[62]

The ties of comradeship binding groups of men therefore served a range of functions, structured by the contradictory demands of a polarising society. The group provided a forum for the rituals of excess, through which assertions of masculinity associated with pushing appetite to its limits were validated. Conducted alone, such behaviour would have held very different meanings, and lost the agency afforded by the endorsement of the group. It was fraternal bonds that enabled the rejection, if not the complete inversion, of the norms of self-restraint and deference expected to govern men's behaviour and interaction, and in their most extreme forms they were deemed threatening to the patriarchal order. Yet they also pasted over some of the cracks in a society in which the social and economic forces dividing men were putting more pressure on the ties that bound them, creating an uneasy relationship between fraternity and patriarchy.

In all their manifestations, these were not the lasting bonds of mutual knowledge, trust or reciprocity, but the shallower and mostly temporary ties of mutual recognition that facilitated the collective performance of certain forms of male identity. They were no less potent as a result, however, nor devoid of the potential for male intimacy. It is possible that, on occasion, such ties fleetingly, and unthreateningly, permitted the subtle elision of the homosocial and the homoerotic – which, as Eve Sedgwick has argued, have not always existed in opposition.[63] The incident with which this chapter opened involving the Dorset butcher and a servant pissing into a chamber pot and then sharing its contents is an extreme example of the intimacies afforded by the male culture of excess. It is impossible to know, however, how representative such an event was, although it is worth recalling that it was the alehouse-keeper who was deemed the principal offender rather than the men involved. It is likely that the alehouse offered opportunities for bodily intimacy that were unacceptable in other contexts, not only between men and women but also between men themselves. Alehouses were often condemned as sites for illicit sexual encounter, sometimes involving genital exposure by men, and more occasionally, women.[64] Men also appear to have exposed themselves in order to urinate in alehouses, such as the Worcestershire clerk Edward Pearce, who reportedly 'played so long in an alehouse at a game called "Fox myne host" and drank so hard that he pissed under the table', before again urinating into the fire when his demand for more drink was not met quickly enough.[65] Drinking rituals involved men's familiarity with each other's bodies, from the gestures of camaraderie, such as linking arms or slapping backs to more transgressive moves, such as that performed by a man from Somerset who was charged with pulling out 'the privy member of Thomas Lane, being asleep' and resting it 'upon a child's shoe'.[66] Occasionally they were deliberately violatory, as when John Pulford 'took out' Robert Lyle's genitals and rolled them on a table, in full view of the alehouse company, calling Lyle his 'whore' and declaring he meant to 'use' him 'as if he had been a woman'.[67]

It is extremely difficult to probe the precise meanings of such actions to the men involved when scrutinising shards of evidence through the distorting lens of regulatory records. It is nonetheless evident that fleeting physical intimacies were afforded by men's drinking rituals. The gestures involved may have variously signified as either homosocial or transgressive (in either a sexual or a social sense), or as homoerotic in a way that was rendered at least temporarily permissible by the solidarities of excess. The manhood associated with the excessive display of appetite was rooted in prodigality, bravado and collectivism, in contrast to the more clearly patriarchal imperatives of thrift, industry, individual responsibility and order. The only hierarchy unthreatened by men's drinking rituals was the gender hierarchy, and one of the functions of the bonds of comradeship was undoubtedly to exclude women. However, while shoring up this particular pillar of patriarchal relations, the camaraderie of excess increasingly served to reinforce rather than offset the divisions between men, particularly on the basis of incipient class identities as well as inter-generational conflicts. This may have contributed to the withdrawal of the 'respectable' from alehouses over the course of the seventeenth century and also to the more explicit associations drawn between cultures of excess and the condemnatory framework of sodomy in the Reformation of manners campaign of the later seventeenth century.[68]

Comradeship involved as many complexities as male friendship in early modern England, sometimes serving to elide the homosocial with the homoerotic unproblematically, and sometimes signifying social and/or sexual transgression. It is possible that these potential contradictions became more difficult to sustain over the course of the period. What is clear, however, is the potency of male bonds established through comradeship. In contrast to the lasting ties of friendship founded on mutual knowledge and reciprocal obligation, it was a form of self-fulfilment based largely on self-effacement: in order to partake, men submerged their individual identities and instead adopted the mantle of manhood offered by the group. Like friendship, comradeship was a potent form of bonding between men in early modern England; unlike friendship, however, this was often not because it was an especially meaningful form of male subjectivity, but precisely because (albeit in carefully studied ways) it was not.

Notes

1. J. Hart, *KΛINIKH, Or the Diet of the Diseased* (London, 1633), pp. 128–30.
2. Ibid., pp. 131–2.
3. J.H. Bettey (ed.), *The Case Book of Sir Francis Ashley J.P. Recorder of Dorchester 1614–1635* (Dorchester: Dorset Record Society, 1981), p. 45.
4. Ibid., pp. 45–7.
5. A. Bray, 'To Be a Man in Early Modern Society. The Curious Case of Michael Wigglesworth', *History Workshop Journal*, 41 (1996), 155–65.

6. A. Bray, *Homosexuality in Renaissance England* (London: Gay Men's Press, 1982).
7. P. Lyman, 'The Fraternal Bond as a Joking Relationship: A Case Study of the Role of Sexist Jokes in Male Group Bonding', in M.S. Kimmel and M.A. Messner (eds), *Men's Lives* (London: Collier Macmillan, 1989), pp. 171–81; R.A. Strikwerda and L. May, 'Male Friendship and Intimacy', in L. May and R.A. Strikwerda (eds), *Rethinking Masculinity: Philosophical Explorations in Light of Feminism* (Maryland: Rowman & Littlefield, 1992), pp. 95–110. For a fuller discussion of this distinction, see A. Shepard, *Meanings of Manhood in Early Modern England* (Oxford: Oxford University Press, 2003), pp. 95–6.
8. D.M. Halperin, 'Introduction: Among Men – History, Sexuality, and the Return of Affect', in K. O'Donnell and M. O'Rourke (eds), *Love, Sex, Intimacy and Friendship between Men, 1550–1800* (Basingstoke: Palgrave Macmillan, 2003). Cf. G.E. Haggerty, *Men in Love: Masculinity and Sexuality in the Eighteenth Century* (New York: Columbia University Press, 1999) and A. Bray, *The Friend* (Chicago: University of Chicago Press, 2003).
9. Bray, *The Friend*, ch. 4.
10. E.K. Sedgwick, *Between Men: English Literature and Male Homosocial Desire* (New York: Columbia University Press, 1985). A. Bray, 'Homosexuality and the Signs of Male Friendship in Elizabethan England', *History Workshop Journal*, 29 (1990), 1–19; idem, *The Friend*. See also B.R. Smith, *Homosexual Desire in Shakespeare's England: A Cultural Poetics* (Chicago: University of Chicago Press, 1991).
11. A. Bray and Michel Rey, 'The Body of the Friend: Continuity and Change in Masculine Friendship in the Seventeenth Century', in T. Hitchcock and M. Cohen (eds), *English Masculinities 1660–1800* (Harlow: Longman, 1999). See also L. Roper, *Oedipus and the Devil: Witchcraft, Sexuality and Religion in Early Modern Europe* (London and New York: Routledge, 1994), ch. 5.
12. For a discussion of the ways in which this distinction has (mis)informed the history of homosexuality, see D.M. Halperin, 'Forgetting Foucault: Acts, Identities, and the History of Sexuality', *Representations*, 63 (1998), 93–120. See also A. Shepard, 'Just Good Friends? Same-Sex Intimacy in Early Modern Britain and Europe', *History Workshop Journal*, 58 (2004), 289–96.
13. M. DiGangi, 'How Queer was the Renaissance?', in O'Donnell and O'Rourke (eds), *Love, Sex, Intimacy and Friendship*, pp. 128–47.
14. Sir W. Raleigh, *Sir Walter Raleighs Instructions to his Sonne and to Posterity* (London, 1632), p. 81; F. Lenton, *Characterismi; or, Lentons Leasures* (London, 1631), sig. E12; T. Young, *Englands Bane; or, The Description of Drunkennesse* (London, 1617), sigs F2^v–F3. See also W. Vaughan, *Directions for Health, Both Naturall and Artificiall* (London, 1617), p. 48.
15. P. Stubbes, *The Anatomie of Abuses* (London, 1583), sig. I4.
16. T. Kingsmill, *The Drunkards Warning* (London, 1631), pp. 32, 33.
17. *The Seconde Tome of Homelyes...Set Out by the Aucthoritie of the Quenes Maiestie: and to be Read in Every Paryshe Churche Agreablye* (London, 1563), fol. 111.
18. Stubbes, *Anatomie of Abuses*, sig. I4; Lenton, *Characterismi*, sig. F.
19. B.H., *The Glasse of Mans Folly, and Meanes to Amendment, for the Health and Wealth of Soule and Body* (London, 1615), pp. 3, 13.
20. *Seconde Tome of Homelyes*, fol. 111^v; Young, *Englands Bane*, sig. D^v.
21. *Glasse of Mans Folly*, pp. 3, 7. See also Hart, *ΚΛΙΝΙΚΗ*, p. 132.

22. K. Wrightson, 'Alehouses, Order and Reformation in Rural England, 1590–1660', in E. Yeo and S. Yeo (eds), *Popular Culture and Class Conflict, 1590–1914: Explorations in the History of Labour and Leisure* (Brighton: Harvester, 1981), pp. 1–27.

23. A.L. Martin, *Alcohol, Sex, and Gender in Late Medieval and Early Modern Europe* (Basingstoke: Palgrave, 2001), pp. 62–6.

24. Young, *Englands Bane*, sig. F.

25. See, e.g., Raleigh, *Sir Walter Raleighs Instructions*, pp. 90–1; *Keepe within Compasse; or, The Worthy Legacy of a Wise Father to his Beloved Sonne* (London, 1619), sig. C5ᵛ; Young, *Englands Bane*, sig. Cᵛ.

26. Hart, *ΚΛΙΝΙΚΗ*, p. 135.

27. W. Whately, *A Bride Bush; or, A Direction for Married Persons* (London, 1623), p. 103.

28. M. Bateson (ed.), *Records of the Borough of Leicester. Being a Series of Extracts from the Archives of the Corporation of Leicester, 1509–1603* (Cambridge: Cambridge University Press, 1905), pp. 108–9.

29. *Glasse of Mans Folly*, p. 4.

30. J.A. Sharpe, 'Plebeian Marriage in Stuart England: Some Evidence from Popular Literature', *Transactions of the Royal Historical Society*, 5th ser., 36 (1986), 69–90.

31. Young, *Englands Bane*, sig. F3.

32. *Glasse of Mans Folly*, p. 8.

33. Bray, 'To Be a Man in Early Modern Society'; DiGangi, 'How Queer was the Renaissance?'.

34. *Glasse of Mans Folly*, p. 12.

35. Shepard, *Meanings of Manhood*, pp. 27–8.

36. Young, *Englands Bane*, sigs D4ᵛ–E.

37. Shepard, *Meanings of Manhood*, pp. 162–6. See also E.A. Foyster, *Manhood in Early Modern England: Honour, Sex and Marriage* (Harlow: Longman, 1999), pp. 40–1.

38. Cambridge University Library, Cambridge University Archive, V.C.Ct.II.12, fol. 2.

39. A. Shepard, 'Manhood, Credit and Patriarchy in Early Modern England, c.1580–1640', *Past and Present*, 167 (2000), 75–106, on pp. 83–5.

40. Martin, *Alcohol, Sex, and Gender*, p. 7.

41. M. Douglas (ed.), *Constructive Drinking: Perspectives on Drink from Anthropology* (Cambridge: Cambridge University Press, 1987).

42. For examples, see Shepard, *Meanings of Manhood*, p. 101.

43. T. Gataker, *The Decease of Lazarus Christ's Friend* (London, 1640), sig. A4.

44. C. Muldrew, 'The Culture of Reconciliation: Community and the Settlement of Economic Disputes in Early Modern England', *Historical Journal*, 39 (1996), 915–42. See also B. Kümin, 'Useful to Have, but Difficult to Govern: Inns and Taverns in Early Modern Bern and Vaud', *Journal of Early Modern History*, 3 (1999), 153–75.

45. P. Clark, 'The Alehouse and the Alternative Society', in D. Pennington and K. Thomas (eds), *Puritans and Revolutionaries: Essays in Seventeenth-Century History Presented to Christopher Hill* (Oxford: Clarendon Press, 1978), pp. 47–72. See also J. Warner, 'Historical Perspectives on the Shifting Boundaries around Youth and Alcohol. The Example of Pre-Industrial England, 1350–1750', *Addiction*, 93 (1998), 641–57.

46. Wrightson, 'Alehouses, Order and Reformation', pp. 7–8; P. Clark, *The English Alehouse: A Social History 1200–1830* (London: Longman, 1983); P. Griffiths, *Youth and Authority: Formative Experiences in England, 1560–1640* (Oxford: Clarendon Press, 1996), pp. 209–12.

47. East Sussex Record Office, Rye 1/5, fol. 18^v.

48. Shepard, *Meanings of Manhood*, pp. 102–3. See also B.A. Tlusty, 'Crossing Gender Boundaries: Women as Drunkards in Early Modern Augsburg', in S. Backman, H. Künast, S. Ullmann and B.A. Tlusty (eds), *Ehrkonzepte in der Frühen Neuzeit: Identitäten und Abgrenzungen* (Berlin: Akademie Verlag, 1998), pp. 185–97.

49. Cambridge University Archive, V.C.Ct.III.32, no. 59.

50. Cambridge University Archive, V.C.Ct.III.14, no. 105. Shepard, *Meanings of Manhood*, pp. 105–6.

51. *Worcestershire County Records: The Quarter Sessions Rolls*, vol. I: *1591–1643*, comp. J.W.W. Bund (Worcester: Baylis, 1900), p. 310.

52. *Case Book of Sir Francis Ashley*, p. 48.

53. P. Griffiths, 'Meanings of Nightwalking in Early Modern England', *The Seventeenth Century*, 13 (1998), 212–38; Shepard, *Meanings of Manhood*, pp. 96–8.

54. S.A.H. Burne (ed.), *The Staffordshire Quarter Sessions Rolls*, vol. 5: *1603–1606* (Kendal: Titus Wilson & Co., 1940), p. 238.

55. *Case Book of Sir Francis Ashley*, p. 87.

56. Shepard, *Meanings of Manhood*. See also M.E. Weisner, '*Wandervögels* and Women: Journeymen's Concepts of Masculinity in Early Modern Germany', *Journal of Social History*, 24 (1991), 767–82.

57. Shepard, *Meanings of Manhood*, pp. 111–12; eadem, 'Contesting Communities? "Town" and "Gown" in Cambridge, *c.*1560–1640', in A. Shepard and P. Withington (eds), *Communities in Early Modern England: Networks, Place, Rhetoric* (Manchester: Manchester University Press, 2000), pp. 216–34.

58. B. Howard Cunnington (ed.), *Records of the County of Wilts, Being Extracts from the Quarter Sessions Great Rolls of the Seventeenth Century* (Devizes, 1932), p. 113.

59. *Worcestershire County Records*, 1: 345. See also p. 323.

60. Trinity College, Cambridge, Trinity College Archives, Admissions and Admonitions, 1566–1759, p. 396. See also p. 397.

61. For a summary of these trends, see K. Wrightson, *Earthly Necessities: Economic Lives in Early Modern Britain* (New York and London: Yale University Press, 2000), part 2, esp. pp. 221–6.

62. For a fuller discussion of the impact of these economic and demographic trends on male identities and social relations, see Shepard, *Meanings of Manhood*, and idem, 'From Anxious Patriarchs to Refined Gentlemen? Manhood in Britain, c.1500–c.1700', *Journal of British Studies*, 44 (2005), 281–95.

63. Sedgwick, *Between Men*. See also Smith, *Homosexual Desire in Shakespeare's England*.

64. See, e.g., the accusation that Dorothy Dugresse 'did shew hir arse in an alehouse' as part of drunken exploits, Cambridge University Archive, V.C.Ct.II.32, fol. 112.

65. *Worcestershire County Records*, 1: 53. See also the complaint against such habits in *Glasse of Mans Folly*, p. 2.

66. G.R. Quaife, *Wanton Wenches and Wayward Wives. Peasants and Illicit Sex in Early Seventeenth Century England* (London: Croom Helm, 1979), p. 166. See also Martin, *Alcohol, Sex, and Gender*, ch. 5; Roper, *Oedipus and the Devil*, ch. 5.

67. L. Gowing, *Common Bodies: Women, Touch and Power in Seventeenth-Century England* (New Haven and London: Yale University Press, 2003), p. 1.

68. Clark, 'The Alehouse'; R. Trumbach, 'The Birth of the Queen: Sodomy and the Emergence of Gender Equality in Modern Culture, 1660–1750', in M.B. Duberman, M. Vicinus and G. Chauncey (eds), *Hidden From History: Reclaiming the Gay and Lesbian Past* (London: Penguin, 1989), pp. 129–40; idem, 'London's Sapphists: From Three Sexes to Four Genders in the Making of Modern Culture', in J. Epstein and K. Straub (eds), *Body Guards: The Cultural Politics of Gender Ambiguity* (New York: Routledge, 1991), pp. 112–41; idem, 'The Heterosexual Male in Eighteenth-Century London and His Queer Interactions', in O'Donnell and O'Rourke (eds), *Love, Sex, Intimacy and Friendship*, pp. 87–127.

6
The Politics of Women's Friendship in Early Modern England

Laura Gowing

Friendship, it has become clear, was one of the pivotal points of communication, power, and intimacy in early modern society. Alan Bray's examination of the emotional and physical dynamics of male friendship showed how, in the great houses of sixteenth- and seventeenth-century England, intimate body practices were located outside the marital relationship. Habits of touching, eating, and sleeping were shared between men, in public and in private; shared kisses, meals, and beds were imbued with all the power that gifts traditionally held in this society. For the intimate male friends of the early seventeenth century, the body was a gift like others, a means of binding by favour and obligation. By the late seventeenth century, Bray argues, the uncomfortable threat of sodomitic readings of friendship made men withdraw from the physical intimacies of friendship, and put it on a more formal footing.[1] As the household became the nuclear family, the gift of the body became one suitable only for exchange between a man and a woman.

This is a story dependent on the political, public roles of elite men and their aspiring servants: the gestures of friendship were made for public consumption, and they marked out hierarchies of preference and priority for the world. And, as the great households with their heavily masculine companies have left the best evidence of this world of public intimacy, it is also premised on the relative absence of women from the closer circles of those households. That absence, asserted firmly by Bray in *The Friend*, is a problematic assumption. The presence of women is often unequally registered in the early modern archive; in the case of the great houses, for example, women servants were likely to be less formally employed and more mobile, their labour less visibly recorded than that of men.[2] Nevertheless, in a world of men, male alliances were highly visible and heavily symbolic. It seems at first rather obvious that

131

Bray's narrative of friendship does not work for women, for two reasons: the political invisibility of women's friendship and the social and legal invisibility of female sodomy, or lesbianism. Both these assumptions are now coming to seem less secure.

Women's friendships had few of the explicitly political implications that charged intimate bonds between men. They have often been invisible to the historian's eye, and to those of literary critics. Derrida's impassioned call for a return to the pre-Enlightenment political ethics of friendship leaves women out of it, as many early modern men did.[3] To contemporaries, the ethical amity that was the ideal of male friendship was simply unavailable to women. As Montaigne's English translator put it: 'the ordinary sufficencie of women, cannot answere this conference and communication, the nurse of this sacred bond: nor seeme their mindes strong enough to endure the pulling of a knot so hard, so fast, and durable'.[4] Impossible, apparently, to construe as companions in amity, women feature in the stories of male friendship largely as facilitators, or enemies, of male bonding.[5] The friendships they dreamed and wrote most about, it seems, were spiritual, more than practical: relationships that stepped beyond gender and sex into a world in which bodies did not matter.[6]

But the reasons for telling the tale of pragmatic, political friendship, with its dangerous closeness to sexual deviance, as a story only about men are becoming problematic. Recent work on political alliances, matchmaking, the queens' courts, and patronage has begun to explore women's part in the bonds of generosity, hospitality, and obligation by which men made their way in the world.[7] If elite women were very often an object of exchange between men, they also played their part in making marriages, promotions, and clientages. Barbara Harris has shown how aristocratic Tudor women, like the men of their world, maintained relationships with a group of 'friends', who were often distant or closer kin: they gave them places in their houses, help at court, private favours, and public preference.[8] Marriage and domesticity brought new relationships which enhanced the ties of the natal families and gave them access to a range of local political roles. At the courts of queens, friendships between women were likely to be pivotal to political manipulations. The early eighteenth-century tensions around the relationships between Queen Anne, Sarah Churchill and the woman who replaced Churchill as Anne's favourite, Abigail Masham, were played out in printed satires; they were preceded by more private intimacies and disruptions among sixteenth- and seventeenth-century court women.[9] A re-evaluation of the political roles of friendship for women is overdue.

At the same time, a new history of same-sex relations between women is demonstrating that, far from being invisible or unknown, sexual acts between women were described in a range of seventeenth-century texts and in different ways. Seventeenth-century texts defined sodomy as a crime that could be committed between women as well as between men.[10] Travellers' tales described the enlarged clitorises that prompted women to use their organs with other women, as if they were men; the earliest pornography prefaced scenes of heterosexual sex with lesbian initiations. The apparent innocence of texts of female friendship has come to be seen as a studied manoeuvre, enabling women writers to avoid the dangerously sexual meanings that might be associated with female intimacy.[11] Valerie Traub's examination of the meanings of lesbianism in the seventeenth century traces the overlapping histories of deviant female sexual figures: the tribade, the female friend, the cross-dresser, the female husband.[12] For Traub, as for Bray, the privatization of the conjugal couple in the late seventeenth century means an important shift: heterosexual desire was more explicitly constructed, and more firmly defined against the perverse. The dangerous convergence of the figures of tribade and friend meant that as the normal was defined, the abnormal was distinguished against it. By the late seventeenth century, in women's writing, at least, intense female intimacy was not necessarily innocent.

This moment of crisis is, of course, not a new idea: the genealogical history of modern lesbianism has identified a whole series of key moments at which relations between women lose their innocence, and become suspect; at which lesbianism, beginning to be named, starts to haunt the purity of chaste friendships. Fixing the precise chronology of such a shift may, in the end, be impossible and unhelpful. Traub's careful delineation of the different histories of particular figures and models of female sexuality suggests a continuing tension between innocence and knowledge, purity and deviance. Annemarie Jagose's reading of lesbian representations construes invisibility as an important rhetoric: lesbian desire can be both visible and rhetorically impossible.[13] In this, it has a cultural meaning quite different from that of male sodomy, whose dangerous possibilities were, in the early modern period, made repeatedly explicit. The peculiar cultural presence of lesbianism demands its own discursive frame.

In that frame, the place of the friend is an awkward one. Bray's avowed intent, to write a history of same-sex relations that would 'play a part in toppling King Sex from the throne he has occupied for too long', cannot have the same radical effect on women's history as it has on men's.[14] The early modern history of women's relations has for so long been defensively asexual that the study of friendship can seem, simply, to reinstate a great many of the suppressions and oppressions of desire that have troubled women's historians.

Evidently, chaste friendship can no longer be read as as a forerunner or substitute for modern lesbianism: it demands examination on its own terms. Likewise, the explicit representation of sex between women in travel literature, midwives' books and erotica suggests a much wider understanding of its possibilities than was once assumed. The history of lesbianism has so often been, in Jagose's words, 'a problem of representation' that this is a promisingly radical rupture.

But the wider context of friendship, explored recently with such power in Bray's last book, does have something important to teach us about the intimacies of female friendship. In early modern England, in Bray's words, 'bodily intimacy became an instrument by which social relationships could be established and given meaning'.[15] It is worth considering whether this is truer for men, than for women; and if so, why. More specifically, a deepening understanding of the tensions of friendship should compel historians to unpack notions of the relationship between homosociality and perversity, sodomy, and intimacy. All this can enable us, in indirect but productive ways, to think about the meanings of women's friendship, and about the meaning of physical intimacy between women. In what follows, I want to use these ideas to consider the acts of friendship that were exchanged between female bodies. These were acts that were indeed deeply political, but rarely in the same way as the intimacies between men.

For men, close friendship very often brought with it demonstrations of physical intimacy. As Bray points out, in early modern England a great deal of bodily life took place in public and outside the household. Bathing, sleeping and eating were public activities, and sharing them had symbolic power as well as practical uses. This was most obvious for men, but it was true for women too. The early seventeenth-century diaries of Lady Anne Clifford record some of the meanings of such intimacies as they changed over a lifetime. In her teenage years, Clifford shared both rooms, and beds, with the friends and patrons who loomed large in her life. Some were relatives, like her aunt, the Countess of Warwick. Looking back to 1603, to the Christmas before the death of Queen Elizabeth, when Clifford was thirteen years old, she recalled that:

> I used to go much to the Court & sometimes I did lie at my Aunt Warwick's Chamber on a Pallet, to whom I was much bound for her

continual care & love of me, in so much as if Queen Elizabeth had lived she intended to prefer me to be of the Privy Chamber for at that time there was much hope and expectation of me as of any other young Ladie whatsoever.[16]

The binding, marked by sharing a room, had both a private meaning and a public one for Anne's future, and her memory.

In the following years, as a new queen's court was established, binding ties by sharing beds and rooms became even more important. In August 1605, Clifford's mother sent her to Oxford with Arbella Stuart: although Stuart, a distant claimant to the throne, ended up imprisoned after marrying without permission, in 1605 she would have been a useful connection at the new court. However, in this instance the Clifford parents, often at odds, were divided on their plans for their daughter, and Anne wrote to her mother regretfully that her father had stopped her sharing Arbella Stuart's room: 'I thought to have gone to Oxford, according to your Ladyship's desire with my Lady Arbella, and to have slept in her chamber, which she much desired, for I am the more bound to her than can be.'[17]

Other bedmates in Clifford's young life were more intimate friends. The night that she lay with her cousin, Frances Bourchier, and Mistress Mary Carey was 'the first beginning of the greatness between us'. This 'greatness' meant emotional and physical intimacy: to have it recorded mattered. Once, Anne's mother, angry at her riding ahead of her during the day with a man, had ordered her to sleep alone, 'which I could not endure'; Frances got the key of her room and lay with her, 'which was' (Anne wrote) 'the first time I loved her so very well'.[18]

There are few records of intimate encounters like this. Anne Clifford was exceptional, perhaps not in remembering the gestures of binding friendship, but in recording them in a document meant for some kind of public consumption. The 'Great Books' in which her diary was kept recorded her role in her family, her pursuit of her inheritance, and her place in the social world of the seventeenth-century aristocracy, and they were presented and preserved with care for her children and their descendants. Evidence of her closeness to her patrons and friends had a public meaning, as well as a personal one.

Later in life, it was Clifford who played the part of generous patron. In the last years of her life, she spent much of her days retired in her chamber in Brougham Castle. There, in 1676, the year in which she died, a series of neighbours, tradesmen and their wives, and dependants came to visit. Clifford's diary records their entertainment with care. Her guests ate, with the household, in the 'painted hall'; she kept to her own rooms. After they had eaten, she received them in her own room. There, even her gestures are recorded. The men were taken by the hand; the women, and sometimes the men, were kissed. In January of 1676, 'Mr Thomas Samford's wife . . . and her eldest son and daughter' came: Clifford recorded 'after dinner I had them into my Chamber & kist them and took him by the hand and talked a good while with them, and I gave her 2 pares of buckskin gloves, and each of them one pare'. The physical gestures are as important as the gifts, and as carefully recorded. On Shrove Monday Clifford saw 'Dorothy Wiber, the deaf woman of my almshouse in Appleby . . . after dinner I had her into my chamber and kissed her'. No-one reciprocates the kisses or the hand-shakes: Clifford's tenants are, at least in her eyes, the humble recipients of physical generosity.

These kisses were not simply gifts of charity: they marked a relation-ship that also enabled Clifford to berate her visitors for their inappro-priate expectations of their patron. Dorothy Wiber, the deaf woman from the almshouse, had brought with her five dozen yards of bonelace to sell, and was reproached angrily for bringing too much; Mrs Willison, a wine-merchant's wife from Penrith, was kissed and taken by the hand, but told 'I would have no more wine off her husband because he used me so badly.'[19] These exchanges, physical, emotional, and economic, were part of Clifford's parting from her world in the few months before her death in March. They surely also represented habits of touch, inti-macy, and distance that had been cultivated over a lifetime's patronage and friendship. Such gestures are a world away from the sworn friend-ships that bound some elite men together. They functioned, though, in the same context, where gifts of the body marked power, patronage, and protection.

If, as an adult, Clifford had more intimate friends, whose physical touch marked a closer or more reciprocal relationship, she left no record of it. While intimacies between men seem, Alan Bray has argued, to hover dangerously close to the boundary between safety and sodomy, women's friendships often seem to happen in the silences between the lines of the story of male friendship, in a space where such dangers are barely imaginable and rarely articulated.[20]

There is an exception to this world of silence, and it comes when we turn from the body, to the heart. If the archives are largely quiet about early modern women's exchanges of touch, they have a little more to say about what it meant for women to share their time, their inclin-ations, and their company. In a culture in which so much of female identity was meant to be mediated through men, intimacies between women could be threatening in rather different ways than those between men.

In the court books of London's house of correction, the Bridewell, in the early seventeenth century, is a puzzling entry. It notes the presentment of two women for 'keeping company' together. In its entirety, the entry says simply, 'Anne Bowell examined saith she dwelleth in Beardes Alley in Fleete streete. Brought in for keeping company with another mans wief, kept till farther order be taken.'[21] This is not, apparently, a clerical mistake: one of the officials who brought in suspicious women and men to the Bridewell, usually thieves, vagrants, and prostitutes must have received word of Anne Bowell's behaviour, and responded to it.

Keeping company with another woman is not an offence recognizable from any other court records; 'keeping company' was generally used to refer to suspicions of adultery or fornication between men and women. It is possible that here, too, keeping company has a sexual meaning. But it is more likely that what is being raised are other dangers of company between women. Bridewell's governors were much concerned with the origins and structure of prostitution in the city; they often questioned women about how they fell into whoredom, and who had corrupted them. Obligingly, women responded with details of other women: their mistresses, or their friends, they said, had persuaded them to meet a man in an alehouse, or go to strange houses, or serve drinks to 'gentleman' and sit about with them afterwards. Mary Routon, questioned in 1561, told the court that Joan Smith 'enticed her from her master and promised her to help her to a good service and ever sithe she hathe kepte her in a chamber wher she hathe had the company of twelve men at the lest by the said Joane Smithes appointment'.[22] In 1574, Margaret Rogers confessed to 'evil life' with a man, saying 'That Margaret Wrighte envegled hir to lewdnes and wolde not suffer hir to be in quiet but alwaies entisinge hir to lewdnes.'[23] It was in the company of women that the sins which undermined orderly society were nurtured. In this context, the patronage and support that women offered each other, translated into a context of sin and promiscuity, made friendship the cause of corruption and moral collapse. Chastity, as Laurie Shannon has noted in her study of Renaissance friendship, was an associative term for women; female friendship could keep women safe.[24] But so was its reverse. Unchastity could infect women, spreading from mistresses to servants, between neighbours and friends.

The world of the women known as Bridewell's 'guests' was miles away from the great houses and courts where Clifford and her peers met, ate, and slept. The gulf between includes the great mass of the female population – the largely respectable, unrecorded spinsters, wives, and widows, who rarely came across the law and rarely left any written record. How their bodily and emotional worlds were negotiated we can only hope to glimpse. But there is something in common across the divide. Women's friendship has political uses: it enables advancement and patronage, or surveillance and supervision; and those uses make it suspicious in a world where advancement is expected to be mediated by men.

One of the places this became most explicit was in the early eighteenth century at the court of Queen Anne. For Renaissance friends, Laurie Shannon has argued, the Aristotelian ideal of friendly similitude provided an egalitarian counter to the hierarchical world of political order.[25] This may have been as true for women as it was for men. But the court world was full of people who were not, and could not be, private people. Like kings and princes, queens and princesses indulged in the creation of private personas for friendship, using pet names, pseudonyms, or fictional characters; but the fantasy of common ground was belied by the real dangers of intimacy between monarchs and commoners. When the private friendship of Mrs Morley and Mrs Freeman, Queen Anne and Sarah, Duchess of Marlborough, broke down, and Anne transferred her affections and friendship from Sarah, Duchess of Marlborough, to Abigail Masham, manuscript propaganda and letters by Sarah and by others presented the queen's fondness for her new bedchamber woman as socially absurd, publicly dangerous, and sexually suspect. In the 1680s, James II had already described his daughter's relations with Sarah Churchill as an immoderate passion; early in the next century, Sarah Churchill was describing Anne's affections for Abigail Masham in the same terms.[26]

Alongside the covert references to sex, and the more explicit references to class, was an understanding that erotic relations between such women interrupted the flow of political influence: women, after all, were expected to be the conduits of male political transactions and the objects of male friendship. Sarah Churchill's intimations, in a letter of 1708, that Anne's reputation was unlikely to be preserved by her 'having no inclination for any but of one's own sex' brought such fears neatly together.[27] That court circles were expected to share these concerns suggests the extent to which such disinclination for male society could constitute a recognized undercurrent to women's political relationships.

There is, here, a tension around female intimacy which suggests rather more than a fear of sapphic relations. To be too fond of women, simply, got in the way of marriage. Countless discourses – legal and ecclesiastical amongst the foremost of them – presented married women as their husband's subjects, their personhood mediated through the role of wife. In law, a discourse of coverture with which women and men were thoroughly familiar limited women's financial, legal, and political status. Like streams running into rivers, as some commentators put it, they were part of a greater whole.

What space did this convention leave for intimate friendships between women? Amongst the elites, the very isolation that marriage could bring made friendships, often nurtured through letters, vital. Lady Anne North's letters to her daughter testify to her concern that, particularly while pregnant, her husband's absence did not leave her too much alone. As her daughter neared her delivery date in January 1681, she wrote that, despite her husband being abroad, 'you are in a place where you have good neighbours & those that have been formerly with you & you are well acquainted with, which no doubt will be very kind & carefull of you', and a week later, 'you live in so sociable a towne that I hope your Neighbours will not lett you be too much alone'.[28] For another elite woman, the social freedoms of poor women were the subject of envy. Lady Anne Dormer, whose letters to her sister record every strain of her painful isolation in marriage, found herself cut off from her neighbours, and wrote wistfully: 'a poore woman that lives in a thatched house when she is ill or weary of her work can step into her neighbour and have some refreshment but I have none but what I find by thinking writing and reading'.[29] Every emphasis, here, is on the casual: the kind of friends that women need are acquaintances, reliable, honest women. The kind of women's speech – 'gossip' – that was so derided in contemporary satirical literature was the foundation of community life for women from the elites to the poor. But for women and men of reputation, intimate friends could never be made casually, and for women more than men, bad company and immodest intimacies threatened reputation.

Amongst the elite women of early modern England, marriage often provided a model for female friends; it also constituted its opposite. Katherine Philips's late seventeenth-century poetry depicts a world of female friendship quite apart from men and marriage, in which women's intimacy is consciously, carefully chaste and innocent.[30] At a time when, in some circles, it was argued that those who married should also be friends, it was important to negotiate the boundaries of female friendship with care. For women friends, one question increasingly recurred: was it possible for friendship and marriage to co-exist? Valerie

Traub quotes *The Ladies Dictionary* of 1694 on the question of 'Friendship contracted by single Persons, *may it continue with the same Zeal and Innocence if either Marry?*': the text concludes that if the marriage is happy, the friendship must be diminished; tenderness for a friend should never outweigh, or even match, that for a spouse.[31]

In 1667, Mary Beale's manuscript discourse on friendship, couched in the form of a letter to her 'deare friend' Elizabeth Tillotson, described friendship as 'the nearest union, which distinct soules are capable of'. Her vision was Aristotelian and Erasmian in its origin, but it stretched further, to encompass a place for women and for heterosexual friendship. Her ideal friends were spouses: if husband and wife could love as friends, the bond of marriage would be restored 'to its first institution', the time before sin.[32] This was a utopian vision familiar to a generation who remembered the wild radicalism of the Revolutionary years. But few, in the late seventeenth century or in the 1650s, shared the idea that marriage could be freed of its hierarchical nature. Montaigne's description of 'a covenant that hath nothing free but the entrance' was echoed by the earliest feminist writers in the seventeenth century.[33] Margaret Godolphin and John Evelyn, in the late seventeenth century, imagined a free platonic union which stood outside the relation of marriage, and yet was imbued with its own erotic power.[34] It was this vision of unworldly, unsexed friendship of which Alan Bray also wrote, and in which he saw something that might help the modern church rediscover the traditions lost with modernity's obsession with identity and sex. But in the seventeenth century there were serious doubts as to whether women could ever attain that freedom of friendship – particularly with each other. Conjugality demanded of women a commitment of body and soul that inhibited their capacity for the love that was free to men.

One way around this was to see female friendship as a nurturing-ground for marital relations. In 1635, Constance Fowler, daughter of a Catholic gentry family in Staffordshire, wrote to her brother, Herbert Aston, several pages about the woman he hoped to marry. Constance had, she wrote, followed his request in managing to make Katherine Thimelby's acquaintance; and very shortly, after an exchange of letters of 'complimental friendship' and a providential dinner meeting where they conversed by 'silent expressions' and 'the prettiest words', they declared a passionate friendship, based on the secret of the relationship between Herbert and Katherine. Constance was the keeper of the secret, the sponsor of the marriage that was to come: by declaring her love for Mrs Thimelby, she wrote herself into her brother's marriage. She wrote:

'she has made me mistress of her heart, and therefore I could only dispose of it'. Her relations with Katherine were described exactly as a falling in love, the necessity for secrecy adding to the drama, and the letters between Katherine and herself constituting herself as mediator to Katherine's relationship with Herbert. Describing their affection for each other, Constance wrote:

> I believe I am blest with the most perfectest and constant lover as ever woman was blest with. Oh, if you would know the story of our affection, you must come hither and read volumes of it, afore you can be able to understand half the dearness of our love. I keep them apurpose for your sight, and no creature breathing but my self ever saw them or knows of them else. You will say, I am certain, when you peruse them that there was never any more passionate affectionate lovers than she and I, and that you never knew two creatures more truly and deadly in love with one another than we are.... For after I had made known to her by letters how infinitely I honoured her, and how I had done so since I first saw her here, she writ me the sweetest answers, that from that very hour I confess I have been most deadly in love with her as ever lover was...

She went on, later in the same letter:

> For you two are dear partners in my heart, and it is so wholly divided betwixt you, that I have so much ado to get leave of it to place any other friend of mine there. Oh then, in pity of this heart which has been so faithful to you, and which has suffered so extremely for you, do what you can to compass that happiness for yourself which I so thirst after, that my dearest friend and you being united in one, your hearts may likewise be come one, and so I may keep them with more ease in my breast than now I can, they being divided.[35]

As Valerie Traub has observed, such language reflects the ways that love, friendship, and kinship overlapped: Constance signed her letter to her brother 'Your dear affectionate lover'.[36] For these two elite women, their intense friendship was not so much a competitor to marriage as a preparation for it, a way of integrating Katherine Thimelby into her new family before the conjugal bond itself was made: the love of her suitor's sister was to pave the way both for the marriage and for their future relation as sisters-in-law. Like lesbian scenes in erotica, too, the exchange of pacts of love between the two women serves as an enabling preamble to heterosexual consummation. But it does raise the question, at least, of whether there was any language left sacred to heterosexual love. Constance herself was in one of those ambiguous situations typical of elite marriages: probably in her late teens at this point, she had already been married to Walter Fowler, but was not, apparently, yet living with him, and their first child was not born until nearly ten years later.[37]

Renaissance friendship, Laurie Shannon argues, was triangulated not only by the heterosexual love interest, but by the ultimate object of loyalty: the sovereign.[38] Before Anne was queen, she was part of another network of royal and common friendships. At the court of James II in the late seventeenth century, the relative power of royal blood, friendship, and marriage was tested in the epistolary intimacies between James's two daughters, and their close friend, Frances Apsley. As young women in the 1670s, Mary Stuart, later wife and queen of William of Orange, and Anne shared their friendship with Frances. The daughter of Allen Apsley and a member of the royal household, she was nine years older than Mary and twelve years older than Anne. All we know of their friendship comes from the letters between them, an epistolary romance in which each took parts, named from contemporary plays and masques, that enabled them to articulate a special form of intimacy. Anne wrote to Frances as her male suitor, Ziphares, and Frances was the 'fair Semandra'. Mary and Frances called each other by two female names, Clorine and Aurelia, but also wrote to each other as husband and wife, with Frances the husband and her princess the wife. And Anne, of course, went on to be Mrs Morley to Sarah Churchill's Mrs Freeman.[39]

Across these multiple roles, in which both Anne and Frances, if not Mary, got to play the adoring male, love between women was measured, tested, and compared. To early readers, including Hannah More, the bundle of letters between Mary and Frances looked like letters from Mary to her husband; to later ones they were 'grotesque protestations of love'.[40] At the start of the surviving letters in 1676, when Mary was fourteen and Frances twenty-three, Mary writes to Frances:

> what can I say more to perswade you that I love you with more zeal then any lover can I love you with a love that ner was known by man I have for you excese of friandship more of love then any woman can for woman and more love then ever the constantest lover had for his Mrs you are loved more then can be exprest by your ever obedient wife vere afectionate friand humbel sarvent to kis the ground where one [whereon] you go to be your dog in a string your fish in a net your bird in a cage your humbel trout.[41]

The rhetoric of excessive friendship was well established: in it, affection always exceeded all other kinds of love, and every model for it – the lover to his mistress, the woman to her woman friend, the dog on a string, the humble trout – is insufficient. Every disagreement, slight, or missed letter provided the prompt for further reassurances.

But Frances and Mary were also particularly preoccupied with the precise affective significance of each model they used. In another letter the same year Mary declared: 'I love Mrs Apsley better than any woman can love a woman but I love my dear Aurelia as a Wife should doe a husband nay more then is able to be exprest.'[42] Mary and Frances were both single, and both would be married shortly; for Mary, in particular, her status and the approach of marriage made precision about friendship within court circles particularly necessary.

In 1677, Mary's marriage to William of Orange took her away from London to Holland. From then, letters constituted the basis of her relationship with Frances, and the epistolary exchange became the focus of their emotional drama, with letters revolving around the frequency of writing, the etiquette of address, and the disclosure of the news of Mary's pregnancies. Neither seems to have considered abandoning the old play of husband and wife: indeed, they actively engaged with the peculiar relationship between the old husband, Frances, and the new. In doing so, they used a language in which marriage was the best way of describing an intense, interdependent relationship; but which also suggested some deep tensions in that relationship's definition. Frances's first letter to Mary after her marriage – the only one that survives, because she kept a draft of it – records her struggle with what Mary's marriage meant:

Syns it was my hard fate to loose the greateste blessing I ever had in thys worlde, which was the deare presenc of my most beloved wife, I have some comfort that shee is taken from mee by so worthy and so greate a prince for so hee is in the oppinnion of all goode men. yr Highness has putt a harde taske upon mee to treate you with the same familiarity as becomes a fond husband to a beloved wife he doates uppon, whom I ought to reverence and adoare as the greatest princes now alive, when I flatter myselfe with the blessing god and thyselfe have given mee in so deare a wife I thynck what the scripture ses thatt man and wife are butt one body and then your hart is myne, I am sure myne is yours. Butt if I behave myselfe to you as I am bound in duty to yr Hyghness I muste aske yr pardon for my presumption, yett synce my life dependes uppon it for I can live no

longer then your favour shynes uppon mee, itt wil bee a great char-
ritye in yr Hyghness to continnue your love and bounty to a
husbande that admyres you and doates uppon you and an obedient
servantt thatt will alwayes serve and adoare you.[43]

There is humour here: the obsequious courtier blends with the slavishly
devoted lover. But there is also a very real sense of the dangers of familiarity between princess-wife and friend-husband. And if 'man and wife
are one body', whose is Mary Stuart's body now, and why is it not still
Frances's? At the same time, Frances's role as a husband to Mary enables
them to negotiate some of the inequalities of friendship between a
subject and a princess: both of them become 'subjects', bound to each
other. To write this letter meant considering, even in jest, at least some
of the ramifications of a woman calling a princess her husband. It
would indeed be a 'hard task' for Frances to treat Mary with both the
familiarity she demanded and the reverence she was owed.

Mary's reply returned immediately to the conjugal bond, as emblematic of affection and duty: 'I am very much ashamed that my dearest
husban should ritt to me frist ... it was my dutty as wife to have ritt
frist', she wrote, and she signed it with both her names, 'Mary Clorin',
adding – 'you se tho I have another husban I keep the name of my
first'.[44] The next year, in August, 1678, Mary wrote with important
news.

I have a hundred thousand pardons to beg of my dear dear husband,
who if I did not know to be very good and hope she loves me a little
still, I could not so much as hope to be forgiven ... but if anything in
the world can make amend for such a fault, I hope trusting you with
a secret will ... It is what I am ashamed to say but seeing it is to my
husband I may, though I have reason to fear because the sea parts us
you may believe it is a bastard but yet I think upon a time of need I
may make you own it, since 'tis not out of the four seas. In the mean-
time, if you have any care of your own reputation consequently you
must have of your wife's too, you ought to keep this a secret since if
it should be known you might get a pair of horns and nothing else
by the bargain, but dearest Aurelia you may be very well assured tho'
I have played the whore a little I love you of all things in the
world ...

This is where Mary and Frances's role playing reaches its strange height,
and Mary is compelled to write an elaborate apology to her husband/

friend, for being pregnant by her husband/spouse. Indeed, she threatens both to make her husband/friend own her child's paternity, and to publicize her cuckoldry. What is really being threatened is Frances's dismissal from Mary's intimate circle: she is important enough to hear the secret, but only if she can keep it to herself. All of this, if it does lead to some convoluted rhetorical explanations, is entertainment; but the last sentence reminds us of the persistence with which Mary and Frances compare one husband to another. 'Though I have played the whore a little', Mary says of her marriage, 'I love you of all things in the world.' Did other married women write to each other as husband and wife? Pseudonymous friendships of course made excellent sense for royal women, preserving secrecy and creating a world in which royal status could be, to some degree, put aside. For these two, using marriage as a model for their friendship also meant construing it, if only in jest, as its antagonistic competitor.

Only after Frances married, when she was 29, did Mary stop calling her husband. The change is noticeable in one letter in particular, when Mary, in her turn, is desperate to know whether or not Frances is pregnant:

> your kind letter dear Aurelia puts in a strange impatience to know what it is you dare not writ & I believe it must be of great importance since you ad presently after that you woud put your life into my hands. for gods sake put me out of my pain & lett me know it, if ever you have loved me, if ever you have loved your prince, if ever you have loved or do either fathere mothere sister brothere, & last of all if you love your dear husban I conjure you to lett me know it & yt quikly...[45]

For once, the husband in the letter is a legal, male husband, Frances's spouse. They remained Clorine and Aurelia until almost the end of the letters, in 1688 when Mary returned to England to take the throne. And Anne and Frances continued as Semandra and Ziphares throughout.

The secret of pregnancy, the news that Mary and Frances most wanted to know about each other, was important: for marriages like these, childbearing was vital, and the news of it – particularly, of course, in Mary's case – of huge political importance. Reproductive secrets were strong currency in court circles. Mary confided her early pregnancies to Frances, and begged Frances for her own news in return; she predicted, correctly, that Frances's first pregnancy would be twins, but they died shortly after birth. At the same time as she was speculating whether

Frances would have another child, and hoping it would live, Mary was exchanging the letters with her sister Anne, which called into question the veracity of the pregnancy of her father's second wife, Mary of Modena, and were to provide such public ammunition against the heir who was eventually born. Anticipations of pregnancy provide endless stuff for Mary and Frances's letters – tooth-ache, illness, silence all provide possible evidence for suspicions of another pregnancy. The same was true, later, of Queen Anne and Sarah Churchill. But one of the consequences of all this was to make the real marriage one about child-bearing, and the letters the place for love, jealousy, and fidelity.

These are only a few of the contexts in which women's intimacies carried political and social weight. But they suggest a tension in women's friendships that is not there for men. Male friends share the body, and the heart. Women friends, once they are married, cannot – should not – give both away. Marriage is one of the keys to the ways that the relationship between friendship and sexuality diverges for men and women.

Alan Bray and Valerie Traub have both argued that the seventeenth century brought shifts in conjugality, which made companionship and friendship part of heterosexual marriage in a way that had not been evident before. If couples are meant to be friends, friendship outside marriage becomes less possible, less central to the social fabric of the early modern world. This is a change which is manifested most clearly in the new discourses in which marriage is portrayed from the late seventeenth-century on: personal writings, family portraits, prescriptive literature. Social historians, increasingly unwilling to follow the dramatic chronology for the history of family life laid down by Lawrence Stone and others, have been less ready to postulate so radical a shift, or to date it to this point. Nevertheless, it is clear that the seventeenth century brought, at the very least, a new rhetoric of family love, playing on domesticity, affection, and conjugal companionship. This may well, as Bray argues, have affected the verbal and physical languages men had to make bonds of friendship. But its effects were not symmetrical: it may not have had the same impact on women. Both the position of women in marriage and the justifications for their inequality in marriage remained largely unchanged by the effects of the Reformation, the Civil Wars, and the reformulation of family politics by theorists from Locke to Filmer.[46]

In theory, marriage already gave a woman a new identity, making her a part of her husband, and intimating that the heart and the body were no longer hers to give away. The practical and emotional ramifications of that principle were not inescapable, but they could cut deep. Anne Clifford wrote most about her body and the ways she shared it with others in her childhood, and in her widowhood: as a wife she often lived in some physical and social isolation. Women's bodies, more so than men, are supposed not to be given without reference to the parameters of a heterosexual relationship. Heterosexual relations also monopolize women's time, or are meant to: time spent with other women, particularly after marriage, is perceived as unproductive if not actually degenerate. If demonstrations of physical affection between women could often pass unremarked, the time and talk that women shared raised tensions of their own.

The tensions of female friendships, then, are unlikely to be best observed in the realm of the sexual, or even the erotic. More so for women than for men, a fondness for one's own sex may have existed as an opposition to marriage long before heterosexuality and homosexuality are supposed to have been invented: not because of sexual identity, but because of the power of marriage. If heterosexuality only became compulsory for men when marriage changed, it was already much more compulsory for women. Always, in a patriarchal system, marriage seems to require women's full attention, to aspire to absorb their whole identity. In this context, women's friendships are unquestionably conducted within different parameters and against different constraints than those of men. Like men's bonds, they had political meanings that might support or undermine structures of power; like men's, they could also be threatening. If the figure of the tribade, coming into sharp focus in the seventeenth century, constituted one risk to chaste friendship, the looming, overarching structure of marriage had always already made bonds between women hard to assert.

Notes

Thanks to Nicole Pohl for her comments and suggestions.

1. A. Bray and M. Rey, 'The Body of the Friend', in T. Hitchcock and M. Cohen (eds), *English Masculinities 1660–1800* (Harlow: Longman, 1999); see also A. Stewart, *Close Readers: Humanism and Sodomy in Early Modern England* (Princeton: Princeton University Press, 1997).
2. A. Bray, *The Friend* (Chicago: Chicago University Press, 2003), p. 157.
3. J. Derrida, *The Politics of Friendship* (London: Verso, 1992).
4. M. de Montaigne, *The Essays*, trans. J. Florio (London, 1603: facsimile, Menston: Scolar Press, 1969), p. 91.
5. Bray, *The Friend*, p. 175; L. Hutson, *The Usurer's Daughter: Male Friendship and Fictions of Women in Sixteenth-Century England* (London: Routledge, 1994);

E. Kosofsky Sedgwick, *Between Men: English Literature and Male Homosocial Desire* (New York: Columbia University Press, 1985), ch. 3.

6. See for example F. Harris, *Transformations of Love: The Friendship of John Evelyn and Margaret Godolphin* (Oxford: Oxford University Press, 2002). On friendships between women, P. Crawford, 'Friendship and Love between Women in Early Modern England', in A. Lynch and P. Maddern (eds), *Venus and Mars: Engendering Love and War in Medieval and Early Modern Europe* (Perth: University of Western Australia Press, 1995).

7. B. Harris, 'Women and Politics in Early Tudor England', *Historical Journal*, 33 (1990), 259–81; P. Wright, 'The Ramifications of a Female Household 1558–1603', in D. Starkey *et al.* (eds), *The English Court* (London: Longman, 1987); S. Mendelson and P. Crawford, *Women in Early Modern England, 1550–1720* (Oxford: Oxford University Press, 1998), ch. 7.

8. B. Harris, *English Aristocratic Women 1450–1550: Marriage and Family, Property and Careers* (New York and Oxford: Oxford University Press, 2002), ch. 8.

9. On Churchill's relationship with Anne, see in particular F. Harris, *A Passion for Government: The Life of Sarah, Duchess of Marlborough* (Oxford: Oxford University Press, 1991); R. Weil, *Political Passions: Gender, the Family and Political Argument in England, 1680–1714* (Manchester: Manchester University Press, 1999), ch. 8.

10. V. Traub, *The Renaissance of Lesbianism in Early Modern England* (Cambridge: Cambridge University Press, 2002), p. 277.

11. H. Andreadis, *Sappho in Early Modern England: Female Same-Sex Literary Erotics, 1550–1714* (Chicago: Chicago University Press, 2001); see also E. Donoghue, *Passions between Women: British Lesbian Culture 1668–1801* (London: Scarlet Press, 1993).

12. Traub, *The Renaissance of Lesbianism*.

13. A. Jagose, *Inconsequence: Lesbian Representation and the Logic of Sequence* (Ithaca: Cornell University Press, 2002), Introduction.

14. A. Bray, *Homosexuality in Renaissance England* (2nd edn, New York: Columbia University Press, 1995), p. 118.

15. Bray, *The Friend*.

16. *The Diaries of Lady Anne Clifford*, ed. D.J.H. Clifford (Stroud: Sutton, 1990), p. 21.

17. G.C. Williamson, *Lady Anne Clifford* (Kendal: T. Wilson & Son, 1922), p. 76.

18. Williamson, *Lady Anne Clifford*, p. 69.

19. *Diaries of Lady Anne Clifford*, pp. 249, 260.

20. Bray, *The Friend*, p. 199.

21. Guildhall Library, London, Bridewell Court Book 5, fol. 17^v, 6 March 1605 (microfilm).

22. Guildhall Library, London, Bridewell Court Book 1, fol. 143, 9 July 1561.

23. Guildhall Library, London, Bridewell Court Book 2, fol. 56, 3 December 1574.

24. L. Shannon, *Sovereign Amity: Figures of Friendship in Shakespearean Contexts* (Chicago: Chicago University Press, 2001), p. 7 and ch. 1.

25. Shannon, *Sovereign Amity*, p. 9.

26. James's words were 'une passion demesurée': Andreadis, *Sappho*, p. 173.

27. Weil, *Political Passions*, p. 210.

28. North Letters, BL, Add. MS 32500, fols 54–5.

29. 5 April 1688: Trumbull Papers, BL, Add. MS 72516.

30. On Philips, see Traub, *Renaissance of Lesbianism*, ch. 7; E.S. Wahl, *Invisible Relations: Representations of Female Intimacy in the Age of Enlightenment* (Stanford: Stanford University Press, 1999), ch. 3; Andreadis, *Sappho*, ch. 3.
31. Traub, *Renaissance of Lesbianism*, p. 309.
32. M. Beale, 'Letter to My Deare Friend' , BL, Harl. MS 6828, fol. 510.
33. Montaigne, *Essays*, p. 91.
34. Harris, *Transformations of Love*.
35. *Tixall Letters; Or the Correspondence of the Aston Family, and their Friends, during the Seventeeth Century*, ed. A.R. Clifford, 2 vols (London: 1816), 1: 107ff.
36. Traub, *Renaissance of Lesbianism*, p. 186.
37. http://human.ntu.ac.uk/research/perdita/fowler.htm, 1 April 2004.
38. Shannon, *Sovereign Amity*, p. 9.
39. See n. 9, p. 148.
40. *Letters of Two Queens*, ed. B. Bathurst (London: R. Holden & Co., 1925), Introduction.
41. Ibid., p. 60.
42. Ibid., pp. 63–4.
43. Ibid., p. 83.
44. Ibid.
45. Ibid., p. 156.
46. See, amongst others, C. Pateman, *The Sexual Contract* (Cambridge: Polity, 1988) and Weil, *Political Passions*.

7
Friends and Neighbours in Early Modern England: Biblical Translations and Social Norms

Naomi Tadmor

'Neighbourhood' was a key concept in early modern England. Most people lived their entire lives in small communities, where human interaction took place first and foremost among neighbours. When people moved away – as they often did in their youth or later in life – they were only likely to find themselves once more living in local communities, surrounded by new yet structurally similar sets of neighbours and neighbourly relationships. Indeed, neighbourliness was a crucial norm.[1] Neighbours were to live in peace and avoid conflict and strife. Clergymen were to extol among their neighbours and parishioners 'charity in loving walking and neighbourly accompanying one another, with reconciling of differences'.[2] In the Elizabethan parish of Swallowfield, Berkshire, neighbours even got together to draw articles which were to guide them in living 'in good love & lykinge one another'. They promised 'th[a]t non of us shall disdayne one another, nor seeke to hynder one another nether by woordes nor deedes, But rather to be helpers, assisters & councellors of one another, And all o[u]r doyinges to be good, honest, lovynge and iuste'.[3] Neighbours joined by love were thus depicted like a strong bundle of sticks which cannot be broken if bound together fast.[4]

John Bossy confessed in 1973, '[h]ow far these aspirations corresponded with reality I have no idea'.[5] Historians still question the extent to which the norms of neighbourliness were realised in early modern England – and I shall return to that question later.[6] But the fact that the aspirations of neighbourliness were anchored in the language of the Holy Scriptures no doubt helped to promote them in early modern culture. The Ten Commandments, for example, invoked the language of neighbourliness: 'Thou shalt not bear false witness against thy neighbour. Thou shalt not covet thy neighbour's house, thou shalt not covet thy neighbour's wife . . . nor any thing that is thy neighbour's' (Exodus 20:16–17). With the onset of Protestantism, the moral code of the Ten Commandments increasingly replaced the medieval ethos of the seven deadly sins. The biblical rules of neighbourliness were inscribed on church walls and recited in catechisms.[7] However, the most important rule of Christian neighbourliness was 'love thy neighbour'. 'Master, which is the great commandment in the law?' asks one of the Pharisees. 'Thou shalt love the Lord thy God with all thy heart, and with all thy soul, and with all thy mind', replies Jesus. 'This is the first and great commandment. And the second is like unto it, Thou shalt love thy neighbour as thyself' (Matthew 22:36–9).[8]

These two commandments of the New Testament were drawn from the Hebrew Bible. The first forms the opening of what became known as the Jewish creed, *Shema Israel* (Deuteronomy 6:4–5). The second appears in Leviticus 19:18.[9] These two commandments, alongside the Ten Commandments, form the foundations of Mosaic law, just as they subsequently became central in the later English tradition. One important difference, however, is that whereas the English commandments are rendered in the language of neighbourliness, the original Hebrew commandments are coined in the language of amity and friendship.

The Hebrew word *re'a*, rendered in the English commandments as 'neighbour', covers a range of meaning, from 'friend' and 'companion' to 'fellow man' or 'every man', including a fellow man who is an enemy.[10] Although *re'a* can also be applied to a person living in near proximity, there is nothing in it to denote near-by habitation. That relationship is described in Hebrew with the word *shakhen*. Likewise, the word 'neighbour' covers a range of meanings from a person living next door to fellow man. However the original sense of this ancient Saxon word was 'one who dwells nearby'.[11] The first known usage of 'neighbour' as denoting fellow man dates from the 1300.[12] By the early modern period, then, *re'a* and 'neighbour' shared a common sense of 'fellow man', but the notion that that fellow man might also be a near-by co-resident in a local community remained embedded in the word 'neighbour' in a way that was absent from the Hebrew original. My point is that by rendering the word *re'a* as 'neighbour' in the biblical translations, the moral relationship of the biblical injunctions was conceived of in the English text as taking place in a social world shaped by local communities. This helped to underpin contemporary norms of Christian neighbourliness and endow them with fresh significance. The process of translation, however, reveals a semantic shift. Generally, Christian teaching is seen as emphasising the universal aspects of the biblical moral code rather than its practical commandments. In this case a shift has taken place in the opposite direction, away from universalism and towards parochialism. Protestant culture is often also associated with individualism, but the findings of this study point to a Protestant ethos of communalism in the making.

This chapter has been composed in memory of Alan Bray, whose scholarship has greatly enriched our understanding of both social ties and devotional life in early modern England. Its first section traces the formation of the semantic shift in biblical translations from the Hebrew language of amity to the English idiom of neighbourliness. The second examines the ways in which the language of neighbourly love was further propagated in the early modern period in a key theological and didactic genre, the catechism. The third suggests its broader dissemination in early modern society and culture both textually, and as a possible directive for social action.

I

A crucial move, which facilitated the semantic shift from the Hebrew language of amity to the English idiom of neighbourliness took place almost a millennium before the first English translation. By the third century BC there were Jewish congregations who required a biblical translation. The most significant ancient translation, the *Septuagint*, was prepared for the Greek speaking Jews of Alexandria, Egypt, from the third century BC onwards. According to the tradition, it was written by 72 elders who worked separately but produced identical texts, a testimony of divine inspiration.[13] This version translated the Hebrew word *re'a* with the use of more than one Greek word. Significantly, it drew a distinction between usages of *re'a* referring to particularly near relationships, and other usages. For example, when God speaks to Moses 'face to face', as a man might speak to his friend, the word *re'a* is translated as *philos* (Exodus 33:11). The proverbial words of wisdom 'Thine own friend, and thy father's friend, forsake not' (Proverbs 27:10) also render *re'a* as *philos*.[14] In describing the relationship between Amnon and his *re'a* Jonadab in II Samuel 13:3, the *Septuagint* uses the word *hetairos*, meaning a comrade, mate, partner, or friend. But in Genesis 11:3, where the descendants of Noah tell one another to go and make bricks in order to build a high tower (later known as the tower of Babel), the word *re'a* is translated as *plesion*, meaning 'near', 'close to', 'compatriot', 'member in the same community', and also 'neighbour'.[15] When Moses intercedes in a struggle between two Hebrews, asking one why he is hitting the other, *re'a* is also rendered as *plesion*. In the biblical moral injunctions of the Ten Commandments *re'a* is translated systematically as *plesion*.[16] Most importantly, in Leviticus 19:18 *re'a* becomes *plesion*.

Eventually Jewish communities ceased to use the *Septuagint*, but the significance of this ancient translation did not decline. The *Septuagint* was the version of the Hebrew Bible used by the early Christians, and it was quoted more in the New Testament than the Hebrew text itself.[17] Thus, when St Jerome was commissioned by Pope Damasus in the fourth century to produce a new Latin version of the Bible, both the Hebrew and the Greek were used. A division in the meaning of *re'a* was thus also retained in the crucial Latin biblical version ascribed to Jerome, the *Vulgate*, suggesting once more some distinction between fellow human beings thrown in near proximity for various reasons, and those bound by particularly close ties. Both relationships were largely also seen as different from the relationship established among people by virtue of close habitation (as in *shakhen*), and designated in the *Vulgate* with the word *vicinus*.[18] The moral injunctions of the Ten Commandments were thus rendered with the word *proximus*, suggesting that they apply to all human beings who may come together in near proximity, whether familial, communal, or geographical. In contrast, Amnon's friend Jonadab was described as *amicus*.[19] 'Thine own friend, and thy father's friend, forsake not' was rendered as 'amicum tuum et amicum patris'. The longed for friend in Psalm 88:19 was described with both words, 'amicum et proximum'.[20] 'Love thy neighbour' in Leviticus 19:18, however, was translated as 'diliges amicum tuum sicut temet ipsum', namely 'love thy friend'.

In the next stage in the development of the semantic shift we find John Wyclif. When Wyclif instigated the translation of the Bible around 1370, he turned to the *Vulgate*.[21] His aim was to find a proper vernacular mode for rendering the holy Latin text. Latin usages of *amicus* were thus generally translated in the Wycliffite Bible as 'friend', *proximus* as 'neighbour'.[22] Usages of *vicinus*, however, were also rendered as neighbour, as were a few related expressions. And so Jonadab was described as the 'freend' of Amnon. The interpersonal relationships in Proverbs 27:10 were described as 'thi frend and the frend of thi fadir'. Following the *Vulgate*, Leviticus 19:18 was also translated as 'thou schalt loue thi freend as thi silf'. In contrast, the Ten Commandments were translated with the use of the word 'neiybore'.[23] The longed for friend in Psalm 88:19 was described as 'frend and neiybore'.[24] The people who turned to one another to build the tower of Babel were also described with the word 'neiybore',[25] as was *vicinus* in 'Betere is a neiybore nyy than a brothir afer',[26] or those described as *qerovim* (near ones) in Isaiah 33:13.[27] The result was that usages of 'neighbour' encompassed a number of different senses. At the same time, the difference in meaning between a close or nearby person or fellow man, and a person who resides nearby in the same community was obliterated, for both were rendered equally as 'neighbour'. A semantic shift has thus occurred: the biblical world of interpersonal relations was rendered in the language of manorial and parochial life.

This would not have been the only time that the Bible 'went native'. In one medieval version of the biblical translation the word 'cider' ('sidir') was used for strong drink, probably to make the text more comprehensible for the people of the apple producing region of Hereford, where the 'Cider Bible' is still kept. In a rendition of the story of Genesis, Adam and Eve discovered they were naked and proceeded to sew themselves 'breeches'.[28] Of course, in medieval and early modern visual iconography, the transposition of biblical scenes to contemporary settings was a widely practised convention. In a similar way, it was probably most natural for Wyclif and his followers to imagine interpersonal relationships (and the moral injunctions associated with them) within the context of local communities. Indeed, the understanding of interpersonal relations within concrete or local contexts is also evident in the Wycliffite Bible in the way in which the language of neighbourliness was sometimes infused with the language of citizenship and kinship. In a passage from Jeremiah, *shakhen* and *re'a* (*shakhen vere'o*) were rendered as 'neghebore and cosyn', then changed to 'neiybore and kynseman' (Jeremiah 6:21). The *re'a* and 'brother' described in Deuteronomy 15:3 as involved in a debt relationship are referred to first as 'citeseyn and nyy kyn', then as 'citesyn and neiybore'. The 'stranger' or 'foreigner' in the same context (*nokhri*) is also understood within a contemporary world view as 'pilgrim and comelyng'.[29] Finally, it was not only that Wyclif and his followers understood the Bible in terms of their own social horizons, they also justified their understanding theoretically. Wyclif 'regarded English as straightforwardly equitable with Latin'.[30] The first Wycliffite translation aimed to 'reproduce as exactly as possible Latin idiom and vocabulary in English'.[31] It was only when this early version proved unsatisfactory that the Latinate idiom was corrected. Yet at the same time Wyclif believed that language 'was a *habitus*: whatever the language, whether Hebrew, Greek, Latin, or English, the same gospel message should and could be delivered'.[32] In this case, then, the message was evidently seen to be delivered through an extensive use of the language of neighbourliness.

In subsequent versions the semantic boundaries between 'friend' and 'neighbour' were both tested and consolidated. With the fall of Constantinople in 1453, an influx of Greek and Latin texts reached the West, and after the expulsion of Jews from Spain in 1492 there was a rise in the scholarly interest in Hebrew throughout Europe.[33] In religious life new ideas were stirring. By 1534 Martin Luther had completed a German translation of the Bible based not on the Latin *Vulgate*, but on the original Hebrew and Greek.[34] English-speaking Protestants wished to bring a similar version of the holy word to their own people. Between Tyndale's translation of the Pentateuch, completed in 1530, and King James's Authorized Version of 1611, no fewer than seven versions of the Bible were produced. They drew on earlier traditions and increasingly on one another, yet they also aimed to transmit the original true word as first coined in the Hebrew and Greek.[35]

Drawing semantic boundaries between friendship and neighbourliness, however, was no easy task. The subtle differences in the translation of particular usages of *re'a* in early modern English Bibles reveal how difficult it was for the learned translators to agree on the exact meaning of this broad ranging Hebrew word. In II Samuel 15:37 Hushai the Archite was described as King David's 'friend', in I Chronicles 27:33 he was designated as his 'companion'. When Moses interceded between the two Hebrews, *re'a* was translated first as 'brothir', and subsequently as 'fellow' (Exodus 2:13).[36] The 'frendis' of the High Priest in Zachariah 3:8 (*re'im*) were also described as 'fellows'.[37] The estranged 'frendis' and 'neiyboris' of the Wycliffite translation of Psalms 37:12 (38:12) turned to 'louers & frendes' in Coverdale's version, and remained so in the Great Bible, the Geneva Bible, and the Authorized Version. But a similar expression in Psalm 121:8 (122:8) was translated in the Wycliffite Bible as 'brithren and my neiyboris',[38] turned to 'brethren and companions' in Coverdale's version, remained so in the Great Bible, became 'brethren and neighbours' in the Geneva Bible, and finally turned back to 'brethren and companions' in the Authorized Version. Some of the variations were not very significant, others were. In the contemporary context of growing poverty and changing practices of poor relief, the wise proverb 'Riches make many frendes but the poore is forsake of his owne frendes' (Coverdale's Bible, Proverbs 19:4), probably sounded different from 'riches gather many friends: but the poore is separated from his neighbour' (Geneva Bible, Proverbs 19:4).[39] From what we know about early modern credit relations, the advice to a lender who found himself defrauded to seek the help of his 'neighbour' no doubt had a different resonance from the advice that he should humble himself and solicit his 'friends'.[40] 'Better is a neighbour that is nere than a brother farre of' (Proverbs 27:10) was not the same as 'Better is a frende at honde, than a brother farre of.'[41] And finally, beyond the interpretative variations there were further extrapolations. In the Wycliffite version of Jeremiah 22:13 the prophet condemns he who oppresses 'his frend in veyn'; by the time of the Authorized Version, a more explicit censure appears of he who 'useth his neighbours seruice without wages, and giueth him not for his worke'.

Despite the many variations, conventions were established, which further confirmed the semantic shift discussed so far. It was clear to the translators that Job's faithful *re'im* were his 'friends', or that the wise phrase 'thine own friend and thy father's friend forsake not' would make little sense if rendered with 'neighbour', 'fellow', or 'companion'. At the same time, there was broad agreement that the right word for using in moral injunctions concerning fellow man, such as the Ten Commandments, was 'neighbour'. This understanding of the semantic field was clearly evident in Tyndale's first and highly influential Protestant translation of the Pentateuch, which in time came to have a major impact on the Authorized Version.[42] Following this logic, Tyndale set out to weed the few remaining usages of 'friend' in moral contexts. In Deuteronomy 23:26 (25) one was allowed to pick corn from another man's field but not to enter it and harvest the corn with a sickle. Following the *Vulgate*, the Wycliffite text designated that field as 'corn of thi freend'. Tyndale changed it to 'neighbour'.[43] In an injunction concerning accidental death *re'a*, previously translated as *amicum eius* and 'freend', was changed by Tyndale to 'neighbour' (Deuteronomy 19:5). Another injunction concerning debt was translated broadly in the *Vulgate* and in the Wycliffite Bible using the words 'freend', 'neiybore', and 'brother' (Deuteronomy 15:2). Tyndale removed 'friend'.[44] When describing practices of judgement, previously rendered with a relational phrase 'bytwixe hem', the word 'neyboure' was added (Exodus 18:16).[45] Most importantly, 'loue thi freend as thi silf' in Leviticus 19:18 became in Tyndale's Bible 'loue thy neghboure'.

Other translators followed. The result was that between Tyndale's version and King James's, the English Bible was placed firmly in the neighbourhood context. Of the usages of 'neighbour' in the Authorized Version's Old Testament 31 per cent were recent additions.[46] No fewer than 29 usages of *re'a*, translated as 'friend' in the Wycliffite Bible, became 'neighbour' in the Authorized Version; 13 additional usages of other words also became 'neighbour'.[47] At the same time only eight usages of 'neighbour' in the Wycliffite version became 'friend' in the Authorized

Version.[48] Of the 69 usages of 'friend' in the Authorized Version, 49 had their origin in *re'a* and 12 more came from the Hebrew root *a-h-v*, meaning 'love', highlighting the affective weight of the term 'friend'.[49] At the same time, 103 of the 135 usages of 'neighbour' in the Authorized Version were derived from *re'a*, and 17 more came from the word *shakhen*, meaning a near-by dweller.[50]

And so the semantic shift had been completed. The Protestant translations of the Hebrew Bible achieved greater consistency in dividing the semantic field and drawing the boundaries between friend, neighbour, and fellow man. In the case of 'love thy neighbour', they also achieved consistency with the New Testament (especially Matthew 22:37–9), which used the word *plesion*, interpreted as 'neighbour'. Only in the Catholic Bible some old complexities remained. Faced with the Protestant translations, the Counter Reformation Council of Trent declared the *Vulgate* as the sole authentic edition of the Bible for public reading, disputations, and explanations. It was only in the middle of the twentieth century that official papal policy changed, leading to the publication in 1952 of the *New American Bible* and the *Jerusalem Bible* in 1966.[51] The Catholic Rheims-Douay Bible, published fully by 1609, had in effect more resemblances with than differences from existing English translations,[52] but it retained important Wycliffite usages of 'friend' and 'neighbour', including 'loue thy freind' in Leviticus 19:18. If neighbourliness was a norm emphasised in the Bible in English in the Wycliffite version, therefore, the choices made in the early modern Protestant versions emphasised it yet more.

II

While neighbourhoods and neighbourliness were highlighted in English biblical translations, in contemporary life they were coming under strain. Confessional changes altered communal rituals, the dissolution of religious houses quickened the land-market, and at the same time population growth and increasing poverty imposed new strains on neighbourhoods and ideals of neighbourliness.[53] Migration was pervasive.[54] Local studies reveal how communities in Tudor and Stuart England were greatly affected by contemporary processes of social re-structuration and polarisation.[55] However, norms of neighbourliness remained crucial and the political aspect of local life was even reinforced.[56] Religious devotion and regulation were still focused on parish life. Interpersonal conflicts continued to be tempered by neighbourly arbitration and mediation.[57] Moreover, with the institutionalisation of the poor laws, parochial government was invested with new powers of taxation, strategic enforcement, and regulation. State formation in early modern England was not simply imposed on the localities; it emerged from localities, which, in turn, formed component parts of the state.[58] 'The parish state' was to rule for centuries.[59] Even in the eighteenth century, '[f]or most English people their only contact with the world of officialdom and their only experience of political authority came through parish officers'.[60]

In this highly localised social and political context, the inculcation of norms of neighbourliness was of great importance. The language of neighbourly love – however naturalised by the sixteenth century – could not be taken for granted. It had to be taught, learned, re-interpreted, and continually reminded. One important medium through which it was strongly reinforced was the catechism. The Ten Commandments, the staple of Protestant teaching from the very outset, were referred to in contemporary catechisms as either the moral law or its summary.[61] Divided into two tables, the first listed the duties owed to God, the second 'to our neighbours or to man' (thus also corresponding to Christ's two commandments).[62] Catechisms then interpreted the Commandments broadly, a logic evident already in the sixteenth century and systematically applied in the seventeenth century.[63]

The moral impetus of the Ten Commandments was thus consistently understood in Tudor and Stuart catechisms within the context of contemporary life, as experienced most typically in neighbourhood communities. This served to reinforce the language of neighbourliness and drive home the message of neighbourly love. The interpretative emphasis of local experience was evident in the teaching of the first four commandments, which were seen to postulate not only the relationship between God and man but the institutionalisation of public worship. The first commandment to worship God and God alone was taught with reference to private and public worship, as practised routinely in community churches. One was told to honour God 'with all service and obedience', and this was to take the form of both 'inward and sincere godliness of heart' and 'open confession'.[64] The interpretations of the second commandment, prohibiting the making of 'any graven image', however contentious, were directly related to the outward appearance of contemporary churches and their ceremonial practices. The postulation of a community was particularly evident in the teaching of the fourth commandment to remember 'to keep holy the Sabbath day'. This was interpreted as a directive for the keeping of regular public worship and church attendance, as well as the regulation of work, commerce, and public amusements in local communities on the Sabbath day. Calvin's catechism, for instance, referred to the order of keeping the Sabbath as a 'politique order', in which one was bound 'to come together and to geve diligente eare to the woorde of God and make open profession of their faith and religion'.[65] A crucial aspect of public worship was the administration of the sacrament, which bound together the communicants in bonds of reconciliation and Christian love. In the order of Communion in Edward VI's Second Prayer Book the worshipers were told explicitly to 'perceive offences against God and neighbour and reconcile themselves unto them', also reciting the Ten Commandments.[66] The notion of 'love thy neighbour' was thus tied intimately with the idea of Christian love, instituted and re-enforced in public worship among nearby dwellers and fellow-worshipers.[67]

Local contexts and neighbourliness were emphasised further in early modern catechisms in the interpretation of other commandments. The sixth commandment was extended to address not only an injunction against murder, but the maintenance of peace, order, and good will in local communities. Anger, variance, contention, and revenge, which could lead to aggression in community life, were condemned.[68] Fighting, mocking, and quarrelling were prohibited, well-wishing and neighbourly love promoted: 'we should not only try to preserve the lives of our neighbours, but also seek to love them from the bottom of our hearts, be reconciled should any differences arise, and succour them when in need'.[69] Similarly, commentaries on the eighth commandment – against theft – invoked strongly a contemporary economic scene and an economic morality rooted in local contexts. Catechumens were told that they should not gain by their neighbour's loss or weakness, take excessive profit or undercut rivals with low prices, conceal faults in a commodity, engross commodities to enhance their price, neglect the payment of just debts or wages, engage in vexatious litigation, or initiate 'unjust enclosure'.[70] The words of Deuteronomy 27:17 are mentioned in this context, warning not to move a neighbour's landmark (i.e. *re'a*) so as to change wrongly the boundaries of his plot.[71] Even depriving the poor of due relief was understood as a form of theft.[72] In the expanding economic sphere of the period, with its mounting and locally felt strains, these commentaries were no doubt highly resonant. On the basis of his study of a great number of catechisms, Green observed that as the seventeenth century wore on, the list of 'economic crimes' in catechisms grew longer and catechumens were increasingly encouraged to seek honest employment.[73] Richard Sherlock's discussion of the Commandments, for instance, concludes with the catechumen's humble promise 'to get my own living'.[74]

The moral language of neighbourliness was also strongly evident in the teaching of the ninth commandment, as was the localisation of context. 'Thou shalt not bare false witness against thy neighbour' was interpreted as a commandment for maintaining agreements, honour, and reputation, concepts of vital importance in early modern society. As the commentary of the popular catechism written by Alexander Nowell, the Dean of St Paul's, explains this commandment was not simply an injunction against perjury, but against any breaking of oath, or faith, lying, slandering, backbiting, and evil speaking, 'whereby our neighbour may take loss or harm or lose his good name and estimation'.[75] 'The law, therefore, forbiddeth us to be inclined so much as think evil of our neighbours, much less to defame them', this text concludes.[76] The last commandment, where one is taught not to covet 'any thing that is thy neighbour's' (Exodus 20:16–17) was likewise interpreted as a justification of the highly hierarchical and deferential contemporary social order and cheerful acceptance of one's lot within it. 'I am commanded to be content with my present state and condition whatever it be, and in order hereunto to be diligent, industrious in the duties of my calling, both for my own support and the relief of others', instructs Sherlock in his commentary on the tenth commandment.[77] 'The summe of all in general is to love my neighbour as my self to express this love by doing unto all men as I would they should do unto me', he concludes his discussion of the second table of the Commandments. He then emphasises humility: to 'do my duty in that state of life whereunto it shall please God to call me'.[78]

Finally, to ensure that the morality of neighbourliness was fully understood, the extension of the term 'neighbour' was specifically explained: 'Now what syest thou of the love of our neighbour?' asks the master of his scholar in Nowell's catechisms. 'Christ's will was that there should be most straight bonds of love among Christians', answers the scholar, drawing a parallel between neighbourly love and broader notions of Christian love. 'How far extendeth the name of neighbour?' asks the master, checking that the scholar has fully understood the broad extension of the term. 'The name of neighbour containeth not only those that be of our kin and alliance, or friends, or such as be knit to us in any civil bond or love, but also those whom we know not, yea, and our enemies', replies the scholar diligently. 'For though any man hate us, yet that notwithstanding, he remaineth still our neighbour ... And thereby it may be easily perceived that holy Scripture hath appointed charity or love to be one of the principal parts of religion.'[79]

The inculcation of the language of neighbourly love in the teaching of the Ten Commandments in early modern catechisms thus highlighted the importance of neighbourliness at that time. Local contexts were taken as given by contemporary commentators, and community morals were emphasised. At the same time, the moral language of neighbourliness had to be repeatedly defined, explained, and taught. It was then also propagated in other religious texts. 'Whatever you would that men should do unto you, do ye even so unto them: for this is the Law of the Prophets' was the subject of one among several sermons, published in 1687 under the title *The Duty of a Christian towards his Neighbour Confided in a Sermon*.[80] If we turn to some other contemporary discourses, however, we can see that the efforts of the learned moralists were at least in some ways successful. Though it needed constant reinforcement and explication, the language of neighbourly love found its way to some common contexts. People's behaviour in early modern England no doubt fell short of the morals of neighbourly love as instilled in contemporary catechisms. But the language of neighbourliness nonetheless postulated a powerful ideal which was not only propagated textually, but which also served in contemporary discourses as a medium for understanding and negotiating conflict and dispute.

III

In 1583 two most cruel and bloody murders were committed in Worcestershire. In one case a man had 'unnaturally murdered his neighbour, and afterwards buried him in his celler'.[81] The deed was all the more horrid because the victim was the murderer's 'frendly neighbour'. In another case a wife and housekeeper had 'carnally acquainted'[82] herself with her handsome male servant and then persuaded him to kill her husband, an honest man 'very well reputed among his Neighbours'.[83] The guilty servant was hanged in chains. The wife was executed by burning until her 'wretched carkas ... dissolved in to ashes', the punishment reserved for a wife condemned of 'petty treason' against her husband. The horrid events were described in a chapbook printed in London in the same year. Before introducing the reader to the gory and salacious details, however, the chapbook's preface invokes pious contemplations. The aim of this narrative, as the preface explains, is not to excite the reader but to invite self-examination of 'our negligence of duetie to our God, as also our lacke of looue to our neighbour'. 'Three thinges reioyce me, and by them am I beautified before God and men: the virtue of Brethren, the looue of neighboures, & a man and wife that agree together', declares the preface, quoting the words of Ecclesiasticus 25:1. 'Beloued, let us looue one another for loue commeth of God and everie one that looueth, is borne of God', the preface explains quoting the words of the Evangelist. 'But he that loueth not, knoweth not God, for God is Loue.'[84]

The use of the biblical language of neighbourly love in this chapbook shows how deeply this discourse had penetrated into contemporary popular culture. Evidently, this language was known and accepted to the point that it could be used as a matter of course in a low brow publication. There it presented a moral to be bolstered, and a measure against which acts of transgression were to be judged. The language of neighbourly love was also evident in other records. Investigating parish records from Elizabethan London, for example, Ian Archer noted that they 'are soaked in the rhetoric of neighbourly unity'.[85] The representation of neighbours bound by love as a bundle of sticks which cannot be broken, mentioned at the start of this essay, was in fact penned by an Elizabethan parish clerk, who composed the following lines:

Even as sticks may easily be broken
So when neighbours agre not then ther is confucion
But a great many of stickes bound in one boundell will
   hardly be broken
So neighbours being ioned in love together can never be severed.[86]

Similarly, parish vestry records reveal vestrymen addressing one another as 'your loving neighbours and friends'. Parish funds were used to subsidise dinners to maintain unity and amity among neighbours.[87] Individual observers also recorded popular rites of neighbourly love. John Aubrey was impressed by the way in which the parishioners of Danby Wisk in the North Riding of Yorkshire went to the alehouse, after receiving the sacrament, to drink together, 'as a testimony of charity and friendship' and 'for the increase of mutuall love': in doing so they followed a long tradition of popular celebrations of Christian neighbourliness.[88] The godly minister Richard Leake condemned a similar rite among his Westmoreland parishioners.[89] But, as Wrightson observed, what could be seen by some as 'inordinate tippling' in a 'disorderly alehouse' could be seen by others as a manifestation of 'good fellowship and good means to increase love among neighbours'.[90]

Historians working on early modern legal documents also highlighted the importance of neighbourliness and the desire to achieve 'love' among neighbours. Early modern English society was extremely litigious, but the commonplace idea was 'that the operation of the law was at best a makeshift for the true exercise of Christian charity'.[91] The language of neighbourly love was thus employed in legal contexts not only as an ideology but as a language of negotiation and persuasion and a possible directive for social action, for it was invoked to encourage moderation and arbitration among litigants (who were often also neighbours). Focusing on litigation related to credit and contract, which formed 80–90 per cent of the cases coming before most common law tribunals, Muldrew argues that 'the primary means of dealing with disputes was to attempt to initiate a community negotiated Christian reconciliation between the disputing parties in order to maintain peace and concord'.[92] The 'constantly repeated Christian stress on the need to love one's neighbour' was not simply descriptive. Rather, it was an active attempt at rhetorical persuasion.[93] Evidence from personal documents, such as diaries, shows that historical actors described economic disputes in terms of virtue and Christian morality, and used the same terms in explaining their own actions throughout the seventeenth century and as late as the middle of the eighteenth century. In the course of this period, Muldrew argues, neighbourly sanctions needed to be increasingly bolstered by formal authority in order to protect the multiple chains of credit relations. But despite the growing complexity of the economy, communities based on extensive and informal networks of personal trust continued to exist and historical actors continued to use the language of neighbourly love in understanding social and economic action and moderating disputes.

The importance of idioms of neighbourly love has also been emphasised by historians working on legal cases of defamation and slander, which increased in volume in the early modern period and accounted for a large part of the cases brought before the ecclesiastical courts.[94] Focusing on the ecclesiastical court of York, for instance, Jim Sharpe argues that the system of ecclesiastical justice in Tudor and Stuart England encouraged amicable settlement between litigants to the point that the initiation of a suit for defamation could in itself be seen 'as the first step towards bringing neighbourly tensions to a close, as well as symptoms of such tensions as already existed'.[95] For women, Laura Gowing explains, slander was a way to maintain 'honesty in the neighbourhood'.[96] Thus in London women outnumbered men in bringing slander suits before the ecclesiastical courts at a rate of five to one.[97] Yet Gowing estimates that only one-fifth to one-third of these cases actually reached the point that witnesses were called, and 80 per cent of litigants settled or abandoned their case long before formal conclusion.[98]

The legal records also shed some light on the ways in which the language of neighbourly love was actively employed in the processes of negotiation and arbitration. In one case brought before the ecclesiastical court in York, for example, neighbours in dispute accepted 'the arbitrament of frend[es] by whose mediation they...were made lovers and frend[es] and thereupon drunke and eate together and did then and there remitte and release the one to the other all...controversies whatsoever from the beginning of the world until this time'.[99] In another case a witness told the court that 'she loved no suit nor troubles and if her friend[es] were so contended and her husband recompensed, she would find in her harte that all were lovers and frend[es]'.[100] Evidently, then, the concept of Christian charity among neighbours was relevant not only to contemporary divines, but to the population at large.[101] Conflict and strife were seen as 'a breach of neighbourly ethics',[102] and litigants were encouraged to make every effort to restore love and amity among neighbours and put an end to dispute. The idea of neighbourly love was actively invoked in these processes of mediation, and the public declaration of 'love' by opponents symbolised the end of the dispute.

Finally, in the course of our period the language of neighbourly love was used not only for mediation and reconciliation, but to negotiate exclusion. In 1618, for example, inhabitants of Taunton complained before the Quarter Session of one of their townsmen, a blacksmith, who had set up a forge in the marketplace to the 'nuisance and damage of his neighbours'.[103] Clearly, in this case 'neighbours' was a term of not only inclusion but also exclusion and accusation. The language of neighbourly love was employed powerfully in contexts of religious exclusion. Prayer book and handbook advised clergymen to exclude from the Christian rites of neighbourliness those who would not reconcile themselves to their neighbours 'by love', or who did not partake in the catechical learning, which instilled not least norms of neighbourliness.[104] In this way, Agnes and Francis Foster were turned away from receiving communion in Elizabethan London 'because of a quarrel with a neighbour', whereas John Barker was sent away for 'absenting himself from the catechisme'. John Dod described vividly how the minister should subject unworthy communicants to 'the shame of departing from the table without the sacrament: all the congregation looking on them, and the minister passing them by'.[105]

Exclusion in the name of neighbourly love was not only the punishment of the ignorant or the quarrelsome few. As 'the physical and moral thresholds of the parish community were reinforced', poor members of the neighbourhood were marginalised, whereas 'the better sort' came to see themselves not merely representatives of the community, but as the very community.[106] Traditional values of reciprocity and solidarity thus remained, Steve Hindle explains, but in a socially restricted way, while the language of community was also used to cloak harsh policies in the name of 'the parish' against the poor. In the parish of Allhallows Staining in Elizabethan London, for example, the desire to increase brotherly love and unity was cited in support of the establishment of select vestries, which excluded the majority of parishioners from the institutions of parish government and concentrated power in the hands of the local elite.[107] Behind the address to his 'good neighbours and loving parishioners', written in 1631 by a Hertfordshire vicar, lay a vitriolic attack against some nearby dwellers who were poor, incomers to the neighbourhood, and burdened with many children.[108] Clearly some 'neighbours' counted more than others, and the migrant poor were castigated most. Yet the poor still maintained some power of negotiation rooted, not least, in the norms of neighbourliness. In Elizabethan London, community sentiments and the rhetoric of neighbourhood were still important because they continued to provide a framework of values to which the poor could appeal, albeit while also satisfying the demands of the godly.[109] Poor folk with little access to education may have also been comforted by the fact that many clergymen made sure that the minimum acceptable knowledge for religious inclusion 'was set fairly low'.[110] Beyond that, there could be room for interpretation: one parishioner argued before the London Archdeaconry court that although he 'hath ben at variance' with a neighbours, he 'beareth him no malice', thus suggesting there could be different opinions as to the type of neighbourly dispute meriting exclusion from communion.[111] At the same time, parishioners' petitions to allow poor neighbours to build cottages on plots of land, although they lacked the four acres required for such a development, suggest the possible force of neighbourly inclusion.[112] Even the decision of a seventeenth-century Somerset Quarter Session to deny the settlement of one inhabitant and prevent him from getting relief on the grounds that he was not a member of the congregation and was not in communion with his neighbours suggests that participation in the neighbourly rites of Christian love could consolidate a claim for settlement and poor relief.[113]

IV

Historians of late medieval and early modern England emphasise the importance of localities and neighbourly relationships in the period. The consolidation and expansion of the language of neighbourliness in English biblical translations from Wyclif to King James's bears this emphasis out. In translating the Hebrew Bible, English divines transposed on to the Hebrew vocabulary of social relations the contemporary language of manorial and parochial life. They based their reading on the *Vulgate* and subsequently on the *Septuagint* and the Hebrew original, but they further filtered the biblical concepts through their own world view. The language of neighbourliness, introduced to English religious discourse around 1300, thus became habituated in the Wycliffite translation of the *Vulgate* and considerably augmented in Protestant translations from Tyndale's to King James's, where nearly one-third of the usages of the word 'neighbour' appeared as recent additions. This language was also further propagated and interpreted in a range of religious and secular texts. When the learned translators of the Authorized Version introduced their magisterial text as being 'translated out of the original tongues: and with the former translations diligently compared and revised', they were therefore also presenting in this case a missed opportunity. The misreading of the Hebrew *re'a* as 'neighbour' was not corrected, but largely augmented and canonised. The Hebrew language of amity was re-inscribed as the English discourse of neighbourly love.

This takes us to the historical significance of this semantic shift. Whereas some historians emphasise a culture of reconciliation and neighbourliness in early modern England,[114] others present a more negative view. However many optimists and pessimists also share a broad interpretative framework in which ideals of charity and neighbourliness in early modern England are broadly seen as being in decline. This interpretative paradigm, also evident in the works of pioneering historians such as R.H. Tawney, Christopher Hill, Keith Thomas, and Lawrence Stone, can be traced to the influence of the 'founding fathers' of social thought, who saw the sixteenth and seventeenth centuries as a transitional period in the development from 'community' to 'society'.[115] In 1992, Eamon Duffy's influential book on the decline of traditional communal Christianity in England gave this interpretative paradigm a new thrust. In describing the ideal of parochial charity and neighbourly love in pre-Reformation Catholic ritual, Duffy observes that it 'was often just that, an ideal', though he emphasises that it was 'a potent one, carrying enormous emotive and ethical weight',[116] until traditional Christianity was eroded by the forces of the Reformation. Focusing on the period 1550–1650, Steve Hindle concludes (quoting Duffy's words) that despite its 'enormous ethical weight' the ethos of neighbourliness became 'just that – an ideal', increasingly divorced from the fragmented visions of neighbourliness that emerged in the highly polarised communities of the century after 1550.[117]

The evidence examined here, however, suggests that the language of neighbourly love in the early modern period was neither a waning relic of the pre-Reformation era, nor necessarily a declining ethos. If social relations in local communities in the sixteenth and seventeenth centuries became polarised and fragmented as the 'better sort' drew together and the 'meaner sort' were increasingly marginalised, the very same period also saw the augmentation and canonisation of the language of neighbourliness in the most holy of early modern English texts, the Bible, as well as its further propagation in a range of texts and contexts, and its continued use as a language of negotiation and a possible directive for social action. The augmentation of the language of neighbourliness and its discursive uses were thus carried out in our period both despite growing social and economic rifts, and because of them. In early modern society mobility was ubiquitous, 'as much a natural part of the life cycle as being born or dying'.[118] Conflict and litigation were rife. Traditional religion was challenged and 'Protestant identities'[119] were sought and fought. An unprecedented culture of print was spreading, as well as new forms of governance. In this society neighbourliness could never be a straightforward reflection of an organic experience: it had to be forged and continually recreated. Future research may clarify further how exactly the language of neighbourliness mutated and changed in the course of the early modern period itself. The idiom of neighbourliness, however, was clearly a vibrant one. Neither empty nor dying, it suggests an early modern ethos of communalism in the making, however complex and self-contradictory.

Notes

This chapter was first presented at 'Alan Bray and "The Friend" ', Birkbeck College, London, 20 September 2003. Versions were also delivered in a colloquium on the Politics of Friendship at the Menzies Centre for Australian Studies, the Cambridge Early Modern History seminar, and the History Work in Progress Seminar at the University of Sussex. I am grateful for the comments I received on these occasions. I am also indebted to the friends and colleagues who have read drafts of this chapter and particularly Brian Cummings, David Feldman, Adam Fox, Sara Japhet, Steve Hindle, Miri Rubin, Alexandra Shepard, Moshe Sluhovsky, Richard Smith, and Keith Wrightson.

1. K. Wrightson, 'The Politics of the Parish in Early Modern England', in P. Griffiths, A. Fox and S. Hindle (eds), *The Experience of Authority in Early Modern England* (Basingstoke: Macmillan, 1996), pp. 10–46, on p. 18.
2. *The English Works of George Herbert*, ed. G.H. Palmer I (Boston and NewYork, 1915), p. 316, quoted in J. Bossy, 'Blood and Baptism: Kinship, Community and

Christianity in Western Europe from the Fourteenth to the Seventeenth Centuries', in D. Baker (ed.), *Sanctity and Secularity: The Church and the World*, The Ecclesiastical History Society (Oxford: Blackwell, 1973), pp. 129–43, on p. 143. See also K. Thomas, *Religion and the Decline of Magic: Studies in Popular Belief in Sixteenth and Seventeenth-Century England* (Harmondsworth: Penguin, 1991; first pub. 1971), pp. 182–3.

3. 'The Swallowfield articles', 4 and 7, in S. Hindle, 'Hierarchy and Community in the Elizabethan Parish: The Swallowfield Articles of 1596', *Historical Journal*, 42 (1999), 835–51, on p. 849. Swallowfield contained four manors. From 1845, the entire parish was brought under the jurisdiction of the county of Berkshire, ibid., pp. 837–8.

4. I. Archer, *The Pursuit of Stability: Social Relations in Elizabethan London* (Cambridge: Cambridge University Press, 1991), p. 84; Wrightson, 'Politics of the Parish', p. 18.

5. Bossy, 'Blood and Baptism', p. 143.

6. See e.g. Muldrew's emphasis on 'the culture of reconciliation': C. Muldrew, 'The Culture of Reconciliation: Community and the Settlement of Economic Disputes in Early Modern England', *Historical Journal*, 39 (1996), 915–42, and compare e.g. Hindle's emphasis on polarisation and strife in S. Hindle, 'A Sense of Place? Becoming and Belonging in the Rural Parish, 1550–1650', in A. Shepard and P. Withington (eds), *Communities in Early Modern England* (Manchester: Manchester University Press, 2000), pp. 96–113; S. Hindle, *The State and Social Change in Early Modern England, 1550–1640* (Basingstoke: Palgrave, 2000), pp. 56–8, 94–6. See also references in these works to earlier discussions, and further discussion below.

7. J. Bossy, 'Moral Arithmetic: Seven Sins into Ten Commandments', in E. Leites (ed.), *Conscience and Casuistry in Early Modern Europe* (Cambridge: Cambridge University Press, 1988), pp. 215–34, and references there. As Bossy argues (and also discussed further below), some shift towards the Decalogue was evident in the fifteenth century. This developed greatly with the Reformation. By the middle of the sixteenth century, the importance of the Decalogue was also emphasised in Catholic teaching associated with the Counter Reformation. See also I. Green, *The Christian's ABC: Catechisms and Catechising in England c. 1530–1740* (Oxford: Clarendon Press, 1996), ch. 10.

8. See also 'love thy neighbour' in Matthew 19:19; Mark 12:31; Luke 10:27; Romans 13:9; Galatians 5:14; James 2:8.

9. The commandments of Leviticus 19 relate to the Decalogue: M. Weinfeld, *The Decalogue and the Recitation of 'Shema': The Development of the Confession* (Tel Aviv: Hakibbutz Hameuchad, 2001), pp. 21–5.

10. Weinfeld, *The Decalogue and the Recitation of 'Shema'*, p. 90. In other words, *re'a* refers to persons with whom one is – or should be – bound in a relationship of well-wishing and amity. Such relationships are imagined as taking place in time and space, but the word *re'a* contains no specification as to the type of space. I include here the by-forms *mere'a* and *re'eh* and feminine and plural forms. See also E. Jenni and C. Westermann, *Theological Lexicon of the Old Testament*, vol. 3 (Peabody Mass. Hendrickson, 1997), pp. 1243–6. The Hebrew transliteration in this chapter follows the modern pronunciation.

11. See 'neighbour' in *OED*: 'one who lives near or next to another; one who occupies a near or adjoining house, one of a number of persons living close to each other, especially in the same street or village'.

12. 'neighbour', *OED*. This reference is taken from the Ten Commandments.
13. See 'Theories of Translation', LXX, in *Anchor Bible Dictionary*, 6 vols (New York: Doubleday, 1992), 6: 513. According to some traditions the number of elders was 70.
14. Interestingly, *shakhen* in this context is also rendered as *philos*. In other instances of the word *shakhen*, however, the *Septuagint* uses *geiton*: e.g. Psalm 79:4, 12 (Septuagint 78:4, 12); 80:7 (79:7); 89:42 (88:42), Jeremiah 12:14, or *geiton* and *plesion* in Exodus 12:4; Jeremiah 6:21.
15. See *philos* and *plesion* in F.W. Danker, *A Greek-English Lexicon of the New Testament and Other Early Christian Literature* (Chicago and London: University of Chicago Press, 1957); *Greek Lexicon of the Septuagint*, compiled by L. Just, E. Eynikel and K. Huspie (Stuttgart: Deutsche Bibelgeselleschaft, 1992–6). I am also particularly grateful to Professor Emmanuel Tov of the Hebrew University for his generous assistance in clarifying this matter.
16. Note also combined usages: the longed for loved one and friend in Psalm 88:19 (or 87:19) is described as *philon kai plesion*.
17. LXX, *Anchor Bible Dictionary*, 6: 513.
18. For example Ruth 4:17; 2 Kings 4:3; Psalm 31:12 (30:12); Psalm 79:4, 12 (78:4, 12); 80:7 (79:7); 89:42 (88:42); Jeremiah 6:21; 12:14.
19. As, for example, was David's friend Hushai, II Samuel 15:37. However, in Job 30:29 *re'a* was translated as *socius*.
20. 87:19 in the Latin computation.
21. The first translation of the New Testament seems to have been completed about 1380, the Old Testament between 1382 and 1384.
22. In describing Moses interceding between the two Hebrews he used the word 'brother', Exodus 2:13, Elsewhere the word 'fellow' was used: see e.g. 'felow', Job 30:29, rendered as *socius* in the *Vulgate* and *hetairos* in the *Septuagint*; 'felowis' in Judges 11:37; II Samuel 2:16. See also Isaiah 34:14, where *re'a* was translated as 'to an other'.
23. Earlier usages of 'neighbour' in biblical texts appear from 1300 (see above n. 12). In Saxon versions the term used was *nextan*, see Matthew 19:19, West Saxon Gospels, 1175, and *nehstan* in Matthew 19:19, West Saxon Gospels 990, *The Bible in English*, Chadwyck-Healey Literature Collections (ProQuest Information and Learning Co., 2005). See also *niechsta* under 'neighbour' and 'next', *OED*. A similar usage is retained in the German: *Nachsten* for the moral relationships of the Ten Commandments, and *Nachbar* for designating a nearby dweller. In French or Italian a similar differentiation is retained in the usage of *prochin* or *prossimo*, as opposed to *voisin* or *vicino*. The transition to 'neighbour' in this context is unique to the English.
24. Psalm 87 in the Wycliffite computation.
25. 'oon seide to his neiybore, Come ye, and make we tiel stonys...' (Genesis 11:3). The Latin was 'dixitque alter ad proximum suum'.
26. See also, for example, Exodus 12:4; Psalm 44:14 (43:14); 79:4 (78:4).
27. See also 'brother, freend, and neighbore' in Exodus 32:27; see also *'amit*, e.g. Leviticus 18:20; 19:15.
28. Genesis 3:7; William Caxton, *The Golden Legend* (1483). This usage is repeated later in one of the most influential Protestant translations, the Geneva Bible, also known as the 'Breeches Bible': see 'Versions, English', *Anchor Bible Dictionary*, 6: 822.

29. *benei amcha* ('thy people' in the Authorized Version), are rendered in the Wycliffite version as 'thy cytesenys' (Leviticus 19:18).
30. A. Hudson, 'Wyclif and the English Language', in A. Kenny (ed.), *Wyclif in His Time* (Oxford: Clarendon Press, 1986), p. 90.
31. Ibid., p. 93.
32. Ibid., p. 90.
33. 'Versions, English', *Anchor Bible Dictionary*, 6: 818. Those include the major translations. For a more detailed computation, see W.J. Chamberlin, *Catalogue of English Bible Translations* (New York, Westport, Ct. and London: Greenwood Press, 1991).
34. The translation of the New Testament was published in 1522 and Luther then set to translate the Hebrew Bible. By 1532 the Prophets were translated and in 1534 the complete Bible appeared.
35. 'Versions, English', *Anchor Bible Dictionary*, 6: 819–23.
36. See 'brothir' in Exodus 2:13 in the Wycliffite version, as see later the Great Bible, the Geneva Bible, and the Authorized Version.
37. They were first designated as 'frendis' in Zacharia 3:8 in the Wycliffite version and 'freds' in the Great Bible, but changed to 'fellows' in the Geneva Bible, and remained so in the Authorized Version.
38. *eḥai ve-re'ai*, Psalm 122:8, 121 in the *Vulgate*, the Wycliffite Coverdale's and Cranmer's computation; translated as 'fratres meos et amicos meos' in the *Vulgate*.
39. See also 'frendes' in Matthew's Bible, and 'neghbore' in the Great Bible. In the Authorized Version the phrase is 'wealth makes many friends, but the poor is separated from his neighbour'.
40. See 'neighbour' in Coverdale's Proverbs 6:3, 'neighbour' and 'friend' and 'friend' and 'neighbour' in the Wycliffite Bible, Geneva Bible, and the Rheims-Douay version, and 'friend' only in the Authorized Version. Note also that 'friend' was used at the time as a kinship term, and see also N. Tadmor, ' "Family" and "Friend" in *Pamela*: A Case Study in the History of the Family in Eighteenth-Century England', *Social History*, 14 (1989), 289–306; N. Tadmor 'The Concept of the Household-Family in Eighteenth-Century England', *Past and Present*, 151 (1996), 110–40; N. Tadmor, *Family and Friends in Eighteenth-Century England: Household, Kinship, and Patronage* (Cambridge: Cambridge University Press, 2001), especially chapter 4 on the language of kinship and chapters 5–7 on friendship, kinship, and social networks.
41. The former was phrased similarly in the Wycliffite Bible, the Geneva Bible, and the Authorized Version, the latter appears in Coverdale's version.
42. Estimates are that 80 per cent of the Authorized Version is due to Tyndale: *Anchor Bible Dictionary*, 'Versions, English', 6: 820. See also E.W. Cleaveland, *A Study of Tyndale's Genesis Compared with the Genesis of Coverdale and of the Authorized Version* (Hamden Conn: Archon Books, 1912). Tyndale published translations of the New Testament, the Pentateuch, and Jonah, and completed drafts from Joshua to II Chronicles, before he was strangled and burned at the stake. These unpublished manuscripts were probably used in Matthew's Bible, see *Tyndale's Old Testament: Being the Pentateuch of 1530, Joshna to II Chronicles of 1537, and Jonah*, ed. D. Daniell (New Haven and London: Yale University Press, 1992), p. ix.

43. *Vulgate*, Deuteronomy 23:25, 'segetem amici tui'.
44. In another borrowing relationship in Exodus 11:2 *re'a* in the female was translated in the *Vulgate* as *vicina* and in the Wycliffite Bible as 'neighbour', whereas her male counterpart was rendered *amico suo* in Latin and 'frend' in the Wycliffite Bible. Tyndale used 'neighbour' for both, perhaps following also the Greek *plesion* used in both cases. Subsequent versions, however, reverted to the gendered differentiation: female 'neighbour' and male 'friend'.
45. 'betwixt every man and his neyboore'. However see the Authorized Version 'between one and another'.
46. The bulk of these were already consolidated in the influential Geneva Bible (1587).
47. Including four expressions translated in the Wycliffite Bible in the language of citizenship, three in the language of kinship, one usage of 'fellow', one of 'any man', and two usages deriving from 'nigh' and rendering derivations of the Hebrew root *q-r-v* ('near'). This is based on an electronic key-word search of the Old Testament in King James's Version in the 'Biola Unbound Bible' website, and manual comparisons of other versions.
48. Seven of which were derived from *re'a*. Eight usages in the language of comfort, love, kinship, knowledge, and council were also rendered as 'friend'. Here there were some noticeable variations between the versions, including the Geneva Bible.
49. One more was *qarov u'moda*, one was *aluf*, and two *anshei shalom*.
50. Nine more were derived from '*amit* (meaning friend, companion, or associate) and three from *qarov*, meaning 'near'. There were also 12 usages of 'fellow' derived from *re'a* and 12 of 'companion'.
51. In 1952 the Old Testament was published in the *New American Bible*, the New Testament in 1970. The *New Jerusalem Bible* was published in 1985, see 'Versions, Catholic', *Anchor Bible Dictionary*, 6: 814.
52. The New Testament published in 1582, the Old Testament in 1609.
53. See, e.g. M. Ingram, 'Communities and Courts: Law and Disorder in Early Seventeenth-Century Wiltshire', in J.S. Cockburn (ed.), *Crime in England, 1500–1800* (London: Methuen, 1977), pp. 110–34, on p. 134: 'the existence of a large and growing number of poor imposed a strain on ideals of neighbourliness', At the same time, old norms of hospitality declined: F. Heal, *Hospitality in Early Modern England* (Oxford: Clarendon Press, 1990).
54. In Elizabethan Buckinghamshire, for example, over 80 per cent of witnesses appearing before the church courts had moved at least once in their lives. In Sussex Weald and Kent 1580–1649 the comparable figures are 77 per cent, and for Suffolk and Norfolk 82 per cent. The population of entire parishes could undergo significant changes: in some places, about half the population could change in the course of a period of 12 years: P. Clark and D. Souden, *Migration and Society in Early Modern England* (Totowa, NJ, 1988), pp. 22, 28, 124, 229. Migration was highly noticeable in urban communities: 'almost certainly the majority of inhabitants in any provincial town had not been born there': P. Clark, 'Introduction: English Country Towns 1500–1800', in P. Clark (ed.), *County Towns in Pre-Industrial England* (Leicester: Leicester University Press, 1981), pp. 1–44, on p. 4. Towns also suffered from pauper migration. For problems related to migration, see also e.g. P. Slack, 'Vagrants and Vagrancy in England, 1598–1668', *Economic History Review*, 27 (1974),

360–79; A.L. Beier, *Masterless Men: Vagrants in England 1560–1640* (London: Methuen, 1985). See also Tadmor, *Family and Friends*, pp. 108–9, 113–14, and notes.

55. K. Wrightson, *English Society 1580–1680* (London and New York: Routledge, 2003; first pub. 1982); K. Wrightson, *Earthly Necessities* (New Haven: Yale University Press, 2000). For local studies, see e.g. K. Wrightson and D. Levine, *Poverty and Piety in an English Village: Terling 1525–1700* (Oxford: Clarendon Press, 1995); first pub. 1979; D. Levine and K. Wrightson, *The Making of an Industrial Society, Whickham 1560–1765* (Oxford: Clarendon Press, 1991); M. Spufford, *Contrasting Communities: English Villagers in the Sixteenth and Seventeenth Centuries* (Cambridge: Cambridge University Press, 1974); G. Nair, *Highley: The Development of a Community 1550–1880* (Oxford: Basil Blackwell, 1988).

56. See especially Wrightson, 'Politics of the Parish'.

57. See Wrightson, *English Society*, pp. 59–65, 163–7. This is seen especially with regard to litigation. See e.g. Ingram, 'Communities and Courts'; M. Clanchy, 'Law and Love in the Middle Ages', in J. Bossy (ed.), *Disputes and Settlements: Law and Human Relations in the* West (Cambridge: Cambridge University Press, 1983), pp. 47–67; J. Sharpe, 'Such Disagreement Betwyx Neighbours: Litigation and Human Relations in Early Modern England', in ibid., pp. 167–87; Muldrew, 'The Culture of Reconciliation'. As Hindle argues, however, ideals of neighbourliness were also enforced by public authority and should be seen in the context of power relations: Hindle, *The State and Social Change*, pp. 94–5.

58. M. Bradick, *State Formation in Early Modern England c. 1550–1700* (Cambridge: Cambridge University Press, 2000), esp. p. 14.

59. John Clare, *The Parish: A Satire*, ed. E. Robinson (Harmondsworth: Penguin, 1985), p. 63. For the parish state and John Clare, see D. Eastwood, *Government and Community in the English Provinces, 1700–1870* (Basingstoke: Macmillan, 1997), p. 47; S. Hindle, 'Power, Poor Relief, and Social Relations in Holland Fen', *Historical Journal*, 41 (1998), 67–96, on pp. 94–6; K.D.M. Snell, 'The Culture of Local Xenophobia', *Social History*, 28 (2003), 1–30.

60. Eastwood, *Government and Community*, p. 47.

61. Green, *The Christian's ABC*, p. 423. In 1281 the Council of Lambeth drew a schema for instructing the laity which also included the Ten Commandments and the dual precept to love God and neighbour. The schema was first translated and adapted for the English Northern provinces in 1357, and in 1425 it was translated by the Bishop of Bath and Wells and placed in every church in his diocese. At the eve of the Reformation, the teaching of the Commandments was thus advocated in a literature for instructing parish priests and in vernacular texts. However, in the period from 1530, catechisms were printed and circulated in impressively large numbers. Between 1530 and 1740, 792 new catechisms are known to have appeared in England; with the addition of related instructive texts, the number of catechetical publications in the period amounted to 1043. See E. Duffy, *The Stripping of the Altars: Traditional Religion in England 1400–1580* (New Haven and London: Yale University Press, 1992), pp. 7, 54; see also references in ibid., p. 56 to *Ordynarye of Crysten Men* (1502) and *Floure of the Commandments* (1510). For the figures on catechisms, 1530–1740, see Green, *The Christian's ABC*, p. 51, and Appendix 1.

See also I.K. Ben Amos, 'Good Works and Social Ties: Helping the Migrant Poor in Early Modern England', in M.C. McClendon, J.P. Ward and M. MacDonald (eds), *Protestant Identities: Religion, Society and Self-fashioning in Post Reformation England* (Stanford: Stanford University Press, 1999), pp. 139–40.

62. Green, *The Christian's ABC*, p. 427, and references there. This was presented in a language that was 'remarkably uniform' throughout a wide sample.
63. Green, *The Christian's ABC*, p. 428.
64. *Nowell's Catechism, or First Instruction and Learning of Christian Religion by Alexander Nowell* . . . (Trans. Thomas Norton, 1570, repr. London, 1846), pp. 11–12. See also e.g. Wake's catechism: 'How are we to worship God? . . . With all the Powers and Faculties but of our Souls and Bodies: In Public and in Private', W. Wake, *The Principles of the Christian Religion Explained in a Brief Commentary upon the Church Catechism. By the Most Reverend Father in God, William, Lord Arch-Bishop of Canterbury* (5th edn, London, 1731). See also Green, *The Christian's ABC*, p. 431.
65. John Calvin, *The Forme of Prayers and Administration of the Sacraments, Used in the English Congregation at Geneva and Approved by the Famous and Godly Learned Man, John Caluyn* (Geneva, 1556), p. 70.
66. *The Second Prayer Book of King Edward the Sixth* (repr. London, n.d.), pp. 377–87.
67. For this notion in medieval times, see Clanchy, 'Law and Love'; Sharpe, 'Such Disagreement Betwyx Neighbours', esp. pp. 178–80; Duffy, *The Stripping of the Altars*, esp. ch. 3; M. Rubin, *Corpus Christi* (Cambridge: Cambridge University Press, 1991). See also evidence on the continued importance of the Lord's Supper in Protestant and indeed Puritan rituals in A. Hunt, 'The Lord's Supper in Early Modern England', *Past and Present*, 161 (1998), 39–83; C. Haigh, 'Communion and Community: Exclusion from Communion in Post-Reformation England', *Journal of Ecclesiastical History*, 51 (2000), 699–720. See also A. Bray, *The Friend* (Chicago and London: University of Chicago Press, 2003), esp. the section 'Friendship and Traditional Religion', pp. 84–104.
68. See e.g. Richard Sherlock, *The Principles of the Holy Christian Religion, or the Catechism of the Church of England Paraphrased* . . . (11th edn, London, 1673; first pub. 1661), pp. 37–8: 'I am forbidden not only to avoid all manner of murther and blood shed, whether directly or indirectly, but all anger, wrath, hatred, variance, strife, contention, revenge, variance, and reviling of others, though I be provoked thereunto'. See also J. Allaine, *Explanation of the Assemblies Shorter Catechism* (London, 1674), p. 106.
69. Green, *The Christian's ABC*, p. 461, and references to catechisms by Calvin, Nowell, Dering-More, Paget, Ball, Hill, Nicholson, Comber, Vincent, Marshall, Williams, and Wake, where such commentaries appear, as well as the Westminster Larger and Shorter catechisms.
70. Green, *The Christian's ABC*, p. 463.
71. Significantly, it is specified that the mark should not be moved whether 'by Meere stones, Evidence, Records, or the like'. This is seen as being '*cousenage* at the theft': E. Boughen, *A Short Exposition of the Catechism of the Church of England* (London, 1673), p. 55, see also Green, *The Christian's ABC*, p. 463.
72. In Sherlock's commentary on the eighth commandment one promises to be 'just and upright in my doing' and 'charitable that the poor be not deprived of their proper livelihood and subsistence, which is my superfluity': Sherlock,

The Principles, p. 34. In Worthington's short catechism one is said to have the duty to supply one's brother's necessities 'according to his ability', J. Worthington, *A Forum of Sound Words or a Scripture Catechism* (London, 1674).

73. Green, *The Christian's ABC*, p. 463.
74. Sherlock, *Principles of the Holy Christian Religion*, p. 44.
75. *Nowell's Catechism*, p. 26.
76. Ibid., p. 27.
77. Sherlock, *Principles of the Holy Christian Religion*, p. 41.
78. Ibid., pp. 43–4. See also 'that we be truly contended with our own outward condition, and heartily desire our neighbour's good in all things belonging unto him great or small', Green, *The Christian ABC*, p. 465, and see the references to catechisms which make this point in n. 247.
79. *Nowell's Catechism*, pp. 30–1. In Boughen's catechism the definition of 'neighbour' is expanded to include not only kindred and 'such as are near us by acquaintance or habitation or Country; but even those that are of another Nation, and Religion', with particular reference to Luke 10:30. See also, e.g., Calvin, *Forme of Prayers*, pp. 85–6.
80. See also e.g. I. Barrow, *On the Love of God and our Neighbour in Several Sermons* (1680); C. Timmewell, *The Duty of a Christian Towards his Neighbour* (1697); J. Lambe, *Discourse Between a Minister and his Parishioners Concerning the Holy Sacrament: Love to God, to our Neighbour, and to our Enemies* (London, 1690); R. Lucas, *The Plain Man's Guide to Heaven* (Including Instructions for Behaviour to One's Neighbour) (London, 1692). See also *Alphabet of Rules on Christian Practice* (1681, including Behaviour to One's Neighbour); N.N., *A Threefold Alphabet of Rules Concerning Christian Practice . . .* (1681).
81. *A Briefe Discourse of Two Most Cruell and Bloudie Murthers, Committed Bothe in Worcestershire, and Bothe Happening Unhappily in the Year 1583* (London, 1583), title page.
82. Ibid., sig. B3.
83. Ibid., sig. B2.
84. Ibid., sig. A2.
85. Archer, *Pursuit of Stability*, p. 84.
86. Ibid.
87. Ibid.
88. J. Aubrey, *Three Prose Works*, ed. J. Buchanan Brown (Fontwell: Centaur Press, 1972), pp. 141–2, quoted and discussed with additional references in A. Hunt, 'The Lord's Supper in Early Modern England', p. 71.
89. Leake, *Four Sermons*, quoted by P. Collinson, *The Religion of Protestants* (Oxford: Oxford University Press, 1982), p. 214, and in Hunt, 'The Lord's Supper', p. 71.
90. Wrightson, 'Two Concepts of Order: Justice, Constables and Jurymen in Seventeenth-Century England', in J. Brewer and J. Styles (eds), *An Ungovernable People: The English and their Law in the Seventeenth and Eighteenth Centuries* (London: Hutchinson, 1980), pp. 25–46, on p. 25.
91. Ingram, 'Communities and Courts', p. 110. For moderation, see also Wrightson, 'Two Concepts of Order'.
92. Muldrew, 'The Culture of Reconciliation', p. 915.
93. Ibid., pp. 920–1.

94. In the early seventeenth century suites for slander were increasing in all courts. The ecclesiastical courts dealt with sexual slander, however, because it imputed spiritual rather than sexual sin, and the penance and apology imposed as punishment by the ecclesiastical courts were seen as more suitable for dealing with slander and defamation than the financial compensations of the common law: see Sharpe, 'Such Disagreement Betwyx Neighbours', p. 179; L. Gowing, 'Language, Power and the Law', in J. Kermode and G. Walker (eds), *Women, Crime, and the Court* (London: UCL Press, 1994), p. 27.

95. Sharpe, 'Such Disagreement Betwyx Neighbours', p. 178.

96. Gowing, 'Language, Power and the Law', p. 30.

97. Ibid., p. 26.

98. Ibid., p. 41.

99. Sharpe, 'Such Disagreement Betwyx Neighbours', p. 176.

100. Ibid., p. 176.

101. Ibid., p. 178.

102. Ibid., pp. 178, 180.

103. Taunton Quarter Sessions, 7–9 July 1618: *Quarter Sessions Records for the County of Somerset*, vol. 1, James I 1607–1625, ed. J.H. Bates (London: Printed for Subscribers only by Harrison and Sons, 1907), p. 231.

104. Hunt, 'The Lord's Supper', esp. pp. 60–9.

105. Examples taken from ibid., p. 65. Sussex parishioners were presented to the court of the Archdeaconry of Chichester for being able to recite 'none of the Ten Commandments', ibid., p. 67. However, there were parishioners who decided to exclude themselves from communion because they were not 'in perfect love and charity' with their neighbours, while in some rare cases parishioners refused to take communion from a clergyman of 'evil name and fame', and thus excluded him. As Haigh explains, parishioners could be excluded from communion on the grounds of malice and sin against their neighbours, but the act of exclusion was in itself divisive and only led to further conflict and strife: Haigh, 'Community and Communion', and see esp. cases on p. 739. Finally, it is worth noting here that the solemnisation of close friendship by means of communion, though signifying general bonds of Christian love, also confirmed the exclusive bond between two communicants, Bray, *The Friend*, e.g. pp. 241–2, 244–6.

106. Hindle, 'A Sense of Place?', esp. p. 98.

107. Archer, *Pursuit of Stability*, p. 84.

108. Quoted in S. Hindle, *On the Parish? The Micro-Politics of Poor Relief in Rural England, c. 1550–1750* (Oxford: Oxford University Press, 2004), ch. 5: 'Exclusion'. I am grateful to Steve Hindle for directing me to this quotation and letting me use his unpublished text.

109. Archer, *Pursuit of Stability*, p. 93.

110. Hunt, 'The Lord's Supper', p. 67.

111. Ibid., p. 66. For the grounds for exclusion, see Haigh, 'Community and Communion'.

112. *Quarter Session Records for the County of Somerset*, ed. Bates, p. 42 (Session Rolls, 1609–10), for a petition signed by a vicar, collectors of the poor, churchwardens, and other parishioners, and p. 41 for a similar request granted on the grounds that the beneficiary and his children were born in the town.

113. *Quarter Session Records for the County of Somerset*, ed. Bates, pp. 4–5 (Session Rolls, 1607–8).
114. See e.g. references in works by Ingram, Sharpe, Archer, and Muldrew mentioned above. See also Wrightson, 'Two Concepts of Order'. A strong emphasis on notions of neighbourliness and social consensus in early modern attitudes to criminality can be found, for example, in C. Herrup, 'Law and Morality in Seventeenth-Century England', *Past and Present*, 106 (1985), 102–23, and in C. Herrup, *Common Peace: Participation and the Criminal Law in Seventeenth-Century England* (Cambridge: Cambridge University Press, 1987). See the analysis of 'hard' and 'soft' approaches to neighbourliness with particular reference to charity and violence: Hindle, *The State and Social Change*, pp. 56–8, 94–6.
115. A. Macfarlane, *Reconstructing Historical Communities* (Cambridge: Cambridge University Press, 1977); R.M. Smith, ' "Modernisation" and the Corporate Medieval Village Community in England: Some Sceptical Reflections', in A.R.H. Baker and D. Gregory (eds), *Explorations in Historical Geography* (Cambridge: Cambridge University Press, 1984), pp. 140–79. For some similar issues in the context of the history of kinship and the family, see Tadmor, *Family and Friends*, e.g. pp. 7–9, 107–8.
116. Duffy, *The Stripping of the Altars*, p. 95. See also Bossy's view that the transition from the moral code based on the Seven Deadly Sins to that of the Ten Commandments led to a narrower obligation to the neighbour: Bossy, 'Moral Arithmetic', p. 217.
117. Hindle, 'A Sense of Place?', pp. 108–9. See also Hindle, *The State and Moral Change*, p. 96.
118. Clark and Souden, *Migration and Society*, p. 22. See also references above, n. 54.
119. McClendon *et al.* (eds), *Protestant Identities*.

8
Tricksters, Lords and Servants: Begging, Friendship and Masculinity in Eighteenth-Century England

Tim Hitchcock

In Bampfylda-Moore Carew's autobiography, *The Life and Adventures of... the Noted Devonshire Stroller and Dog-Stealer*, first published in 1745, he recounts a tale as old (and probably as spurious) as the genre of rogue literature itself.[1] He tells how in the town of Maiden-Bradley on the road south of Frome in Wiltshire, he came across a fellow mendicant pretending, like Bampfylda himself, to be a shipwrecked sailor begging his way homeward, 'in a Habit as forlorn as his own, a begging for God's Sake, just like himself'. They address each other in canting language, asking about the best places to doss and whether Bampfylda would 'brush into the Boozing-Ken and be his Thrums, that is go into the Alehouse and spend his Threepence with him'. They retire to the pub and in casual friendship, compare notes on the generosity of the gentlemen of the neighbourhood, determining to go out begging as a team. Eventually they come to the home of a Lord Weymouth and approach the kitchen door. Telling their stories, they are frightened by the cook with accounts of the horse whipping and spells in Bridewell meted out to false beggars by the master of the house. Undaunted Bampfylda presses his case and convinces the cook of his sincerity, receiving 'the best part of a shoulder of mutton, half a fine wheaten loaf, and a shilling'.

The two beggars depart from the house well pleased with their day's work, and having traded the food for ready cash at a local inn, take their leave and go their separate ways.

The beggar who plays Bampfylda's temporary companion is Lord Weymouth himself, dressed in rags and determined to test both the generosity of his neighbours and servants, and the honesty of the beggars who constantly solicit food at his door. Having snuck back to his palatial home Weymouth quickly swaps clothes and orders his servants to hunt down the two mendicants. Bampfylda is brought before the Lord and a Restoration comedy of quick-change confusion and misdirection follows, before Weymouth reveals his true identity. Proud to befriend the 'famous' Bampfylda Carew, Lord Weymouth welcomes him into his home as an equal, entertaining him for days on end, providing him with a new suit of clothes and ten guineas in cash besides. He insists on Carew accompanying him to the Warminster Horse Race, where Carew is introduced to Weymouth's many friends, and in the years that follow, Carew claims to have visited Lord Weymouth on many occasions and to have always received a 'hearty welcome'.[2]

This story is at best unlikely, but it does describe perhaps the one place in eighteenth-century literature where friendship, a secure masculine identity and begging all exist together in a single text. At the same time, the lonely and unique character of this dramatic interlude points up some of the tensions that begging and dependency create for historical accounts of friendship and masculinity. In a highly stratified society, the intimate signs and gestures of friendship described by Alan Bray are most easily conveyed over only the lowest of social hurdles. The examples of friendships so eloquently described by Bray are between lovers from almost precisely the same class. And while he locates the history of friendship within a clearly demarcated hierarchy, in which the very acts of friendship play a significant part in defining social difference, the wide gap between Lord Weymouth and a common beggar would seem to defeat any attempt to create an emotional relationship between them. For a man in Lord Weymouth's position, gifts and generosity are full of the patronising superiority of an almsgiver, while a beggar could possess nothing to give. Even the gift of his body, made offensive by the requirements of a begging life, could not normally be given by a beggar to his benefactor. But if class and social divisions complicate the models of behaviour from which the histories of friendship and masculinity are constructed, this is not to say they are irrelevant to the experience of eighteenth-century almsgivers and beggars.

*   *   *   *

This chapter is a preliminary attempt to map friendship and emotional affect onto begging and almsgiving. Using the examples of male beggars and almsgivers, and their relationships with each other, it will suggest that in our headlong pursuit of a history of emotional interiority and gendered identity, we need to retain a perhaps old-fashioned awareness of class. More than this, it is an attempt to suggest some of the ways in which the emotional bonds excavated by Alan Bray can be used to re-invigorate our understanding of social division. It will suggest first that elite masculinity actually required the existence of the beggarly poor, or at least supplicating subordinates. The existence of objects of charity huddled on the street corner allowed elite men publicly to demonstrate their generosity and Christian virtue, qualities necessary to a fully-fledged male identity – itself a foundation stone of male friendship. This chapter will also suggest that older notions of the household, and the signs of friendship and obligation that the structures of the household allowed, frequently confused the role of the beggar for the middling sort and gentle. The interrelationship between rich and poor inherent in domestic service, the requirement to participate in a masculine 'good fellowship' and the real demands of Christian rhetoric all effectively complicated and occasionally overcame the apparently straightforward condescension of the gentleman for the beggar on the street corner. Second, and from the perspective of the beggar, this chapter will suggest that within common conceptions of manliness, there were only a limited number of ways for poor eighteenth-century men to enact their begging roles. They could unselfconsciously appeal to the rhetoric of Christian charity and mutual obligation, creating for themselves a specific and particular form of Christian masculinity. Alternatively, they could adopt the tricks, chicanery and humour so often attributed to beggars in popular writing in order to save themselves from the condescension of the almsgiver, and the otherwise emasculated role of the supplicant. And increasingly over the course of the second half of the eighteenth century, they could appeal to a growing sense of militaristic nationalism. In the process of addressing these developments, this chapter will also suggest that until new attitudes towards friendship, affect and beggars emerged with early Romanticism the requirements of eighteenth-century masculinity ensured that male friendship was only occasionally possible across the chasms of social difference.

Most historical studies of early modern affect and masculinity are remarkably innocent of class division. We are possessed of fine studies of masculine sociability, and foppery, of the import of the three-piece suit, of the anxieties that come with patriarchal authority, and of the power of different types of households and economics to influence and inflect male behaviour.[3] But with the notable exceptions of Alan Bray's work on friendship, of Merry Wiesner's work on sixteenth-century German apprentices, and Michael Rocke's fine volume on Renaissance homosexuality, there are very few studies that take seriously the role of inequality in the construction of a masculine identity or social interaction.[4] And even the few works that do treat inequality seriously tend to present it as gradual and finely gradated, and to assume that the locus of emotional connection will lie between a gentlemen and his closest inferior or superior. And yet the distinction between how a man behaved to socially inferior fellows, and how he conducted himself amongst his near equals was a common topic of contemporary advice literature, and reflects the importance that eighteenth-century men placed on managing and understanding these relationships of inequality. Erasmus Jones, for instance, happily parodied the easy sociability and physical friendship that could exist between men of the middling sort in his scathing volume of advice to the socially aspirant, *The Man of Manners, or, the Plebeian Polish'd*:

> Two low fellows meet in the street, resembling the arms of the hand in hand fire office, accosting one another, with a How fares your best body? Give me thy bawdy fist. Another that hath not seen his friend for some time, Ye son of a whore, where have you been all this while? Where in the name of vengeance have you hid yourself? Cries a third. – While another familiar spark says to his friend, damn ye you dog how dost do? Give me thy honest paw, come g'is it heartily.

Jones then contrasts these enthusiastic gestures and bombast with a stinging critique of the behaviour of his nouveau riche audience when dealing with beggars:

> I have seen some people as they have pass'd open-handed enough; but then they dispensed their charities with so unhandsome a grace, that methought they did ill in doing good, and refus'd an alms while they gave one; they seem'd to insult over a poor creature's misery, and seldom open'd their purse, till they had vented their gall. This is not to relieve the indigent, but to throw shame upon want, and confusion upon necessity; 'tis to hang weight to their burthen and to fret poverty with contempt...[5]

Clearly, in Jones's view, the ability to deal properly with requests for alms, to respond easily to the whining cry of suffering on the street corner, was a central act in the pantomime of gentle masculinity he advised his socially aspirant readers to play. And yet the secondary literature on charity and hospitality in this period has concentrated almost exclusively on charity at the kitchen door, or by institutions, rather than given casually on the street corner.[6] Even in Alan Bray's work, generally so focussed on relationships between individuals, it is the structures and behaviour dictated by great institutions (large medieval households and early modern university colleges) that provide the context for his understanding of charitable behaviour.[7] For Bray charitable giving entailed personal restraint at table, allowing sufficient food to be set aside for both junior members of the household, and eventually beggars at the kitchen door. Cold cash given anonymously on the street does not fit into this economy of giving through restraint. And yet it is clear that contemporaries were frequently more concerned with the practices and implications of casual street corner charity, than they were with any other sort. Thomas D'Urfey brackets both types of charity but gives precedence to the casual street-corner variety, when in *Collin's Walk Through London* he has his simple, yet virtuous Jacobite Major proclaim:

> I came ... of a good kind,
> so much to Charity Inclin'd,
> That even Vagabonds and Mumpers,
> Have from my bounty had full Bumpers,
> The blind and cripples in the street,
> I've oft reliev'd with broken meat;
> And many a Christmas Wassail Bowl,
> Has felt the largess of my Soul.[8]

In a similar vein Addison reserves his greatest admiration in *The Spectator* for the casual charity to a common beggar in Grays Inn Walks practised by his country friend, Sir Roger De Coverly:

> I was touched with a secret joy at the sight of the good old man, who before he saw me was engaged in conversation with a beggar man that had asked an alms of him. I cou'd hear my friend chide him for not finding out some work; but at the same time saw him put his hand in his pocket and give him six pence.[9]

There is also evidence for the importance of casual charity amongst the artefacts of recorded behaviour. It was probably for this same purpose of almsgiving that William Matthews, a gentleman down to his very undergarments, had about him three separate hoards of cash, when he went out riding in Hyde Park on a Spring morning in 1770. In his right-hand waistcoat pocket, next to his body linen, he had a substantial amount, 1 guinea, five shillings and three pence, as befitted a gentleman out for a ride, while in his left-hand breeches pocket, handy but not readily accessible, he kept eight shillings, probably to pay for a quick drink or the common expenses of the day; but in his right-hand coat pocket, the pocket most easily reached, was squirreled his small change, always ready to give out to any beggar who caught his fancy.[10]

To be able to chat amiably to the beggar by the roadside, to give money and heartfelt advice to the needy while avoiding appearing to participate in the beggar's social world, was an important masculine skill. You needed to be both sociable, to be able to talk easily with a beggar, and yet not 'friendly' in the way of near equals. This was in part a specifically eighteenth-century phenomenon, the existence of which reflects Alan Bray's late seventeenth-century transition in the culture of friendship and signs of affect. In the peculiarly constructive space opened up between the social model of Mr Spectator at the beginning of the eighteenth century and early Romanticism at its end, institutional giving could be allowed to proceed with little comment, while external and public acts of charity attracted ever-closer scrutiny. This was a social pantomime that needed to be practised, its every gesture repeated before a mirror, before being assayed on the streets of Britain's great cities. But once the off-hand sympathy, chiding words and overly elaborate gestures of charity had been mastered, it seems an easy expression of authority, and a constant reminder of the location of real power. But, it could and did become much more complicated than this. There were times, for instance, when the beggar could turn that condescending sociability on his benefactor. 'Mr Sturdy', described by Richard Steele in *The Spectator*, was clearly using the measured sociability that should exist between almsgiver and supplicant to subvert the relationship and radically narrow the social distance between a gentleman and a beggar:

> at the corner of Warwick-Street, as I was listning to a new ballad, a ragged rascal, a beggar who knew me, came up to me, and began to turn the Eyes of the good Company upon me, by telling me he was extreme poor, and should die in the Streets for want of Drink, except I immediately would have the Charity to give him Six-pence to go in the next Ale-house and save his Life. He urged, with a melancholy Face, that all his Family had died of Thirst. All the Mob have Humour, and two or three began to take the Jest; by which Mr. Sturdy carried his Point . . . [11]

Steele was six pence the poorer, and immediately quit the scene in a Hackney carriage, his masculine pride tarnished. What 'Mr Sturdy' had done was use humour to claim the authority of good fellowship, to present himself as a good fellow, rather than a simple and pitiable beggar, and in the process had backed Mr Spectator, that epitome of eighteenth-century gentle manliness, in to an uncomfortable corner.

* * * *

Casual charity had its pitfalls for eighteenth-century men, but it was in circumstances in which the structures of the household became involved – that millennium-old template for social behaviour – that giving to the poor became most frequently confused with the social obligations of friendship and loyalty. When the beggar was an old servant, or an erstwhile equal down on his luck, when he ceased to be that heap of inhuman whining rags so common in the advice literature, the issue of how to treat the supplicating poor became more difficult.

Robert Hughes was a victualler and owner of the Kings Arms Inn, near Holborn Bridge in London, and a charitable man. He first met Thomas Shaw when he employed him as a porter in the early 1780s. By 1786 Shaw had moved to the Peacock in the Minories.[12] He was an alcoholic and eventually lost his job and his home, ending up begging about the streets. By the early 1790s, Shaw was homeless and alcoholic on the streets of London. For over two years, however, he was given permission to sleep in the barns of Robert Hughes' inn. In the depths of January 1792, Hughes came across Shaw collapsed in a doorway. He gave him hot gin and water, before arranging for him to be taken to the New Compter, a local holding prison, prior to his being passed to his parish of settlement. In this instance it seems clear that a notion of obligation existed between Hughes and Shaw that went beyond casual charity. Despite the limited and temporary nature of Shaw's employment by Hughes, there remained a sense of master and man about their interactions, with all the patriarchal obligations and attenuated friendship contained therein.[13]

The historiography of service has always emphasised its role in the construction of early modern and eighteenth-century households, and has concentrated on the forms of service that seem most solid and reliable.[14] But, at least a large minority of services provided in the eighteenth century came in the form of casual labour. Like Daniel Defoe's eponymous hero in *Colonel Jack*, each street and ally had its pauper ready to go on errands and its beggar ready to lend a hand in exchange for a bit of food, or access to a place to sleep. Colonel Jack describes how:

> the People in Rosemary-Lane, and Ratcliff, and that Way knowing us pretty well, we got victuals easily enough, and without much Begging. For my particular Part, I got some Reputation, for a mighty civil honest Boy; for if I was sent of an Errand, I always did it punctually and carefully...some of the poorer Shope-Keepers, would often leave me at their Door, to look after their shops, 'till they went up to Dinner...[15]

These casual relationships added a new component to the exchanges between the almsgiver and his object of charity. They ensured that long-standing notions of household solidarity combined with gentle and also middling sort notions of virtuous charity, to give ever-stronger rhetorical support to the claims of one man on another.

The tensions that these ambiguous relations could generate are well illustrated in the case of Thomas Shaw's casual friend and fellow mendicant, a black man named John Peazy.[16] Both had worked on and off for John Granger at the Peacock in the Minories, but Peazy had been turned off by Granger, who suspected him of carrying on an affair with his wife. Peazy found a new place with an apothecary, and every Sunday for a month he and his ex-mistress would secretly meet for a walk through the fields around London. Peazy had a problem with alcohol and eventually lost his new place. Broke and begging, he returned to the Peacock and was allowed to sleep in a back kitchen by Mrs Granger. The following morning Peazy begged a handful of small change taken from the till in the tap room and an early morning shot of gin, before leaving the Peacock to get drunk at the nearby Three Kings alehouse. Like Robert Hughes and Thomas Shaw, John Granger and John Peazy had a relationship in which their old roles of master and servant should have supported Granger's patriarchal authority and informed his treatment of this old servant down on his luck. But the little issue of Peazy's sexual relationship with Rebecca Granger complicated this picture. John Granger had Peazy arrested and thrown in to the Poultry Compter for theft of the money a jury later believed to have been given him by Rebecca. The interview between Granger and Peazy in the keeper's parlour at the Poultry Compter reflects the tensions of patriarchal authority and the limits of male friendship. Granger accused Peazy of theft, to which he replied, self-consciously using the language of service, 'I did not rob you master, I have no more than my mistress gave me.' Granger replied,

'If you will confess what concern you have had with my wife, I will forgive you', before demanding, 'how many times have you laid with my wife'. Granger had beaten Rebecca repeatedly during the course of their married life together, and while he was berating John Peazy at the Compter, Rebecca left the family home out of fear of John Granger's violence. Peazy begged him to pay the bail and secure his release, and Granger refused, saying how 'very sorry' he was for his actions.[17]

The point of this story and the examples so far is that begging and the response to beggars on the part of the elite and middling sort suggest that Alan Bray's model of friendship as a series of structured gift relations is only partially applicable. It is clear that giving to other men down on their luck was a largely unproblematic obligation that supported gentle manliness as long as the object of charity could be kept at a sufficient distance, could be defined as a disconnected, largely inhuman, 'other'. It was both an act of eighteenth-century 'politeness', and inherently at odds with 'friendship'. It is also certain that once the personal and complicating issues of real knowledge, or human contact, were inserted between the beggar and his benefactor, this easily enacted abstract virtue of public charity became much more difficult to practise, became a much more rugged geography through which to navigate. In these instances the gestures and content of friendship as a series of gifts frequently conflicted with the polite behaviour expected of a gentleman patronising his inferior.

* * * *

If well-to-do men could find the process of distributing alms challenging, beggars were in an even more invidious position. It is now clear that most men, from the middling sort upwards constructed their self-identities in this period out of the bricks and mortar of honesty, religious sincerity, a reputation for good fellowship, generosity and to cap it all, the ability to lead and discipline a patriarchal household. For working men, it is equally clear that their constructions of manliness were made from their skills as craftsmen, their ability to do physical work, their strength, and sexual and physical vigour, combined again with honesty, religious sincerity and good fellowship. For all men (with the possible exception of the gentry, who happily lived off others for most of their lives) financial independence and self-reliance were also structural elements in the creation of a secure masculine identity. Beggars were denied almost all of these. And without them beggarly men were subject to the contempt of their fellows; a contempt that precluded friendship.

The very difficult choices presented to poor men is clearly reflected in Francis Place's recollection of his attempts to set up as a tailor towards the end of the eighteenth century:

> the most profitable part for me to follow was dancing attendance on silly people, to make myself acceptable to coxcombs, to please their whims, to have no opinion of my own...I knew well that to enable me to make money I must consent to submit to much indignity, and insolence, to tyranny and injustice. I had no choice between doing this and being a beggar, and I was resolved not to be a beggar...In short, a man to be a good tailor, would be either a philosopher or a mean cringing slave whose feelings had never been excited to the pitch of manhood.[18]

For Place even the relative subservience of the tailor threatened his sense of self-reliant manliness, while the dependence of a beggar represented a pit of failed masculinity into which he refused to fall. In either condition, cringing tailor or subservient beggar, manly friendship between equals seemed impossible.

Perhaps the only characteristic that beggars could claim (and did claim) from among this jig-saw puzzle of masculine attributes was religious sincerity. It is clear that many beggars, from Bampfylda-Moore Carew to murderous beggars like Samuel Badham – hanged for strangling his common law wife in 1740 – used 'a great many scripture words' with great success.[19] In other words, they appealed self-consciously to a tradition of Christian charity in formulating their requests. Certainly the anonymous author of the 1744 *Trip to St James's* thought so. In describing the language used by a male beggar, he says: '...the greatest profligate of them flies to Religion for Aid, and assists his cant with a doleful tone, and a study'd dismality of gestures'.[20] At the same time it is also clear that many poor men in desperate circumstances felt their own sincerely held religious beliefs helped to justify their appeals to the benevolence of their co-religionists. Certainly, James Dawson Burn remembered with real admiration the sincere religiosity of his otherwise drunken, beggarly and improvident step-father, William McNamee, in his *Autobiography of a Beggar Boy*:

> It is true, and strangely so, whether McNamee was drunk or sober, he never forgot to pray, morning and evening: and it was an amiable trait in his character that, whether in prosperity or adversity, he never let any of us forget the duty we owed to God, and our dependence on his Divine will.[21]

Although slightly after our period, perhaps the most striking instance of religion being used to help support the self-image and struggles of a beggar can be found in the autobiography of John James Bezer. A recently married shoemaker and porter, Bezer was a devout Methodist and when his luck ran out he determined to 'sing a hymn or two for bread and wife and child'. The internal struggle his poverty caused him is heart rending. Having determined to begin, he went through the city:

> stepped into Thomas Street for that purpose, and then stepped out again; and thus I acted in several streets along the Borough. However, I would commence, that I would...But no, courage failed again, and on I travelled. – I will not weary my reader as I was wearied by recounting my repeated trials, and my repeated failures, till I got right on to Brixton....Here goes – 'God moves' – begin again – 'God moves in a' out with it, and so I did, almost choking, 'God moves in a mysterious way, His wonders to perform.' Just before I had concluded singing the hymn, a penny piece was thrown out...[22]

Bezer's approach to begging reflected a genuine and heartfelt appeal to Christian charity, while his emotional stage fright, his inability to actually commit himself to the act of begging, reflects the extent to which the role of the beggar was fundamentally at odds with his self-image as a man.

Most beggars did not have Bezer's deeply felt religious conviction. For them the use of 'scripture words', the appeals to God and Christian charity were simply a normal language of supplication from which no substantial masculine identity was likely to emerge. So, the question remains how did beggars retain their sense of self-respect, how did they manage to construct a positive self-image? If all the normal ways of defining one's masculine identity are denied to you, how do you find a way to feel good about yourself? And if the ideal of manly friendship demanded a relationship between equals, or at least the absence of outright contempt, how did beggars, the most unmanned of men, make friends?

For many the question simply did not arise. There is an incontrovertible point in many lives when the practicalities of survival overwhelm the niceties of culture. People mired down in alcoholism and dying of painful diseases – people dying from cold and hunger on the streets – found it difficult to formulate strategies for the maintenance of their self-respect. When, in late April 1764, Robert Griffiths was left 'on his backside by a door in...Windmill Street' at eleven o'clock at night, to die of starvation and cold, he was not in position to formulate a strategy, or worry about his masculinity.[23] But many beggars did self-consciously construct a personae that actively engaged and subverted the characteristics historians have associated with masculinity in this period.

The most commonplace beggar personae was that of the 'trickster'. This is a stereotype that is largely restricted to male beggars and which exists both in elite commentary about begging and in the rarer accounts by beggars themselves.[24] The idea of a 'trickster' persona is familiar from the histories of slave and Black culture in North America and the Caribbean, and there is a well-developed literature that relates this phenomenon to the conditions of relative powerlessness associated with enslavement and racial abuse.[25] It is also a fragment of a larger body of behaviours associated with resistance to over powerful and dominant authorities by the least powerful – it is a cultural extension of what James C. Scott has characterised for peasant societies as the 'weapons of the weak'.[26]

In relation to English beggars, characters such as Bampfylda-Moore Carew exemplify this tradition and highlight both the reality of the 'trickster' character for the poor, and its manipulation and deployment by the better off. Written first as the legitimate autobiography of a real individual, Carew's 1745 *Life and Adventures* gives detailed descriptions of a whole series of tricks and cunning plans designed to encourage the generosity of the rich. The story with which I started this chapter is simply one variety of 'trick', in that instance a trick in part played against Carew. On page after page of the autobiography Carew describes his *modus operandi*. Cross-dressing (with the occasional borrowed infant for verisimilitude), pretending to be a shipwrecked sailor, feigning withered limbs and a broken body were all tricks that Carew played and described in his own words. And throughout, these tricks are used to reinforce the image of Carew as a famous and wonderfully clever man. One aspect of the story of Carew's encounter with Lord Weymouth that was not noted above is that Weymouth only accepted Carew into his house as an equal after having brought an old school friend of Carew's to verify his identity as the 'King of the Beggars'. It was in part his fame as a 'trickster' that made Carew the social equal of a lord.

And it is not just within the leather bound covers of published accounts of begging that these practices can be found. In criminal records numerous examples of beggars pretending to be blind or deaf and dumb in order to elicit the sympathy of their contributors can be located. On 18 December 1750 Michael Lince was taken up in the parish of Allhallows Lombard Street in the City of London, 'with his leg tied up, pretending to be lame & afterwards running away from the constable'. On the very same day William Maxwell was arrested in St Brides parish, 'with a false, forged and counterfeit pass pretending to be deaf & dumb'.[27]

More common still were men who walked a tightrope between real physical suffering and a 'trickster'-like self-presentation. Samuel Badham, for instance, seems to sit uncomfortably in both camps. In around 1732 he was struck down by an unidentified illness that meant he could no longer wear shoes. He had been trained as a shoemaker so his condition did not preclude him continuing to follow his profession. But after his wife's death and with 'a thick bundle of rags tyed under the soles of his feet, and with a stick in each hand', he set himself up as a beggar. The pattern of his life was soon well established. He would go out for several days at a time, staying in cheap lodgings at night and begging about the streets of London in the day time, 'picking up what I could get in the Way of Charity', by using 'a great many Scripture words'. For the next eight years he was able to pursue a regular and untroubled career, until in 1740 he murdered Susannah Hart, his common law wife, with his bare hands, was tried at the Old Bailey and hanged at Tyburn.[28]

But if beggars themselves used a 'trickster' persona to provide mental succour in difficult circumstances, their social superiors also deployed the idea with equal alacrity. Ned Ward included a description of a 'beggars club' in his 1709 *History of London Clubs*:

This society of old bearded hypocrites, wooden legg'd implorers of charity, strolling clapperdugeons, limping dissembers, sham-disabled seamen, blind gun powder blasted mummers and old broken limb'd labourers, hold their weekly meeting at a famous boozing ken in the midst of old street, where by the vertue of sound tipple, the pretenders to the dark are restor'd instantly to their sight, those afflicted with feign'd sickness, recover perfect health, and others that halt before they are lame, stretch their legs without their crutches.[29]

The literary criminals who bawlderised the second edition of Bampfylde-Moore Carew's autobiography under the title of *An Apology for the Life of . . . the . . . King of the Beggars* in 1749 also had no compunction in adding large swathes of ever more unbelievable tricks to the comprehensive account of beggarly tricks given in the first edition.[30]

The difficulty for beggars is that this 'trickster' masculinity was inevitably based on an acceptance of relative powerlessness. It was a contemptuous response to the contempt in which one was held by other men. By the eighteenth century, after generations of rogue literature that essentially retailed and popularised this 'trickster' beggar, it also represented an odd inter-dependant and mutually supporting relationship between elite contempt and pauper strategy. At the same time, as both Carew's account and the fanciful rendition by Ned Ward suggests, 'tricks' provided a shared knowledge upon which easy sociability and friendship rapidly grew. There was nothing more effective in securing the trust of a 'friend' than sharing the secrets of one's own 'trickery'.

There were alternatives that more directly appealed to the notions of manliness valued by this society. One way forward for a professional beggar was to think of themselves as virtuously independent, to appeal to a tradition of self-reliance. When one looks in to the lives of beggars like Nicholas Randall, for instance, he seems anything but subservient, or a 'trickster'. He was an old man and 'a beggar' who regularly stationed himself at the 'pissing place going to Brentford'. He lived by himself in a small house with a garden at Turnham Green. By the side of the highway there, he 'has a little house...and a garden a little distance from it', with 'two pear-trees, a damson tree, and two or three apple trees in it'. On 19 August 1759 a group of young teenage boys from the neighbourhood came by, stealing fruit, and calling that 'they would knock the old son of a bitch down'. Randall, still proud and even more angry, took up his rifle, loaded it with bird shot, and fired at two of the boys, hitting one in the leg and blinding another in one eye.[31]

Samuel Badham strove to live with equal independence. After a long-day begging, he came home to find his wife, Susannah, wearing a 'parish gown'. He said, 'Sukey, there's no body that ever belonged to me ever wore a parish gown.' And immediately 'went out and asked Charity, and with what I got I bought her another gown, and got the other made into a petticoat for her'.[32]

Israel R. Potter's autobiographical account of his life as a street seller in London in the last quarter of the eighteenth century has been used by American scholars to chart the beginnings of an American particularism based on a notion of masculine self-reliance. But the accident of Potter's birth in North America and brief participation in the American War of the 1770s does little to change the fact that his appeals to self-reliance were based on his experience of a long adult life spent as a near beggar on the streets of London. Throughout his autobiography Potter took great pains to describe the strategies he used to avoid absolute dependence, and is careful to cast the profits of his own success as a beggar in the light of unsolicited charity bestowed upon him out of real compassion. At one point he relates how on 'one stormy night of a Saturday' he attempted to sell home-made matches at a local market:

> I remained until the clock struck eleven, the hour at which the market closed and yet had met with no...success!...I was about to return, when, Heaven seemed pleased to interpose in my behalf, and to send relief when I little expected it; – passing a beef stall I attracted the notice of the butcher, who viewing me, probably as I was, a miserable object of pity, emaciated by long fastings, and clad in tattered garments, from which the water was fast dripping, and judging no doubt by my appearance that on no one could charity be more properly bestowed, he threw into my basket a beeve's heart, with the request that I would depart with it immediately for my home, if any I had![33]

This notion of a beggarly masculine self-reliance, so frequently appealed to by Potter, and used by Herman Melville when he fictionalised the autobiography to create 'America's first tragic hero' seems more redolent of the cultures of the labouring poor exposed in the works of William Blake and Francis Place than it does of any specifically American characteristic.

One final element of contemporary masculinities that seems to have been substantially adopted by and adapted to the needs of male beggars is the notion of bravery, and more specifically, martial bravery tied to a new nationalism. Shipwrecked sailors and discharged soldiers had always had a special place in the taxonomy of poverty and need reflected in social policy, and feature as notable exceptions to the censorious regime created for vagrants in the legislation of the sixteenth and seventeenth centuries. But from the 1760s onwards, the self-conscious presentation of one's self as a member of the military seems to have become more common. A typical example can be found in the behaviour of Thomas Dargaval, who was picked up for vagrancy in the City of London on a chill November day in 1782. He was around 23 years old. He had grown up in Liverpool and was apprenticed to the sea at the age of 12. For nine years he served in merchantmen, first as an apprentice, and then before the mast, until he was discharged in around 1780 at Port Royal, Jamaica. At this point he signed on to a ship operating under letters of marque out of Bristol. On the voyage back to Britain, the ship, the Vigilant, was attacked by two French men of war, and Thomas was wounded by canister shot from one of the attacking vessels, losing his right arm to the surgeon's knife. A prisoner in Brest for 11 months, he considered his predicament and asked the ship's carpenter for help. Together they made a small wooden model of the Vigilant and Thomas took it with him when he was finally exchanged. Discharged onto the streets of Dover in February 1782, Dargaval quickly set to work making use of the wooden model. For the next 10 months he travelled about showing the ship to whoever would look and telling his story to whoever would listen and in the process squeezed a modest income from the hard hearts of a war weary populace.[34] In part, Dargaval's strategy appealed to the nascent nationalism of Britain, but in the process he made a claim which substantially intersected with a masculine self-identity. The clear signs of his bravery ensured that other men would listen to his story, and treat him as a notional equal.

This military sympathy had the great advantage of allowing a kind of friendship. On the evening of 15 July 1742 Robert Burns was arrested on a general warrant issued to sweep the streets of Westminster clean of prostitutes and beggars. He was a soldier and was brought to the round-house. And while twenty-four women were confined in a cell, six foot square, without air or water, with the direct result that six of them died during the night, Burns was allowed to sit and drink with the watch-house keeper and constable. The topic of their conversation was 'military affairs', and Burns' ability to discuss them with authority ensured he could keep the attention and sympathy of a group of men who were otherwise happy to sit by while two dozen women slowly died within earshot.[35]

What one is left with after this brief survey of beggarly and charitable masculinities is a picture that seems ever more complex. It is clear that charity, the process of giving to a beggar on the street, was a central attribute of eighteenth-century middling sort and elite masculinity. To be un-generous was to be unmanly. To this extent, the ideology of masculinity required the objects of charity who sat by the roadside and begged for relief. Elite manliness was in part defined by the existence of an unmanned pauper hoard. Dependent, physically incapable, given to trickery, morally uncontrolled and generally pitiable, the poor helped to throw into sharp relief the strength, independence and honesty of elite men. In response, beggars themselves necessarily appealed to other forms of masculine self-regard. The 'trickster' figure must be seen as a way of countering the contempt felt by the elite, at the same time as it reinforced many of the preconceptions about poverty produced in contemporary literature. More than this, religious sincerity, humour, notions of military valour and independence were deployed by the very poor in appeals for respect that helped to both justify their claims to friendship and undercut the contempt felt for beggarly men.

Between and betwixt all of these poles of representation lay a number of attributes and characteristics deeply embedded in notions of masculinity that essentially subverted the apparently irretrievably unequal relationship between the beggar and his benefactor. In the reality of a genuinely felt religious impulse both beggar and Christian almsgiver could find a connection. It is the reality of this religious connection that led to so many complaints about the uncharitable behaviour of the clergy. One proverbial saying suggested that 'Charity in the street may beg two hours of a clergy-man before she will get the tythe of two-pence-half penny to succour her babes.'[36] And while there is no doubt that religious language was used self-consciously by many, it is also clear that many beggars were themselves deeply affected by their own rhetoric. In a similar way the realities of a connection between beggars and their benefactors complicated the exchange between the two. Notions of service and of mutual obligation pervaded this society, even as the theoretical underpinning of this social glue was being attacked by the new political economy. Ex-servants form only one example of acquaintances whose calls for help could not be ignored, and whose poverty could not wash away the indelible imprint of an older relationship. The role of the trickster could also help to bridge the gap between beggar and almsgiver, as could the admiration engendered by the evidence of military valour. As Alan Bray has demonstrated, the history of friendship is located deep within the structures of past societies; it is formed in social practices that define a household, a position and person. The history of eighteenth-century begging and beggars suggests that those structures occasionally helped to provide force and meaning to both the words of the supplicant and the open hand of the giver. But on most occasions friendship and connection was precluded by the failed masculinity of the beggar, and the requirements of the public practice of politeness.

Notes

1. For the history of rogue literature see W.C. Carroll, *Fat King, Lean Beggar: Representations of Poverty in the Age of Shakespeare* (Ithaca, NY: Cornell University Press, 1996); A. Feinberg, 'The Representation of the Poor in Elizabethan and Stuart Drama', *Literature & History*, 12 (1986), 152–63. For useful modern editions of sixteenth- and seventeenth-century rogue literature see G. Salgado (ed.), *Cony-Catchers and Bawdy Baskets: An Anthology of Elizabethan Low Life* (Harmondsworth: Penguin, 1972) and A.F. Kinney (ed.), *Rogues, Vagabonds*

and Sturdy Beggars: A New Gallery of Tudor and Early Stuart Rogue Literature (Amherst: University of Massachusetts Press, 1990 edn).

2. Bampfylde-Moore Carew, *King of the Beggars*, ed. C.H. Wilkinson (Oxford: Clarendon Press, 1931), pp. 86–91. This story is taken from the 1745 edition of *The Life and Adventures of Bampfylde-Moore Carew*, which Wilkinson credits with being a relatively unadulterated autobiography of a real individual. For a recent and comprehensive account of the evidence for Carew's life and activities see G. Morgan and P. Rushton, *Eighteenth-Century Criminal Transportation: The Formation of the Criminal Atlantic* (Basingstoke: Palgrave, 2004), pp. 78–85.

3. For recent literature on masculinity in early modern and eighteenth-century Britain see S.D. Amussen, ' "The Part of a Christian Man": The Cultural Politics of Manhood in Early Modern England', in S.D. Amussen and M.A. Kishlansky (eds), *Political Culture and Cultural Politics in Early Modern England: Essays Presented to David Underdown* (Manchester and New York: Manchester University Press, 1995), pp. 213–33; P. Carter, 'Men About Town: Representations of Foppery and Masculinity in Early Eighteenth-Century Urban Society', in H. Barker and E. Chalus (eds), *Gender in Eighteenth-Century England: Roles, Representations and Responsibilities* (London and New York: Addison Wesley Longman, 1997); P. Carter, *Men and the Emergence of Polite Society: Britain 1660–1800* (Harlow: Longman, 2001); M. Cohen, *Fashioning Masculinity: National Identity and Language in the Eighteenth Century* (London: Routledge, 1996); B. Cowan, 'What was Masculine About the Public Sphere?: Gender and the Coffeehouse Milieu in Post-Restoration England', *History Workshop Journal*, 51 (2001), 127–57; E.A. Foyster, *Manhood in Early Modern England: Honour, Sex and Marriage* (London: Longman, 1999); D. Kuchta, *The Three-Piece Suit and Modern Masculinity, England 1550–1850* (Berkeley and Los Angeles: University of California Press, 2002) and T. Hitchcock and M. Cohen (eds), *English Masculinities, 1660–1800* (London and New York: Addison Wesley Longman, 1999).

4. For works that take the divisions between social class seriously in relation to masculinity see in particular A. Bray and M. Rey, 'The Body of the Friend: Continuity and Change in Masculine Friendship in the Seventeenth Century', in Hitchcock and Cohen (eds), *English Masculinities*, pp. 65–84; A. Bray, *The Friend* (Chicago: University of Chicago Press, 2003); M.E. Wiesner, '*Wandervogels* and Women: Journeymen's Concepts of Masculinity in Early Modern Germany', *Journal of Social History*, 24 (1991), 767–82; M.E. Wiesner, 'Guilds, Male Bonding and Women's Work in Early Modern Germany', *Gender & History*, i, 2 (1989), 125–37; M. Rocke, *Forbidden Friendships: Homosexuality and Male Culture in Renaissance Florence* (Oxford: Oxford University Press, 1996).

5. E. Jones, *The Man of Manners: Or, Plebeian Polish'd* (London, 1737), pp. 2, 3.

6. For two excellent contributions to the history of hospitality see S. Hindle, 'Dearth, Fasting and Alms: The Campaign for General Hospitality in Late Elizabethan England', *Past and Present*, 171 (2001), 44–86, and F. Heal, *Hospitality in Early Modern England* (Oxford: Oxford University Press, 1990).

7. Bray and Rey, 'Body of the Friend', pp. 69–70.

8. [T. D'Urfey], *Collin's Walk Through London and Westminster. A Poem in Burlesque* (London, 1690), p. 27.

9. *The Spectator*, no. 269.

10. Westminster Abbey Muniment Room, Records of the Coroner's Court for Westminster, 19 May 1770, 'William Matthews'.
11. *The Spectator*, no. 454.
12. *Old Bailey Sessions Proceedings* [henceforth *OBP*] 22 February 1786, 'John Peazy', t17860222-126. All quotes from this source are taken from the modern edition of the Proceedings available online at http://www.oldbaileyonline.org, last consulted on 20 September 2004.
13. Corporation of London Records Office, Records of the Coroner's Court for the City of London, 6 January 1792, 'Thomas Robert Shaw'.
14. There is a small but authoritative literature on service in the eighteenth century. See for example: B. Hill, *Servants: English Domestics in the Eighteenth Century* (Oxford: Clarendon Press, 1996); D.A. Kent, 'Ubiquitous But Invisible: Female Domestic Servants in Mid-Eighteenth Century London', *History Workshop Journal*, 28 (1989), 111–28: T. Meldrum, 'London Domestic Servants from Depositional Evidence, 1660–1750: Servant-Employer Sexuality in the Patriarchal Household', in T. Hitchcock, P. King and P. Sharpe (eds), *Chronicling Poverty: The Voices and Strategies of the English Poor, 1640–1840* (Basingstoke: Macmillan, 1997) and T. Meldrum, *Domestic Service and Gender, 1660–1750: Life and Work in the London Household* (Harlow: Longman, 2000).
15. D. Defoe, *The History and Remarkable Life of the Truly Honourable Col. Jacque, Commonly Call'd Col. Jack* (1722, Oxford University Press edn, 1970), p. 8.
16. It is very likely that Peazy's race further complicated matters. For some recent literature on the large black population of eighteenth-century London see: S.J. Braidwood, *Black Poor and White Philanthropists: London's Blacks and the Foundation of the Sierra Leone Settlement 1786–1791* (Liverpool: Liverpool University Press, 1994); G. Gerzina, *Black London: Life before Emancipation* (London: John Murray, 1995); N. Myers, *Reconstructing the Black Past: Blacks in Britain, 1780–1830* (London: Cass, 1996) and N. Myers, 'Servant, Sailor, Soldier, Tailor, Beggarman: Black Survival in White Society 1780–1830', *Immigrants & Minorities*, 12: 1 (1993), 47–74.
17. *OBP*, 22 February 1786, 'John Peazy', t17860222-126.
18. *The Autobiography of Francis Place*, ed. M. Thale (Cambridge: Cambridge University Press, 1972), pp. 216–17.
19. For Samuel Badham see *The Ordinary of Newgate's Account*, 6 August 1740; *OBP*, 9 July 1740, 'Samuel Badham', t17400709-2.
20. *A Trip from the St James's to the Royal-Exchange. With Remarks Serious and Diverting on the Manners, Customs and Amusements of the Inhabitants of London and Westminster* (London, 1744), p. 24.
21. J.D. Burn, *The Autobiography of a Beggar Boy*, ed. David Vincent (London: Europa, 1978), pp. 54–5.
22. J.J. Bezer, 'The Autobiography of One of the Chartist Rebels of 1848', in D.M. Vincent (ed.), *Testaments of Radicalism* (London: Europa, 1977), p. 179.
23. Westminster Abbey Muniment Room, Westminster Coroner's Records, 21 April 1764, 'Robert Griffiths'.
24. For a rare literary example of a female 'trickster' see W. King, 'The Beggar Woman' (1709) reproduced in R. Lonsdale (ed.), *Eighteenth-Century Verse* (Oxford: Oxford University Press, 1984), pp. 79–80.
25. For examples of this extensive literature see J. Roberts, 'Brer' Rabbit and John: Trickster Heroes in Slavery', *Trickster to Badman, the Black Folk Hero*

in Slavery and Freedom (Philadelphia: University of Pennsylvania Press, 1989); L. Levene, *Black Culture and Black Consciousness* (Oxford: Oxford University Press, 1977); H. Tiffin, 'The Metaphor of Anancy in Caribbean Literature', in R. Sellick (ed.), *Myth and Metaphor* (Adelaide: Centre for Research in the New Literatures in English, 1984).

26. J.C. Scott, *Weapons of the Weak: Everyday Forms of Peasant Resistance* (New Haven: Yale University Press, 1985).

27. Guildhall Library, 'Court of Governors, Bridewell and Bethlem. Minutes, 12 January 1737/8 to 4 April 1751', MS 33011/21, p. 470.

28. *The Ordinary of Newgates His Account*, 6 August 1740; OBP, 9 July 1740, 'Samuel Badham', t17400709-2.

29. N. Ward, *The History of London Clubs: Or the Citizen's Pastime, Particularly the Lying Club, the Beggars Club* ... (London, 1709), p. 7. Other powerful literary examples of the beggar as trickster can be found in D. Defoe, *The Compleat Mendicant* (London, 1699); and in F. Coventry, *The History of Pompey the Little: Or The Life and Adventures of a Lap-Dog* (1752), ed. R.A. Day (Oxford: Oxford University Press, 1974), see in particular chs 15–20, pp. 76–105.

30. For a detailed account of the publishing history of this volume and an indication of which sections were added later see C.H. Wilkinson's 'Introduction' to Bampfylde-Moore Carew, *The King of the Beggars* (Oxford: Clarendon Press, 1931).

31. *OBP*, 12 September 1759, 'Nicholas Randall', t17590912-22.

32. *The Ordinary of Newgate, His Account*, 6 August 1740, Appendix 'Samuel Badham's Account of Himself'.

33. I.R. Potter, *The Life and Remarkable Adventures of Israel R. Potter* (1824; New York: Corinth Books 1961 edn), pp. 92–3. See the introduction to this edition for an account of the role of Melville's fictional account of Potter's life in American literary history.

34. Corporation of London Record Office, London Sessions Papers, December 1782, '31 examinations of supposed vagrants', see the examination of Thomas Dargaval, 16 November 1782.

35. *OBP*, William Bird, 9 September 1742, t17420909-37.

36. *T——B——'s Last Letter to His Witty Friends & Companions* [including 'Merry observations upon every month and every remarkable day throughout the whole year'] (1718), p. 69. For a similar complaint see also J. Collier's 1763 poem 'The Pluralist and Old Soldier', reproduced in R. Lonsdale (ed.), *Eighteenth-Century Verse* (Oxford: Oxford University Press, 1984), p. 511.

9
Spinoza and Friends: Religion, Philosophy and Friendship in the Berlin Enlightenment

Adam Sutcliffe

The topic of friendship was widely and vigorously discussed during the eighteenth century, but it was a subject on which no clear Enlightenment consensus emerged.[1] The unrestrained intensity of the Renaissance ideal of friendship – most famously expressed in Michel de Montaigne's elegiac essay, in which he describes his deceased friend as so close to him as to have been barely distinguishable from his own self[2] – could no longer easily be sustained in the eighteenth century, when both changing gender relations and the competitive vigour of commercial society complicated the imagined innocence of intimacies between men. Michel Foucault has argued that it was in this century that homosexuality became a problem in Europe, concomitantly with the decline of traditional models of male friendship and the rise of modern institutions that sought to discipline these intimacies.[3] For Alan Bray, too, it was in this period, in England at least, that premodern traditions of friendship were almost extinguished by the modern rationalization of interpersonal relations demanded by Kantian ethics.[4] The increasing visibility of the pursuit of commercial self-interest also seemed to threaten the selflessness and mutuality on which authentic bonds of friendship were traditionally assumed to be based. Bernard Mandeville's provocative argument, in his *Fable of the Bees* (1723), that 'private vices' produce 'public benefits' was an enduring provocation for the next fifty years, in particular to the leading thinkers of the Scottish Enlightenment, almost all of whom wrestled with Mandeville in their attempts to reconcile a theory of beneficent friendship with a positive analysis of commercial society.[5]

Friendship in the Enlightenment was both a social and a philosophical issue. The changing dynamics of interpersonal interaction in the eighteenth century themselves immediately posed pressing questions concerning the nature of human instincts and passions. At a more abstract level, however, Enlightenment thinkers also explored the significance of friendship for philosophy itself. Enlightenment moral philosophers challenged with increasing confidence the supremacy of religion as a source for ethical guidance in interpersonal relations, and the development of philosophical conceptualizations and models of friendship was of central importance in this intellectual expansion of their terrain.[6] The conceptualization of friendship – its parameters, responsibilities, social function and relationship to other forms of intimacy such as love and kinship – captured the attention of a number of Enlightenment thinkers, from the Marquis d'Argens and Claude-Adrien Helvétius to Adam Ferguson and Immanuel Kant. Related to this project, but distinct from it, was the development of models of philosophical friendship, in which intellectual and interpersonal ideals were brought into alignment with the practice of philosophy itself.

Philosophy, however, has traditionally imagined itself as a very impersonal and solitary activity. In contrast to the collective structures of religious life, and also to the public rituals of experimentation of organized Enlightenment science, western philosophy, at least from the private cogitations of Descartes' *Meditations* onward, has been distinguished by its simple dependence on the supposedly autonomous reflections of the individual thinking mind. If this is so, then how can philosophy provide a model for the social dimension of life?[7] This question intersects with some of the key underlying quandaries of Enlightenment philosophy: including, most profoundly, the relationship of rationalist universalism to the various modes of personal and cultural difference.

These philosophical quandaries were perhaps most succinctly brought together in the figure of Spinoza, and in his charged and contested reputation both during the Enlightenment and since. Starting even before his death in 1677, Spinoza was widely demonized by traditionalists as the most dangerous form of atheist, while being fervently heroized by a small but increasingly influential band of disciples.[8] Even Spinoza's philosophical opponents, however, tended to agree that as an individual Spinoza could not be faulted: in the eighteenth century he became the key specimen of the 'virtuous atheist', paradoxical for some, while for others a straightforward refutation of the smugness of the pious.[9] Spinoza was widely imagined during the Enlightenment as the quintessential philosopher: an identity that was persistently idealized as detached, individual, non-relational and almost inevitably male. However, alongside and intermeshed with this abstracted mode of celebration, he has also inspired a unique intensity of attachment among successive generations of followers. As pure intellectuality he represents the epitome of the philosopher's imagined transcendence of the messiness of human relations. However, despite this, or perhaps because of it, he has retained an almost irresistibly powerful posthumous attraction as a philosophical friend.

By the end of the seventeenth century the term 'Spinozist' was in widespread use, both as a critical term associating Spinoza with atheism and subversion and, more tentatively, as an affirmative label of radical allegiance. The relationship of Spinoza's philosophy to the mix of irreligious, materialist and rationalist ideas loosely proclaimed as 'Spinozist' is complex, and remains today a topic of scholarly controversy.[10] The association of Spinozism with Spinoza, however, was personal as much as it was philosophical. By describing themselves as Spinozists, or at least not rejecting the term when it was accusingly thrust upon them, Early Enlightenment radicals affirmed a relationship of discipleship with their intellectual hero, who offered them a model of how to live a philosophical life. To be a Spinozist, in effect, was to declare oneself a friend of Spinoza. Friendship with a dead person might readily appear to be an absurdity: is true friendship not necessarily based on some form of lived reciprocity? To consider a relationship of philosophical affiliation – a cerebral, impersonal form of connection, one might assume – in terms of friendship is a scarcely less surprising concept. Nonetheless, the philosophical celebration of Spinoza, perhaps uniquely among major philosophers, has been closely associated with his personal idealization as, in effect, the pure embodiment of the perfect philosopher.

Recent biographers have presented a considerably more complicated picture of Spinoza's life than that of the traditional hagiography.[11] However, the iconic Spinoza – whatever its relation to the historical Spinoza – is a symbol of striking and largely autonomous significance. Embedded within his secular sanctification we find a dense and intricate cluster of suppressed contradictions. Most obviously, it is ironic that Spinoza, of all people – a thinker intimately associated with the debunking of the Bible's mythic heroizations, and with a monistic ontology that strikingly de-emphasizes the individual self – should become the focus of such intense personal idealization. More broadly, the figure of Spinoza seems both to affirm and to deny the dominant conception of Enlightenment philosophy as an impersonal practice rooted in the detached application of reason. It is for these philosophical qualities that Spinoza has been so admired; and yet the imagined intimacy into which this admiration so readily overflows highlights the impossibility, and perhaps also the unattractiveness, of total flight from the personal and the particular.

The ambiguous significance of Spinoza's Jewish origins lurks, almost silently, at the core of these paradoxes. This biographical fact, while seldom directly confronted by either his admirers or his detractors, has also very seldom been forgotten. As an unabashed Jewish heretic, Spinoza has, since his expulsion from the Amsterdam Sephardic community in 1656, been widely cast as the quintessential philosophical rebel against theocratic dogmatism. For Christians – and even more intensely for critical or estranged Christians – his rebellion readily appeared to repeat the earlier overcoming of the Jewish legalism and tribalism that supposedly marked the historical emergence of Christianity. However, this subtle Christianization of Spinoza paradoxically sustained an awareness of Spinoza's Jewish origins, and indeed imbued them with significance. It was precisely as an ex-Jew that Spinoza's life echoed, in semi-secular terms, Jesus' exit from extreme particularism into a more philosophical, rarefied universalism.[12]

Willi Goetschel has recently argued that the genius of Spinoza, and his striking modernity, lies in his transcendence of the dichotomy between the universal and the particular. According to Goetschel's reading, Spinoza's Jewishness, which has remained a 'scandal' to successive generations of his readers, provided him with a perspective from which to reimagine the universal and the particular not as exclusive alternatives but as interdependent perspectives, non-hierarchically related to each other within his geometrical philosophical schema.[13] The vexed problem of the relationship between the universal and the particular was thrown into stark focus by the question of friendship, in which abstract ideals of virtuous interpersonal relations awkwardly collided with the inescapably particularist partisanship of private intimacies. In later eighteenth-century German thought Spinoza was a powerful intellectual presence, above all, as Goetschel rightly emphasizes, for the philosophical dramatist Gottfried Lessing, and his close Jewish friend Moses Mendelssohn.[14] Not only did friendship underpin the relationship between these two men; it was also central to their approach to philosophy. With Spinoza, and through friendship, the two men struggled to rethink the relationship between (Enlightenment) universalism and (Jewish) particularism. They did not, this essay will suggest, find a conclusively harmonious resolution of these perspectives. However, their attempts to do so remain immensely stimulating and enriching, and offer a penetrating insight into the challenges of friendship across boundaries of cultural difference.

Lessing, Mendelssohn, and the drama of friendship

The history of Jewish emancipation, as it was mythologized in nineteenth-century Germany, in particular among prosperous, ardently cultured and profoundly patriotic German Jews, was widely seen as having begun with a friendship. The intimacy between Gotthold Ephraim Lessing (1729–81) – philosopher, dramatist, and the figure most power-fully associated with the ideal of tolerance in the German Enlighten-ment – and Moses Mendelssohn (1729–86), the only Jew to gain high intellectual recognition in philosophical circles in mid-eighteenth-century Berlin, and the foundational thinker of the *Haskalah* (Jewish Enlightenment), was feted as an exemplary model of intellectual and emotional intimacy between Christian and Jew. Mendelssohn's intense friendships with many Christian friends are abundantly documented in his surviving correspondence. It was, however, his particular closeness to Lessing that became for later generations what Klaus Berghahn has aptly described as 'the stuff which legends of German-Jewish symbiosis are made of'.[15]

The emblematic sanctification of this friendship is captured in the famous painting of the German-Jewish artist Moritz Oppenheim, *Lavater and Lessing Visit Moses Mendelssohn* (1856). The Swiss theologian Johann Caspar Lavater was in a sense the anti-Lessing of Mendelssohn's life: his challenge, in 1769, that Mendelssohn either refute a recently published demonstration of the truth of Christianity or convert from Judaism brusquely violated the cultivated politeness and warmth of the eighteenth-century 'cult of friendship' in Germany.[16] Oppenheim depicts Lavater rudely interrupting a game of chess between Lessing and Mendelssohn. While Lavater assails Mendelssohn in the foreground of the painting, the abandoned chessboard lies pushed away on the table, behind which Lessing looks on disapprovingly. Mendelssohn's civility is contrasted to Lavater's rudeness: despite the unwelcome nature of his interruption, a woman arrives from the kitchen with refreshments for the uninvited guest. The chessboard, meanwhile, symbolizes the contrasting civility and mutuality of Lessing's intellectual and social relationship with the Jewish philosopher.[17]

It was chess that first brought Mendelssohn and Lessing together. According to their mutual friend Friedrich Nicolai, the two men made each other's acquaintance when Mendelssohn was recommended to

Lessing as a chess partner.[18] The friendship between the two men, who were almost exact contemporaries, soon blossomed into intimacy. Mendelssohn's biographer, Alexander Altmann, ascribes this to the rare intellectual virtues shared by the two men: 'though of entirely different background, temperament, and education, they had much in common: strength of temperament, a free and open mind searching for truth, and a sense of piety and respect for tradition'.[19] The cultural differences between the two were stark. Mendelssohn was the son of a modest Torah scribe from Dessau, who had come to Berlin in 1743 to study Talmud under the auspices of the traditionally pious Jewish community there; Lessing, in contrast, was the son of a Protestant pastor and had studied at the prestigious university of Leipzig.[20] The communalities between the two men, so highly extolled by Altmann, are less clear-cut. The bond between the two was clearly powerful and genuine. However, an attentive reading of their work suggests that for both Lessing and Mendelssohn the idea of their friendship, and its symbolic potency, was at least as important as the relationship itself.

The surviving correspondence between Lessing and Mendelssohn is extensive, regular, and strikingly passionate. They assert the primacy and intensity of their friendship in virtually every letter, signing off and on as 'Best Friend!', 'Dearest Friend!', 'your true friend', 'do not stop loving your constant friend', and other similar formulations. Mendelssohn protested when he did not receive frequent news when Lessing was away from Berlin. 'Best Friend!', he wrote in December 1760, 'In your absence I live, in the middle of this great city, like a hermit.... Write to me regularly, dear friend – so that I will not be deprived of my one remaining pleasure.'[21] At times he portrayed their friendship in virtually amorous terms. In an epistle to Lessing, published anonymously in 1756, Mendelssohn wrote that his friend knew very well how profoundly open his (Mendelssohn's) heart was to the sentiments of friendship: 'You have all too often noted, not without pleasure, the powerful effect on my emotions of a friendly glance from you, which could banish all sorrows from me, and suddenly fill me with happiness.'[22]

The relationship between the two men, however, was not simply based on leisure and pleasure. For Mendelssohn, Lessing was also an indispensable intellectual sponsor, through whom he gained a degree of access to the wider world of Berlin letters that, as a Jew, would otherwise have been impossible for him. For Lessing this friendship was also of a wider public significance. The famous dramatist was politically admired above all as an opponent of prejudice and as a committed advocate of toleration. In his association with Mendelssohn, Lessing was able to enact in his own life the principles of tolerance that he theatrically enacted in his plays. By bringing his private life into visible alignment with his declared principles, this friendship offered Lessing a precious opportunity to emulate his Spinozan ideal of the virtuous philosopher.

In his play *The Jews* (1754), completed before he met Mendelssohn, Lessing pointedly challenged the prevalent stereotypes of his era. This drama revolves around the robbery of a Baron by highwaymen assumed to be Jews, but who are later unmasked as the victim's Christian servants, and whose crime is foiled by an anonymous and virtuous traveller, who is revealed in the play's denouement himself to be a Jew. Lessing thus upbraids contemporary assumptions that Jews are inherently less moral than Christians. The Jewishness of his heroic traveller is effectively invisible: Lessing presents and celebrates him as an ethical universalist, moved to rescue the Baron by his unrestricted 'love of humanity'.[23] Lessing's reputation as a pioneering and passionate friend of the Jews, however, is based above all on his later and much more sophisticated play *Nathan the Wise* (1779), the eponymous hero of which has long been widely assumed to be modelled on Mendelssohn. This play enjoyed immense popularity among nineteenth-century German Jews, some of whom even themselves adopted the surname Lessing in gratitude and homage to their literary hero.[24]

Set in Jerusalem at the time of the Second Crusade, *Nathan* is most famous for the 'parable of the three rings' that constitutes its intellectual core. Nathan, a prosperous Jew resident in Jerusalem, is summoned before the Sultan Saladin and asked by him which of the three great monotheistic religions is the true one. In response Nathan relates his parable: a father, the possessor of a ring representative of religious truth, resolves the problem of which of his three sons should inherit this ring by having two identical copies made and giving each son one of the three, without identifying which one was the original. Later, when the sons dispute over which of their rings is genuine, a wise judge rules that only the behaviour of each owner can attest to their ring's authenticity.[25] This parable, as Goetschel has argued, advances a religious pragmatism that can also be discerned in Spinoza's writings. Nathan recasts the question of absolute truth at another level, repudiating the exclusive validity of any one religion in favour of a praxis-oriented approach in which competing truths are assessed purely in terms of the practical results they produce.[26] However, this argument evacuates from the stage any consideration of the differences between religions. All three rings are equally true, the parable suggests, because in their fundamental characteristics they are identical.

Nathan is a much more developed character than the Traveller of *The Jews*: however, like him, his Jewish identity is without positive substance. In his beliefs he echoes Lessing's own Deism, while his character is presented in deliberate counterpoint to common stereotypes of Jewish insularity and legalistic pedantry. We learn from his adopted daughter, Recha, that he has no love for 'cold book-learning, which / merely stamps dead characters into the brain'.[27] As the nineteenth-century German-Jewish novelist Fanny Lewald aptly noted, Nathan, like the other leading protagonists in the play, sounds curiously Protestant.[28] Like Spinoza – and also, perhaps, like Lessing's selective view of Mendelssohn – Nathan is ultimately a non-Jewish Jew, celebrated for his Jewish difference but simultaneously also for his transcendence of particularity, which empties this difference of any meaningful significance.[29]

The playing of chess is a frequent image in *Nathan the Wise*. We first meet Saladin (who is portrayed, like Nathan, as a counter-stereotypical wise and gentle ruler) deeply immersed in a game of chess with his sister, Sittah. Their game, which is the focus of a whole scene, stands metonymically for their respectful and intellectual friendship across the divide of gender.[30] They are then interrupted – just as Lavater interrupted Lessing and Mendelssohn – by Al-Hafi, a Derwish, who extols the virtues of his friend Nathan: 'He is intelligent; he knows / how to live; he plays good chess.'[31] Friendship, indeed, is arguably the play's most insistent theme, and the playing of chess is its recurrent symbol.

The plot of *Nathan* turns on the rescue of Nathan's beloved Recha from a fire, before the play begins, by a Knight Templar, who owes his own life to the mercy of his captor Saladin. Determined to express his gratitude to the lifesaver of his adoptive daughter, Nathan approaches the Templar, whose disdain for Jews at first leads him to respond grudgingly. He soon realizes, however, that the open-minded and noble Nathan is no typical Jew. Recognizing each other not as Christian and Jew, but as *Menschen* (humans), they warmly declare their friendship to each other: 'We must, must be friends', they eagerly agree.[32] This moment is echoed in the one request that Saladin has for Nathan after hearing his parable: 'Be my friend.'[33]

The urgent, imperative tone in which these exhortations to friendship are expressed is paradoxical. Friendship, as it is commonly understood, is inherently a voluntaristic, spontaneous relationship: what, then, is the meaning of the impulsion that drives the forging of friendship between Nathan and his Christian and Moslem acquaintances? It is Nathan's wisdom, and the universalist humanity that is its core, that seems to make friendship between him and those he meets who share this outlook so irresistible. His friendships dramatically bridge the gulf of difference between Jew, Christian and Moslem – and yet they are predicated on a more fundamental sameness grounded in the wisdom of a consciously shared humanity. It is for this reason that none of the insistently declared friendships in *Nathan* successfully evoke a dramatically credible interpersonal vitality. Despite their vaunted ecumenicism, Nathan's relationships of philosophical concord lack the encounter across difference that animates the passion and the complexity of lived friendships.

The conclusion of *Nathan* suggests, against the grain of the harmonious resolution of its plot, that Jewish difference nonetheless remains puzzlingly unique and indistinguishable. When Recha herself thanks the Templar for his gallantry, he falls in love with her – but fears that Nathan will never allow him to marry her, as he is not a Jew. However, in the play's final scene Nathan reveals that the Templar's father, who 'was my friend',[34] was also Recha's biological father – and moreover that he was neither a Jew, nor, as the Templar had believed, a German, but in fact the lost brother of Saladin. The friendship of all major characters is thus sealed and elevated in a common kinship. Only Nathan is excluded from this familial resolution. An inversion appears to take place between Judaism and Enlightenment rationality: the wisdom of humanity is bound together through a structure of blood relationships more usually associated with Jewish tribalism, while Nathan, the only Jew, finds his outsider status recast in an inverted form, as representative of an overarching God-like universalism, selflessly facilitating the intimacies of others but ultimately himself standing above and outside them. The friend of everybody, Nathan is left, perhaps as an inevitable corollary of this, without a distinctively intense emotional attachment to any other character in the play.

Nathan's anomalous status closely echoes that of Spinoza, who, in both transcending his Jewishness and retaining its trace, was, as we have noted, both uniquely attractive as an imagined philosophical friend and simultaneously seen as impersonally aloof from the untidiness and partisanship of interpersonal relations. The fundamental ambiguity of the Enlightenment notion of philosophical friendship – both universalist in its animating principles and necessarily particularist in its private intimacy – remains in *Nathan the Wise* both unacknowledged and unresolved. To its eponymous hero Lessing unreflectively ascribed the same irresolvable ambiguities that adhered to Spinoza's Jewish status. Nathan's Jewish universalism appears on the surface to reconcile ethnic particularity with philosophical universality. However, on closer examination this illusion dissolves. Like Spinoza, Nathan remains excluded from the intimacies of true friendship, his inverted and trans-valuated Jewishness now standing not as a mark of irrational particu-larism but rather as its opposite: a pure universalism above and beyond the affective bonds of human relationality.

Hannah Arendt, in her lecture 'On Humanity in Dark Times: Thoughts on Lessing', explored the Enlightenment concept of friendship in the aftermath of the most drastic collapse of this Germanic ideal. Delivered in Hamburg in 1959 in acceptance of the Lessing Prize awarded to her by that city, Arendt juxtaposed the universalizing uniformity of fraternity to the 'forever vigilant partiality' of Lessing's notion of friendship: 'He wanted to be the friend of many men, but no man's brother.'[35] The inclusive solidarity of fraternity, she argued, emerges among pariah groups: it is their 'privilege'.[36] Of higher nobility, however, especially in politically 'dark times', is the humanizing gesture of friendship, across barriers of cultural difference and intellectual disagreement. Lessing, Arendt claimed, was always reluctant to end a friendship because of a dispute: he was a relentless humanizer of the world, 'though continual and inces-sant discourse about its affairs and the things in it'.[37]

For Lessing, on Arendt's reading, friendship was paramount. For its sake he sacrifices even the seductive but divisive concept of universal truth.[38] While this is certainly an arguable reading of *Nathan*, it does not take account of the underlying endurance of universalism in the play. The original 'true' ring of Nathan's parable is indeed no longer identifiable – but it and its two identical copies share a uniform sameness, which empties all content from the pluralism of the three religious traditions they represent. Returning to Germany from her exilic home in the United States, Arendt had good reasons to offer an optimistic reading of Lessing in her address. The award of the Lessing Prize to her was in a sense an attempt to keep alive the precious embers of German/ German-Jewish friendship, of which Lessing's relationship with Mendelssohn had stood as the prototype and which Nazism had all but destroyed. In her interpretation of Lessing, written for an occasion cele-bratory of him, it is hard not to suspect that Arendt perhaps deliberately conflated what she wished Lessing had said about friendship with what he in fact did say. The essence of friendship, she declared, is formed 'in the interspaces between men in all their variety'.[39] Such acknowledgement of human variety, however, is absent from Lessing's dramas, and it is precisely this lack that leaves the friendships represented in them so emotionally thin and unconvincing.

Philosophical friendship and the Berlin 'Spinoza Quarrel'

Mendelssohn's close friendship with Lessing, and also his ethnic association with Spinoza, drew him into the most acrimonious squabble of the Berlin Enlightenment: his famous 'Spinoza Quarrel' with another of Lessing's friends, Friedrich Jacobi. In 1783, two years after Lessing's death, Jacobi confronted Mendelssohn with an account of a confidential conversation he had had with Lessing, from which he drew sensational implications. Jacobi claimed that Lessing had revealed to him his admiration for the 'pantheism' encapsulated in Goethe's use, in his poem *Prometheus*, of the Greek phrase *hen kai pan* (one and all). When Jacobi objected that he must therefore be a Spinozist, Lessing replied (according to Jacobi) that 'if I have to name myself after anyone, I know of nobody else'.[40] When Jacobi told his friend that he himself was also familiar with Spinoza's philosophy, Lessing responded in mysterious and almost apocalyptic fashion: 'Then there is no hope for you. Become his friend all the way instead. There is no other philosophy than the philosophy of Spinoza.'[41]

Jacobi's claim that Lessing was at core a 'Spinozist' was not simply an issue of abstract philosophy. His assertion also profoundly challenged Mendelssohn's interpretation of the legacies of both Lessing and Spinoza, and his cherished bond with his deceased hero and patron. Against the model ecumenical friendship of Lessing and Mendelssohn, Jacobi posited a much more ominous vision of a dangerously seductive collectivity of Spinozists, who together accepted a sterile fatalism that erased human individuality and autonomy and was thus the antithesis of all true friendship. Lessing's fall into Spinozism was inevitable, Jacobi argued, because all forms of philosophical deduction, including the Leibniz-Wolffian system of Mendelssohn and (so Mendelssohn thought) Lessing himself, could only demonstrate similarities, and thus remained trapped within a fatalistic determinism that was the essence of Spinozism. The only possible escape from this foundational emptiness was through a transcendental *salto mortale* (somersault) into the acceptance of faith, which Jacobi regarded as the only viable underpinning for 'all human cognition and activity'.[42]

The exchanges between Jacobi and Mendelssohn over the following four years grew increasingly strained, as the significance of their debate broadened into a profound controversy over the nature of philosophy, and its relationship to faith in general and implicitly to Judaism in particular.[43] This dispute took place during a decade of profound transition in German philosophy: 1781, the year of Lessing's death, was also the year of the appearance of Immanuel Kant's *Critique of Pure Reason*. The implications of Kant's radical rethinking of the basis of thought took some time to be assimilated, but they were immediately unsettling both for pre-Kantian 'popular philosophers', such as Mendelssohn, and for critics of Enlightenment rationalism such as Jacobi. In attempting to expose Lessing as a Spinozist, Jacobi was also advancing an early rebuttal of Kantian rationalist idealism.[44] However, emboldened perhaps by the sweeping challenge of Kantianism, Jacobi directed his counter-attack against rationalist philosophy in all its forms. Spinozism, he alleged, represented the ineluctable terminus of all philosophical thought. The 'Spirit of Spinozism' was both philosophically eternal and specifically Jewish: in its modern form it was simply a more abstract expression of the ancient 'emanating *En-Soph*' of the 'philosophising Cabbalists' who were Spinoza's intellectual predecessors.[45] Jacobi thus cast the Enlightenment as a whole as implicitly Jewish, and doubly implicated both Spinoza and Mendelssohn, as rationalist philosophers and as Jews, in what he regarded as the pernicious sterility of modern secular philosophy.

Mendelssohn repeatedly tried to diffuse the polemical charge of Jacobi's attack, and to decouple his association of Spinozism with Judaism. In his reluctant engagement with him he was extremely careful in defining his positions. His first reaction, as Jacobi himself reported, was to question the self-evident nature of 'Spinozism': with precisely which of Spinoza's texts had Lessing expressed his agreement, Mendelssohn inquired, and according to whose interpretation?[46] However, this strategy was rhetorically unsuccessful: the hypostatization of Spinozism, and also its association with Jewishness, were deeply ingrained in eighteenth-century German thought. In his final text, *To Lessing's Friends* (1786), Mendelssohn emphasized instead the responsibilities of friendship. How, he asked, could Jacobi's behaviour be reconciled with his upright reputation? If Jacobi had truly believed that Lessing had revealed to him a private secret, then to have betrayed this confidence after his friend's death was irresponsible.[47] How could Jacobi permit himself to blacken the name of their common friend who was no longer alive to defend himself, and against whom there was no other evidence than his own report of their conversation?[48] In critiquing Jacobi's dishonourable conduct Mendelssohn implicitly presented himself as the true friend of Lessing. In doing so, however, he also mounted an indirect refutation of Jacobi's central charge that supposedly 'Spinozist' philosophy was inherently cold and soulless. Adopting the position of the true upholder of the loyalties and affections of friendship, Mendelssohn turned the tables on his adversary. It was Jacobi, he implied, who privileged argument over interpersonal attachments, and whose manner suggested an inner coldness and lack of feeling.

Jacobi also regarded the question of the nature of friendship as central to the Spinoza Quarrel, but he understood the issue in very different terms. For him, as Jeffrey Librett has shown, the non-rational freedom of the will was the essence of humanity, and all Enlightenment advocates of reason were therefore enemies of humanity. The absolute friend, in contrast – the friend of humanity – must always accept the non-rational paramountcy of faith. He must always insist on this irrational core of friendship, and thus also recognize the stark opposition between friend and enemy. In proto-Schmittian terms, Jacobi defined as his ultimate enemy those who sought to deny this partisan distinction between the enemy and the friend.[49]

Friendship and faith were for Jacobi intimately intertwined. 'True friendship is as certain as that God is truthful', he wrote in 1806, emphasizing that both friendship and religion resided in 'the heart of man', and that both were generated and given constancy by the power of faith.[50] In his epistolary pseudo-novel *Allwill* (1792), the eponymous hero fervently declared Jacobi's own commitment to a profoundly non-rational view of friendship, and his deep hostility to what he saw as the philosophical alternative to this:

> Away with him who says that ... friendship is built on self-interest! The object, the reason why the two friends unite, is for them only the means through which one feels the other; the sense, the organ. It's not the one who does the most for me whom I love the most, but he with whom I can accomplish the most. ... That may be nonsense to your philosophers perhaps! But I know who has it better; I or they.[51]

Jacobi regarded this passionately sensory view of friendship as the absolute antithesis of the calculating instrumentalism inherent in rationalist views of interpersonal allegiances. Lessing and Mendelssohn in fact both regarded themselves as opponents of self-interest-based philosophies: such opinions, associated with such Enlightenment *enfants terribles* as Hobbes, Mandeville and Helvétius, had been widely opposed by many German *Aufklärer*.[52] Nonetheless, Jacobi not altogether unreasonably detected an incipient instrumentalism in Mendelssohn's and Lessing's views of friendship. There was indeed an element of utility in the relationship between these two men; and the friendships represented in *Nathan the Wise* seem more animated by intellectual respect and affinity than by instinctive passion. Jacobi's retreat from these uncertainties led him into a faith-based irrationalism that could not encompass within the bonds of friendship individuals from outside his community of faith: he expresses hostility not only to Jews but also to Africans.[53] His vigorous rejection of Enlightenment rationality constitutes a key landmark in the troubled relationship of ethnic difference to notions of friendship and community in modern German history.[54]

Jacobi's initiation of the Spinoza Quarrel, far from quashing German 'Spinozism', in fact instigated a far greater level of reverential interest in Spinoza than ever before.[55] Respectful attention to Spinoza's thought became, in reaction against Jacobi's violent rejection of him, a totem of reasonableness and sensitivity. Johann Gottfried Herder, in his *God: Some Conversations* (1787), bitingly satirized the second-hand dismissal of Spinoza that he perceived as widespread among intolerant conservatives. Herder's dialogic character Philolaus admits that he has not himself read Spinoza, but asserts that he is nonetheless convinced that he was 'an atheist and pantheist, ... an enemy of revelation, a mocker of religion [and] a destroyer of all states and of all civil society', and therefore fully deserving of 'the hatred and loathing of all friends of humanity and of all true philosophers'.[56] Philolaus' interlocutor, Theopron, and behind him Herder, challenges his friend, critiquing his unthinking dismissal of Spinoza's thought, and arguing for a more measured, open-minded approach, unclouded by the prejudices of popular opinion.[57]

Herder's defence of Spinoza was characteristic of the romantic spirit of the German 'Spinoza Renaissance' that followed in the aftermath of the Spinoza Quarrel, encompassing Goethe, Novalis, Heine and others.[58] It was precisely because of the shrill rejection of Spinoza's ideas by the ignorant and prejudiced, Herder suggested, that his thought deserved to be given considered attention. Aggressive dismissal was the mark of bad conduct and bad philosophy; to read open-mindedly and sensitively, in contrast, defined the true philosopher. For Herder's negative voice, Philolaus, Spinoza should be rejected by 'all friends of humanity' (*Menschenfreunde*). Through the voice of Theopron, Herder rejects this category, also used by Jacobi, which antagonistically cast as implied 'enemies of humanity' all those who did not dismiss Spinoza. In contrast to this dichotomy Herder upholds a practice of philosophy influenced both by his interpretation of Spinoza and by his idealized associations with him.[59] True philosophy, he suggests, must be grounded in sensitivity to the marginalized and a resistance to dogma. Against the binarism of friend and enemy, Herder advances a vision of philosophical exchange infused with a tolerant and inclusive spirit of friendship.

Spinoza and the politics of friendship

During the half-century immediately following Mendelssohn's death the lives of German Jews were transformed more dramatically than those of any other group: forces of political reform unleashed by the French Revolution, though at first very unevenly and fitfully applied, precipitated a Jewish rush toward urbanization and bourgeoisification.[60] Many early nineteenth-century German Jews cherished the memory of Spinoza, which stood for them as emblematic of the aspirations of assimilated Jewry.[61] Among non-Jewish readers too, however, Spinoza continued to inspire an exceptional degree of interest, variety of interpretation and intensity of identification throughout the nineteenth century.[62]

Spinoza's polymorphous appeal has by no means diminished in recent decades. 'Spinoza Societies' exist in North America, the Netherlands, Germany, France, Italy and Japan, all devoted to the celebration of this hero-philosopher. Two of these societies – the French 'Association des Amis de Spinoza' and the 'Associazione Italiana degli Amici di Spinoza' – explicitly announce in their titles a primary orientation toward the fostering of friendship with their sage. A search on the Internet reveals very few traces of similar collective befriendings of other leading philosophers. The only such readily apparent example, the 'Societé des Amis de Marx', in fact provides a telling contrast. Whereas the 'Association des Amis de Spinoza' homepage lovingly presents the image of a graceful, pathos-laden statue of Spinoza, the gruff, prescriptive text of the 'Societé des Amis de Marx' website makes it clear that all interpersonal energies are to be directed not towards Marx, but to the working classes, who must dutifully be befriended so that they can then be cajoled into reading the *Grundrisse*.[63]

What is the nature of this friendship that Spinoza so powerfully and persistently inspires? And why did this issue bring to the fore so much enmity between Moses Mendelssohn and Friedrich Jacobi? Jacques Derrida's *Politics of Friendship* here offers some very useful and insightful pointers. This multilayered text is woven around a sustained interrogation of a puzzling dictum attributed to Aristotle, and revisited by, among others, Montaigne, Nietzsche and Blanchot: 'O my friends, there is no friend.' From this starting-point Derrida teases out the multiple paradoxes and exclusions that have beset the ideal of friendship in the western political and philosophical tradition. The abstract virtue of unselfish loving – the 'what' of friendship – stands in awkward disjuncture alongside the singularity of the 'who': the individual friend.[64] Perfect friendship is unthinkable: while we aspire to emulate perfection, attaining such a God-like ideal would dissolve the interpersonal mortal needs to which friendship responds.[65] Most potently, perhaps, the private intimacy and trust that most profoundly characterizes dyadic friendship awkwardly jars against political ideals of collective friendship, enshrined by the French Revolution in the principle of fraternity. All these visions of brotherhood-based friendship, meanwhile, teeter uncertainly on the rim of homoeroticism, while excluding all other relationalities: friendships between women; friendships between men and women; and friendships across generations.[66]

Alan Bray refers only in passing to Derrida's text – but he identifies it as a kindred study, asking at its core 'the same questions' about the history of friendship.[67] However, Bray's uncompromising disdain for the confining impersonality of the Kantian – and contemporary post-Kantian – universalist paradigm of friendship differs significantly from Derrida's subtle and non-evaluative exploration of the political significance of Kant's notion of friendly respect, which, Kant seems to argue, distinguishes friendship from love.[68] This boundary was profoundly blurry in the late eighteenth century, and its troubling indeterminacy was enmeshed within broader realms of uncertainty concerning the boundaries between private and public, and between dominant and minority cultures. Whereas the implicit emancipatory power of Bray's work lies in the reconstruction of alternative, premodern patterns of intimacy, Derrida suggests that these 'modern' confusions are to some degree transhistorical, and that they cannot be transcended or resolved, but must instead be acknowledged and understood in their inescapable complexity.

Derrida shows that the vexed relationship between the universalism of philosophy (the 'what' questions) and the partisanship of friendship (the question of 'who') in a sense intellectually foreshadows all the ambiguities and dilemmas of human intimacy. In exploring the contours of idealized philosophical friendship through the figure of Spinoza, the leading thinkers of the Berlin Enlightenment were thus also grappling with the second half of this dyad: the private attachments of human intimacy. The Jewishness of Spinoza, shared in fiction by Nathan the Wise and to some degree projected by Lessing and others onto Mendelssohn himself, enabled the apparent elision of the tensions inherent in this binarism. Judaism stood unmistakably as representative of particularity and difference. However, Spinoza and, echoing him, both Nathan and Mendelssohn were cast as archetypical symbols of the transcendence of Jewish particularity, therefore representing, as we have seen, the inverse of this: pure universalism in individual form. The impossible fusion of the universal and the particular was achieved for the Berlin Enlightenment in the embodied resolution of a supposed oxymoron: the Jewish philosopher. The universalized Jew – in a sense, an anti-Jew – could thus be imagined simultaneously as a perfect individual friend (the 'who' of friendship) and as symbolic of idealized friendship in abstract (the 'what').

The intellectualized abstraction of this figuration should not, however, be taken to suggest that imagined friendships with Spinoza had no relation to more concretely bodily desires. Despite the studiedly rational rhetoric of Lessing and of most other eighteenth-century admirers of Spinoza, their powerful idealization of this intellectual hero was at times, particularly in the writings of Goethe and other participants in the 'Spinoza Renaissance', charged with an intensity that overflowed purely intellectual bounds.[69] These passionate attachments to a deceased and semi-imaginary figure pose the question of the proximate relationship between philosophy and fantasy, and also, more specifically, of the accommodation within philosophical friendship of same-sex desire. At a time when, as both Foucault and Bray argue, intimacies between men were newly subject to suppression and suspicion, friendships across ethnic boundaries could to some degree eclipse the usual suspicion of passions rooted in male sameness because race was available to take the place of gender as a legitimating axis of difference. Lessing's attachments to both Spinoza and Mendelssohn – and also, in fiction, to Nathan – were powerfully grounded in both philosophical and emotional identification; but the inextinguishable Jewish otherness of these men remained central to their allure for him. Did the passion invested by Lessing and others in figures of Jewish maleness in some sense give expression to a desire for an alternative to heterosexual intimacy? These attachments to idealized figures of Jewish male universality hovered ambiguously between sameness and difference, and thus silently blurred the foundational boundary on which the imagined fixity of normative heterosexuality was based.

The construction of gender difference has been imbricated with the mutually constitutive opposition of Christianity and Judaism arguably since the emergence of Christianity itself.[70] In early twentieth-century Germany (and elsewhere), stereotypes of effeminate homosexuality were frequently conflated with the image of the bourgeois Jewish man, whose cultural rootlessness and soft domesticity were contrasted with the virile masculinity of nationalistic forms of male bonding, such as the German *Männerbünde*.[71] The long-standing association of Jewish men with womanliness, from the menstruating Jewish men of the Middle Ages to the modern figure of the Jewish homosexual, suggests that Jewish maleness has persistently straddled the demarcation fault-line of normative Euro-/Christian masculinity, and has thus posed a provocative challenge to the presumptive sameness of maleness itself. For thinkers such as Jacobi friendships between Jews and Christians were unimaginable because they introduced difference into a form of relationship he saw as by definition rooted in solidaristic male sameness. Lessing and Mendelssohn elevated this ideology of sameness from the level of religion and nationality to that of philosophical wisdom. However, alongside this transcendental celebration of the intellectualized universalism of pure friendship, their own friendship, and the celebra-tion of friendships between Jews and Gentiles more generally was unambiguously animated by the fact of ethnic difference, which was the key feature that distinguished these friendships from all others. The friendship between Lessing and Mendelssohn was 'hetero' in ethnic terms, and this to some extent displaced the potentially suspect same-ness of its intense homosociality. In disrupting the very distinction between sameness and difference the figure of the Jewish same-sex friend thus profoundly queered normative understandings of intimacy and sexuality, in a manner loosely analogous to other boundary-blurring categories of identity such as the cross dresser (also associated with Jews) or the bisexual.[72]

The late eighteenth century in Germany, far from being a period of interpersonal uniformity and stiffness, was an era in which same-sex friendship was often expressed with great passion, and in which the boundary between homosociality and homoeroticism was extremely unclear.[73] However, as we have already noted, the social and political transformations of the period, in asserting the supposed neutrality of the male public sphere of fraternal citizenry, placed pressure on private male intimacies, while celebrating the power of feminine charm, wit and beauty to regulate behaviour among men. This gendering of polite discourse was also, in Berlin, racially inflected. The intellectual and cultural elite of the city in the period 1780–1806 gathered above all at the homes of Jewish women such as Rahel Varnhagen and Henriette Herz, Berlin's most prominent *salonnières*.[74] The eagerly accepted hospit-ality of Jewish hostesses highlighted the universalist, cosmopolitan openness of the salon gatherings. However, women such as Varnhagen also provided a spark of exotic, even 'oriental' fascination – an exoti-cism that was also frequently associated with Jews in general in this period.[75] The instability of Jewish difference at this time, at the dawn of modern processes of Jewish assimilation and advancement, imbued all relations between Jews and non-Jews – of opposite sexes as well as of the same sex – with a particular charge of intensity, complexity and ambiguity.

Spinoza, for admirers such as Lessing, was cast as the transcendentally perfect friend. However, insofar as he could occupy this status he was also not really a friend at all: his imagined perfection necessarily hollowed out those traces of human imperfection on which all relationships, real or imagined, are based, leaving only a sanctified ideal behind. Moses Mendelssohn's Spinoza was more complex. While indubitably also encompassing elements of idealization, Mendelssohn's friendship with Spinoza started from a more concrete sense of kinship and shared experience. However, he imagined this private intimacy to be in some sense subsumed within a collective and public friendship: the friendship of philosophers. Jacobi and Lessing also understood friendship with Spinoza within a wider context: for both men this was in no sense simply one instance of friendship among many. They both imagined this relationship as the key model and underlying essence of all philosophical friendship. Whereas for Lessing this was a positive model, for Jacobi it epitomized the negative sterility of all philosophy.

Mendelssohn and Jacobi's own friendship, never explicitly terminated by either party, collapsed under the weight of these contrasting perspectives. However, the *Spinozastreit* was never truly an argument between friends. Jacobi's inability to countenance the possibility of an equal and intimate relationship with a Jew clouded their relationship from the outset. Mendelssohn, meanwhile, while stoically ignoring rather than reciprocating the hostility Jacobi directed towards him, was also unable to recognize Jacobi's challenge to Enlightenment rationalism. Neither man had any empathy for the other: moreover, on Jacobi's side an ominous strain of ethnic antipathy is clearly apparent. However, the ideal of interpersonal respect, without which friendship cannot be sustained, remained dimly alive during the *Spinozastreit*. The quarrel was in large measure a public baiting of Mendelssohn into which he was drawn against his will. Nonetheless, it would be unwarranted to condemn Jacobi outright: his provocations, while often dogmatic or aggressive, were also to some degree animated by a genuine desire to achieve engagement and even an element of understanding across a wide gulf of disagreement and mutual incomprehension.

'Respect', Derrida reminds us with relish, is an anagram of 'spectre'. Friendship can never be fully present, never tangible: 'All phenomena of friendship, all things and all beings to be loved, belong to spectrality.'[76]

Spinoza's spectral friendship, however, is particularly alluring, and particularly ubiquitous. His personal biography, of intellectual isolation, communal indifference, and the transgression of boundaries, has persistently meshed with the reception of his philosophy. For more than three centuries the hybrid concoction of ideas and identities associated with him has proven uniquely seductive. Spinoza's spectral ambiguity, impossibly fusing universalism with Jewishness, individualism with collective identification, secularism with theism, and rationalist detachment with political engagement, has made him a particularly compelling and vital figure, not only for Jews in the modern, secular world, but potentially for all of us searching for a friend in our never-ending exploration of seemingly incommensurate identities and values.[77]

Notes

1. The synthetic literature on friendship and the Enlightenment remains thin, but two useful studies exist on France: A. Vincent-Buffault, *L'Exercice de l'amitié* (Paris: Seuil, 1995); F. Gerson, *L'amitié au XVIIIe siècle* (Paris: La Pensée Universelle, 1974).
2. M. de Montaigne, 'De l'amitié' [1580], in *Oevres complètes* (Paris: Gallimard, 1962), pp. 177–93.
3. M. Foucault, 'Sex, Power and the Politics of Identity' [1984], in his *Essential Works, I: Ethics, Subjectivity and Truth* (New York: The New Press, 1997), pp. 163–73, on p. 171.
4. A. Bray, *The Friend* (Chicago: University of Chicago Press, 2003), pp. 212–19.
5. See A.O. Hirschman, *The Passions and the Interests* (Princeton: Princeton University Press, 1997[1977]), pp. 17–19; L. and P. McCarthy, 'Hume, Smith and Ferguson: Friendship in Commercial Society', in P. King and H. Devere (eds), *The Challenge to Friendship in Modernity* (London: Frank Cass, 2000), pp. 33–49; A. Silver, 'Friendship in Commercial Society: Eighteenth-Century Social Theory and Modern Sociology', *American Journal of Sociology*, 95 (1990), 1474–1504.
6. For an excellent overview see J.B. Schneewind, *The Invention of Autonomy: A History of Modern Moral Philosophy* (Cambridge: Cambridge University Press, 1998).
7. For a range of approaches to this question see N.K. Badhwar (ed.), *Friendship: A Philosophical Reader* (Ithaca: Cornell University Press, 1993).
8. See P. Cristofolini (ed.), *The Spinozistic Heresy: The Debate on the Tractatus Theologico-Politicus, 1670–77, and the Immediate Reception of Spinozism* (Amsterdam: APA-Holland Press, 1995); W. van Bunge and W. Klever (eds), *Disguised and Overt Spinozism Around 1700* (Leiden: Brill, 1996); J. Israel, *Radical Enlightenment: Philosophy and the Making of Modernity, 1650–1750* (Oxford: Oxford University Press, 2001), pp. 157–328.
9. See M.L. Lussu, *Bayle, Holbach e il dibatttito sull'ateo virtuoso* (Genoa: ECIG, 1997), pp. 31–7.

10. See, most recently, Israel, *Radical Enlightenment*, pp. 563–703; M. Mulsow, *Moderne aus dem Untergrund: Radikale Frühaufklärung in Deutschland 1680–1720* (Hamburg: Felix Meiner, 2002); W. van Bunge (ed.), *The Early Enlightenment in the Dutch Republic* (Leiden: Brill, 2003).

11. See S. Nadler, *Spinoza: A Life* (Cambridge: Cambridge University Press, 1999).

12. For a development of this argument see A. Sutcliffe, *Judaism and Enlightenment* (Cambridge: Cambridge University Press, 2003), pp. 133–47.

13. W. Goetschel, *Spinoza's Modernity: Mendelssohn, Lessing, and Heine* (Madison: University of Wisconsin Press, 2004), pp. 23–81.

14. Ibid., pp. 85–250.

15. K.L. Berghahn (ed.), 'On Friendship: The Beginnings of a Christian-Jewish Dialogue in the 18th Century', in idem (ed.), *The German-Jewish Dialogue Reconsidered* (New York: Peter Lang, 1996), pp. 5–24, on p. 16.

16. On the friendship cult see ibid., pp. 6–11; for a full account of the 'Lavater affair' see A. Altmann, *Moses Mendelssohn: A Biographical Study* (Philadelphia: Jewish Publication Society of America, 1973), pp. 194–263.

17. On Oppenheim's painting see R.I. Cohen, *Jewish Icons: Art and Society in Modern Europe* (Berkeley and Los Angeles: University of California Press, 1998), pp. 163–6. See also A. Altmann, 'Moses Mendelssohn as the Archetypical German Jew', in J. Reinharz and W. Schatzberg (eds), *The Jewish Response to German Culture: From the Enlightenment to the Second World War* (Hanover, NH: University Press of New England, 1985), pp. 17–31.

18. Altmann, *Mendelssohn*, p. 36.

19. Ibid.

20. Ibid., pp. 3–25; T. Höhle, 'Einleitung' to G.E. Lessing, *Werke*, 5 vols (Berlin: Bibliothek Deutscher Klassiker, 1982), 1: v–xx.

21. Mendelssohn to Lessing, 19 December 1760, in M. Mendelssohn, *Gesammelte Schriften: Jubiläumsausgabe* (henceforth *JubA*), 24 vols (Stuttgart: Friedrich Frommann, 1971–97), 11: 189.

22. Mendelssohn, *Sendschreiben an Lessing*, in *JubA*, 2: 83–96, on p. 90. On this text see Altmann, *Mendelssohn*, pp. 48–9.

23. On this play see R. Robertson, *The 'Jewish Question' in German Literature 1749–1939: Emancipation and its Discontents* (Oxford: Oxford University Press, 1999), pp. 34–6.

24. A. Elon, *The Pity of It All: A History of the Jews in Germany 1743–1933* (New York: Henry Holt, 2002), p. 62; Robertson, 'Jewish Question', p. 34.

25. G.E. Lessing, *Nathan der Weise* [1779], Act 3 Scene 2, in *Werke*, 1: 80–7.

26. Goetschel, *Spinoza's Modernity*, pp. 230–50.

27. Lessing, *Nathan*, p. 142 (Act 5 Scene 2).

28. Robertson, 'Jewish Question', p. 42.

29. See ibid., pp. 37–45; idem, ' "Dies hohe Lied der Duldung"? The Ambiguities of Toleration in Lessing's *Die Juden* and *Nathan der Weise*', *Modern Language Review*, 93 (1998), 105–20.

30. Lessing, *Nathan*, pp. 37–41 (Act 2 Scene 1).

31. Ibid., p. 48 (Act 2 Scene 2).

32. Ibid., p. 57 (Act 2 Scene 5).

33. Ibid., p. 85 (Act 3 Scene 7).

34. Ibid., p. 152 (Act 5 Scene 8).

35. H. Arendt (ed.), 'On Humanity in Dark Times: Thoughts about Lessing' [1959], *Men in Dark Times* (New York: Harcourt, 1968), pp. 3–31, on pp. 29–30. For a thoughtful analysis of this address see P. Fenves, 'Politics of Friendship – Once Again', *Eighteenth-Century Studies*, 32 (1998–9), 133–55, on 144–8.
36. Arendt, 'Humanity', p. 13.
37. Ibid., p. 30.
38. Ibid., pp. 26–7.
39. Ibid., p. 31.
40. F. Jacobi, *'Concerning the Doctrine of Spinoza'* [1785], *The Main Philosophical Writings and the Novel 'Allwill'*, ed. and trans. G. di Giovanni (Montreal: McGill-Queen's University Press, 1994), p. 187.
41. Ibid.
42. Ibid., p. 234.
43. See S. Zac, *Spinoza en Allemagne: Mendelssohn, Lessing et Jacobi* (Paris: Méridiens Klincksieck, 1989); A. Sutcliffe, 'Quarreling over Spinoza: Moses Mendelssohn and the Fashioning of Jewish Philosophical Heroism', in R. Brann and A. Sutcliffe (eds), *Renewing the Past, Reconfiguring Jewish Culture: From al-Andalus to the Haskalah* (Philadelphia: University of Pennsylvania Press, 2004), pp. 167–88, on pp. 175–81.
44. T. Pinkard, *German Philosophy 1760–1860: The Legacy of Idealism* (Cambridge: Cambridge University Press, 2002), pp. 90–6; U. Goldenbaum, 'Mendelssohns schwierige Beziehung zu Spinoza', in E. Schürmann, N. Waszek and F. Weinreich (eds), *Spinoza in Deutschland des achtzehnten Jahrhunderts* (Stuttgart: Fromman-Holzboog, 2002), pp. 265–317, on pp. 310–12.
45. Jacobi, *Doctrine of Spinoza*, in *Philosophical Writings*, pp. 187–8.
46. Ibid., p. 182.
47. Mendelssohn, *An die Freunde Lessings* [1786], in *JubA*, 3(2): 192–3.
48. Ibid., p. 217.
49. J.S. Libbett, 'Humanist Antiformalism as a Theopolitics of Race: F.H. Jacobi on Friend and Enemy', *Eighteenth-Century Studies*, 32 (1998–9), 233–45, on pp. 239–40. See also C. Schmitt, *The Concept of the Political* [1932], trans. G. Schwab (Chicago: University of Chicago Press, 1996).
50. F.H. Jacobi, *Was gebieten Ehre, Sittlichkeit und Recht . . .* [1806], cited in G. di Giovanni, 'Introduction' to Jacobi, *Philosophical Writings*, p. 152.
51. F.H. Jacobi, *Edward Allwill's Collection of Letters* (1792), in idem, *Philosophical Writings*, pp. 418–19.
52. F. Oz, *Translating the Enlightenment: Scottish Civic Discourse in Eighteenth-Century Germany* (Oxford: Oxford University Press, 1995), p. 122.
53. Libbett, 'Humanist Antiformalism', pp. 238–9.
54. On the place of friendship in nineteenth- and early twentieth-century German history see G.L. Mosse, 'Friendship and Nationhood: About the Promise and Failure of German Nationalism', *Journal of Contemporary History*, 17 (1982), 351–67.
55. See F.C. Beiser, *The Fate of Reason: German Philosophy from Kant to Fichte* (Cambridge, MA: Harvard University Press, 1987), pp. 44–5.
56. J.G. Herder, *Gott: einige Gespräche* [1787], cited in C. Schapkow, 'Die Freiheit zu philosophieren': *Jüdische Identität in der Moderne im Spiegel der Rezeption Baruch de Spinozas in der deutschsprachiegn Literatur* (Bielefeld: Aisthesis, 2001), p. 73.

57. Ibid.
58. M. Bollacher, *Der junge Goethe und Spinoza* (Tübingen: Niemeyer, 1969); I. Reimers-Tovote, 'Schaffende Betrachtung: Zur Spinoza-Rezeption bei Friedrich von Hardenberg (Novalis)', in E. Balibar, H. Seidel and M. Walther (eds), *Freiheit und Notwendigkeit: Ethische und politische Aspekte bei Spinoza und in der Geschichte des (Anti-) Spinozismus* (Würzburg: Königshausen, 1994), pp. 143–53; on Heine see Goetschel, *Spinoza's Modernity*, pp. 253–76.
59. On Herder and Spinoza see M. Bollacher, 'Der Philosoph und die Dichter: Spiegelungen Spinozas in der deutschen Romantik', in H. Delf, J.H. Schoeps and M. Walther (eds), *Spinoza in der europäischen Geistesgeschichte* (Berlin: Hentrich, 1994), pp. 275–88, on pp. 276–80.
60. See D. Sorkin, *The Transformation of German Jewry 1780–1840* (Oxford: Oxford University Press, 1987).
61. See Schapkow, 'Die Freiheit zu philosophieren'; Z. Levy, *Baruch Spinoza: Seine Aufnahme durch die jüdischen Denker in Deutschland* (Stuttgart: Kohlhammer, 2001).
62. An extremely wide range of responses to Spinoza are anthologised in W.I. Boucher, ed., *Spinoza: Eighteenth and Nineteenth-Century Discussions*, 6 vols (Bristol: Thoemmes Press, 1999).
63. http://www.aspinoza.com/; http://xnet2.uparis10.fr/pls/portal30/docs/folder/intranet/cdr/revues/amarx/amimarx.htm Both sites accessed on 12 April 2004.
64. J. Derrida, *Politics of Friendship* [1994], trans. G. Collins (London: Verso, 1997), pp. 1–25.
65. Ibid., pp. 221–4.
66. Ibid., pp. 227–70.
67. Bray, *The Friend*, p. 8.
68. Derrida, *Politics of Friendship*, pp. 252–63. For a recent reading of Kant's ethics in relation to heteronormativity and sexuality, see E.O. Clarke, *Virtuous Vice: Homoeroticism and the Public Sphere* (Durham, NC: Duke University Press, 2000), pp. 101–21.
69. On the intensity of Goethe's bond to Spinoza see Schapkow, 'Die Freiheit zu philosophieren', pp. 81–4.
70. See L. Lampert, *Gender and Jewish Difference from Paul to Shakespeare* (Philadelphia: University of Pennsylvania Press, 2004); D. Boyarin, *Border Lines: The Partition of Judaeo-Christianity* (Philadelphia: University of Pennsylvania Press, 2004).
71. J. Geller, 'Freud, Blüher, and the *Secessio Inversa*: Männerbünde, Homosexuality, and Freud's Theory of Cultural Formation', in D. Boyarin, D. Itzkovitz and A. Pellegrini (eds), *Queer Theory and the Jewish Question* (New York: Columbia University Press, 2003), pp. 90–120, esp. pp. 104–8. See also M. Bunzl, 'Jews, Queers and Other Symptoms: Recent Work in Jewish Cultural Studies', *GLQ: A Journal of Lesbian and Gay Studies*, 6 (2000), 321–41; D. Boyarin, *Unheroic Conduct: The Rise of Heterosexuality and the Invention of the Jewish Man* (Berkeley and Los Angeles: University of California Press, 1997), pp. 189–270.
72. See M. Garber, *Vested Interests: Cross Dressing and Cultural Anxiety* (New York: HarperCollins, 1993), pp. 224–33; idem, *Vice Versa: Bisexuality and the Eroticism of Everyday Life* (New York: Simon & Schuster, 1995).

73. See R. Tobin, *Warm Brothers: Queer Theory and the Age of Goethe* (Philadelphia: University of Pennsylvania Press, 2000), esp. pp. 35–9; A. Kuzniar, *Outing Goethe and His Age* (Stanford: Stanford University Press, 1996).

74. See D. Hertz, *Jewish High Society in Old Regime Berlin* (New Haven: Yale University Press, 1988); more generally on women as regulators of Enlightenment discourse see D. Goodman, *The Republic of Letters: A Cultural History of the French Enlightenment* (Ithaca: Cornell University Press, 1994).

75. Tobin, *Warm Brothers*, pp. 62–3; H. Arendt, *Rahel Varnhagen: The Life of a Jewess*, ed. L. Weissberg (Baltimore: Johns Hopkins University Press, 1997), esp. pp. 250–9.

76. Derrida, *Politics of Friendship*, p. 288.

77. On the ideal of detachment in nineteenth-century Britain, and its entwinement with Jewishness, see A. Anderson, *The Powers of Distance: Cosmopolitanism and the Cultivation of Detachment* (Princeton: Princeton University Press, 2001), esp. pp. 119–46.

Index

Abelard, Peter, 52
Addison, Joseph, 181
adultery, 82–3, 137
  and drunkenness, 118
  and priests, 98
Aelred of Rievaulx, 47, 52–3
Africans, 210
alcoholism, 183, 184, 187
alehouses, 116–18, 123–4, 125,
  162, 177
  and 'false-friendship', 118–19
  women and, 121
Allen, Cardinal, 99
Altmann, Alexander, 202
Ambrose, 46, 48
Ami et Amile, 51–2
amicitia, 6, 46, 48
  Christian context, 53
  and marriage, 52
Amsterdam Sephardic community
  at, 200
An Apology for the Life of . . . the . . . King
  of the Beggars, 189
Anne, Queen, 132, 138, 142, 146
anti-Catholicism, 89, 92–3, 94–100
Appel, Schmidt, 70
Appleby, 136
Apsley, Allan, 142
Apsley, Frances, 10, 142–6
Aquinas, Thomas, 52, 57n3
Archer, Ian, 162
Arendt, Hannah, 206
Ariès, Philippe, 5
Aristotle, 4, 138, 140, 211
  Nicomachean Ethics, 45–6, 55
Art d'aimer, 53
Ashley, Sir Francis, 111
Aston, Herbert, 140–1
Aubrey, John, 162
'Aucassin et Nicolette', 52
Augustine, 47, 55
  Confessions, 48–9

Badham, Samuel, 186, 189, 190
Badham, Susannah, 190
Bagshaw, Christopher, 98
Baines, Thomas, 91
Bale, John, 94–5
Barber, Mary, 30
Barker, John, 164
Bartlin, Candler, 69
Baur, Hans, 69, 70, 71, 72, 78, 85n15
Beale, Mary, 140
beggars, 10–11, 177–93
  'beggars club', 189
  bravery amongst, 191–2
  and charity, 187
  and male identity, 179
  and religion, 186–7, 189, 193
  'trickster' persona, 188–90, 192
Behringer, Wolfgang, 68
Berching, 71, 72
Berger, Peter L., and Luckmann,
  Thomas, The Social Construction of
  Reality, 44
Berghahn, Klaus, 201
Bergrheinfeld, 68
Berlin, 201–3, 207, 212–13, 214–15
Betteridge, Tom, Sodomy in Early
  Modern Europe, 93
Bezer, John James, 187
Bible
  'Cider Bible', 154
  Coverdale's, 155
  Geneva, 155
  Great Bible, 155
  Hebrew Bible, 10, 151–3, 157
  Jerusalem Bible, 157
  King James' Authorized Version,
    155, 156–7, 165–6
  Luther's translation, 155
  New American Bible, 157
  Rheims-Douay Bible, 157
  Septuagint, 152, 153, 166
  Tyndale's, 155, 156, 166

Bible – *continued*
  Vulgate, 153, 157, 166
  Wycliffite version, 153–4, 155,
    156–7
Bird, Henry, 99
Bittelmayr, Jacob, 74
Bittelmayr, Margretha, 74–7, 80, 81–2
Blake, William, 191
Blakey, Elizabeth, 121
Blanchot, Maurice, 211
body, the, 23, 25, 91, 131, 147
Boëtie, Étienne de la, 56
Böhm, Anna Maria, 81
Bonschab, Leonhard, 75
Borromeo, Cardinal, 99
Bossy, John, 72, 150
Boswell, John, 9, 23, 50
Bourchier, Frances, 135
Bowell, Anne, 137
Brändl, Veronica, 81
Brandt, Lorenz (Langschneider at
  Eichstätt), 70
Bray, Alan, 15, 45, 71, 78, 112, 113,
    131, 133, 136, 140, 146, 152, 178,
    179, 182, 185, 193, 197, 213
  on charity, 181
  on Derrida, 4, 212
  The Friend, 1, 6, 8, 12, 16–17, 22,
    23–4, 28, 31, 32, 66–7, 77, 83,
    91, 131, 134
  *Homosexuality in Renaissance
    England*, 1, 3, 15–16, 17–18,
    28, 29, 37n34, 90–4
  influence of, 1–2, 12, 15, 16, 17–18,
    40–1n76, 90
  and Roman Catholicism, 9, 91–2,
    104
Bredbeck, Gregory, 90
Bristol, 191
brotherhoods, 7
  sworn brotherhood, 28, 30, 112
Brougham Castle, 135–6
Brown, William, 91
Bryan, William, 124
Burger, G. and S.F. Kruger, *Queering the
  Middle Ages*, 31
Burn, James Dawson, *Autobiography of
  a Beggar Boy*, 186–7
Burns, Robert, 192

C.B., *Puritanism
  Pvritanisme the mother, Sinne the
    daughter*, 88, 89, 100–4, 104n2
Cade (minister), 89
Calvin, Jean, 89, 102, 159
Cambridge, 121, 124
  Christ's College, 91
  St. John's College, 119
  Trinity College, 119, 124
Carew, Bampfylda-Moore, *The Life and
  Adventures of . . . the Noted
  Devonshire Stroller and Dog-Stealer*,
    177–8, 186, 188, 189–90
Carey, Mary, 135
carnival, 67, 79–80
Casparin, Schweizer, 69
catechisms, 152, 158–61, 164
Catholicism, 9, 66
  and Alan Bray, 91–3
  attacks by John Bale, 94
  English, after the Reformation,
    97–100
  and homosexuality, 91–3, 98, 104
  post-Reformation English, 97–100
  seminaries, 99–100
  and sodomy, 89
  see also anti-Catholicism
celibacy, 93, 94, 95
Chambers, Peter, 100
charity, 48, 160, 164, 166, 179, 181
  and beggars, 187
  casual, 181–2, 183
  and masculinity, 192
  refusal to give, 73, 85n26
chastity, 47, 94, 137
childbirth, 73, 145–6
Chitting, Ann, 30
Chramnesind (nobleman), 49–50
Churchill, Sarah (Duchess of
  Marlborough), 132, 138, 142, 146
Cicero, M.T., *Laelius*, 46, 48, 55
Claßner, Georg, 71, 72
Clanvowe, Sir John, 6–7
class divisions, 10, 137–8, 175–80
  and masculinity, 194n4
Clifford, Lady Anne, 30,
    134–6, 147
Clinton, Bill, 20, 36–7n28
Coke, Edward, 92

comradeship, 9–10, 70, 113, 114,
124–5, 126
Constantinople, 6, 155
Counter-Reformation, 9, 66, 67–9
Council of Trent, 157
courts, royal, 145
courts, legal, 163–5
Coventry, Bishop of, 123
Crawford, Patricia, 7
Cromwell, Thomas, 96

Damasus, Pope, 153
Danby Wisk, Yorks., 162
Dargaval, Thomas, 191–2
D'Argens, Marquis, 198
De Coverly, Sir Roger, 181
Définition d'amour, 53
Defoe, Daniel, *Colonel Jack*, 183–4
Derrida, Jacques, 4, 11, 132,
211–12, 215
Descartes, René, *Meditations*, 198
desire, 28, 29, 133
Dessau, 202
Devil, links with, 74–5, 79, 83, 116
diaries, 134–5, 163
DiGangi, Mario, 21–2, 90
Dinzelbacher, Peter, 50
Dod, John, 164
Dolan, Frances, 98
domestic violence, 117–18
Dorchester, 111
Dormer, Lady Anne, 139
Dorset, 122, 125
Dover, 192
drink culture
drinking rituals, 117, 120–1, 122–3
and gender, 121–3
and homoeroticism, 125
and male bonding, 78, 110–30
see also alehouses
drunkenness, 110–30
arguments against, 110, 114–15
and domestic violence, 117–18
and manhood, 115
and sodomy, 119
Dublin, Newman House, 92
Duffy, Eamon, 7, 166
D'Urfey, Thomas, *Collin's Walk
Through London*, 181

Durrant, Jonathan, 9
*The Duty of a Christian towards
his Neighbour Confided in a
Sermon*, 161

eating and drinking, *see* food
and drink
Edmunds, Christopher, 111
Edward IV, 55
Eichstätt
Amerserin, the, 70
Anna, servant, 74
Apothekerin, the, 75, 86*n*33
Beckin, Große, 69
Bonschabin, the, 75
Gelbschusterin, the, 70, 73, 83
Hausmeister, the, 77
Hofrat, 67, 71, 81
Hofwachtmeisterin, the, 81
impact of war on, 68, 84
Landschneider, *see* Brandt, Lorenz
(Langschneider at Eichstätt)
Mosin, the, 70
Oblaierin, the, 81–2, 87
Richelin, the, 75
Schleifferin, the, 81
Schöttnerin, the, 70
weapons ban at, 79–80
Eickels, Klaus van, 50
Eliade, Mircea, 44
Elizabeth, Queen, 134–5
Ellwangen, 67
Elton, Geoffrey, 96
Ely, Humphrey, 99
emotion, 22, 24, 28, 44–5, 52
history of, 3
transcendency of the emotional,
53–7
Enderlin, Haimen, 70
Enlightenment, 11, 17, 197
friendship during, 197–200, 205,
216
rationalism, 207–8, 209–10
universalism, 198, 200, 205–6,
212–13, 214
Erasmus, Desiderius, 140
Erb, Anna, 70
eroticism, 20, 21, 26–7
and friendship, 22, 24, 25, 26–9, 44

Evelyn, John, 4, 140
Exeter, 100

Faderman, Lillian, *Surpassing the Love of Men*, 31
families, 4–5, 17, 117
Feawtrell, Edward, 124
Ferguson, Adam, 198
Filmer, Sir Robert, 146
Finch, Sir John, 91
Fioravanti, Girolamo, 99
Fisher, Robert, 99
Flandrin, J.-L., 15
Florence, 101
food and drink, 50, 71, 72, 74–9, 80
see also drink culture; drunkenness
Ford, Thomas, 111
Foster, Agnes and Francis, 164
Foucault, Michel, 19, 34, 88, 197, 213
Fowler, Constance, 140–2
Fowler, Walter, 142
Frantzen, Allen J., 95
fraternities, 7
French Revolution, 211, 212
The Friend, see Bray, Alan
Friend (organisation), 92, 106n16
friend, meanings of, 4–5
friendship
    Aristotle on, 45–6
    changes in, 19
    cult of, in eighteenth century
        Germany, 201
    Derrida on, 211–12
    during the eighteenth century,
        197–220
    in Eichstätt, 66–87
    Enlightenment concept of,
        205, 206
    equivocal nature, 17
    erotic potential, 23
    and eroticism, 22, 24, 25
    ethical import, 22
    and faith, 209
    'false friendship', 118–19
    female, 7–8, 10, 30–1, 131–49
    in the fifteenth century, 55–6
    German-Jewish, 200–6
    as gift relationship, 185
    male, 3, 4, 15–17, 37n35

and male homosexuality, 21, 22, 26
and marriage, 146
and masculine bonds, 17
medieval, 6
modern analysis, 44
pagan ideal of, 48
philosophical, 198, 207–10
Platonic, 4, 140
pseudonymous, 145
Renaissance ideal, 197
social practices in the Middle Ages,
    49–51
and sodomy, 20, 24
universalist paradigm, 212
Wollstonecraft on, 43

Gabler, Paul, 71, 81, 85n18
Galata, 6
Gataker, Thomas, 121
Ging, Barthlme, 81, 82
Girtenstihl, Michael, 70, 81
Gisors, 50
The Glasse of Mans Folly, 115–17, 118
Godolphin, Margaret, 4, 140
Goethe, Johann Wolfgang von, 207,
    210, 213
Goetschel, Willi, 200, 203
Goldberg, Jonathan, 3, 23, 26, 90
    *Homosexuality in Renaissance
        England*, 16
    Queering the Renaissance, 16,
        27, 31
'good fellowship', 112, 118–19,
    179
gossip, 139
Gowing, Laura, 7, 10, 163
Granger, John, 184–5
Granger, Rebecca, 184–5
Green, Ian, 159
Green, John, 98
Grefencker, Herr, 80
Gregory I, Pope, 94
Gregory VII, Pope, 50
Gregory of Tours, 49, 50
Griffiths, Robert, 187–8

Hackspacher, Margretha, 81
Hakluyt, Mr., 124
Halbmayr, Elisabeth, 82

Halperin, David, M., 28
Hamburg, 206
Hanger, Richard, 119–20
Harris, Barbara, 132
Harris, Frances, 4
Harsnett, Samuel, *Declaration of egregious Popish Impostures*, 98
Hart, James, *KAINIKH, or The Diet of the Diseased*, 110–11, 112, 116–17
Hart, Susannah, 189
Harwood, Edmund, 99–100
Hebich, Dr, 77
Heine, Heinrich, 210
Helvétius, Claude-Adrien, 198, 209
Henry II, King, 50
Henry IV, Emperor, 50
Herder, Johann Gottfried, *God: Some Conversations*, 210
Hereford, 154
Herrmann, Anne, *Queering the Moderns*, 31
Herrup, Cynthia, 23
Hertfordshire, 165
Herz, Henriette, 214
heterosexuality, 3, 5, 20, 21, 147
Hill, Christopher, 166
Hindle, Steve, 165, 166
Hirschberg, 71
History Workshop Journal, 1, 3, 91
Hitchcock, Tim, 10
HIV/AIDS, 32
Hobbes, Thomas, 209
Hochenschildt, Michael, 69, 70, 71, 72, 85n17
homoeroticisnm, 125
homosexuality, 16, 26, 71
  Alan Bray on, 1–3
  attitudes to, 28
  and friendship, 21
  history of, 1–2, 31–4
  male, 71
  and religion, 88–109
  Richard 'the Lionheart', 50
  and Roman Catholicism, 91–3
  and social life, 18
  subcultures, 90, 91, 100–1
  see also lesbianism; sodomy; tribadism

Homosexuality in Renaissance England, see Bray, Alan
Hörmann, Waldburg, 81
hospitality, 180–1
household, 131
Hughes, Robert, 183, 184
Hunt, Arabella, 22
Hunt, Margaret, 27

identity, 11–12, 18, 26, 29
  sexual, 77
incontinence, 96–8
individualism, rise of, 16, 50, 66
intimacy, 23, 24, 29, 113, 125, 135
  between men, 19, 213
  between women, 136–7
inversion, 114
Isabeau, Queen of France, 54
Isham, Francis, 100

Jacobi, Friedrich, 11, 207, 208, 209, 210, 214, 215
  Allwill, 209
Jagose, Annemarie, 133–4
James II, King, 138, 142
Jardine, Lisa, 90
Jerome, 153
Jesuits, 99, 100
John of Salisbury, 52
John the Fearless of Burgundy, 54, 64–5n87
John VIII, Pope, 94–5
Jones, Erasmus, *The Man of Manners*, 180
Judaism, 5–6, 201, 203, 205–6, 208, 210, 211, 212, 213–15
Julius II, Pope, 94

Kant, Immanuel, 198, 212
  Critique of Pure Reason, 208
Kantian ethics, 197
King, Gregory, 120
Kingsmill, Thomas, 115
kinship
  forms of, 83
  ritualised, 7, 67, 69, 70
  'voluntary', 17, 25

kissing, 6–7, 19, 54
  as a religious symbol, 7
  ritual between kings and
    nobleman, 55
  and women, 136
Knab, Walburga, 81

The Ladies Dictionary, 140
Lake, Peter and Michael Questier, *The
    Antichrist's Lewd Hat*, 89, 98, 100
Lane, Thomas, 125
Lanng, Valtin, 77–8
Lavater, Johann Caspar, 201
le Bel, Jean, *Ars d'amour*, 53–5
Leake, Richard, 162
Leibniz, Gottfried Wilhelm von, 207
Leicester, 117
Leipzig university, 202
Lenton, Francis, 114, 115
lesbianism, 27, 29–30, 31–2,
    39–40n67, 41–2n86, 74,
    86n41, 133
  see also tribadism
Lessing, Gottfried
  Arendt on, 206
  Nathan the Wise, 203–6, 209
  relationship with Mendelssohn,
    11, 200, 201, 202, 207, 208,
    213–14, 215
  The Jews, 203, 204
  view of friendship, 206
Lewald, Fanny, 203
Lewinsky, Monica, 20, 36–7n28
Lewis, Owen, 99
Librett, Jeffrey, 209
Lince, Michael, 188
Lister, Anne, 23, 25, 30
Liverpool, 191
Locke, John, 146
Lollards, 95, 107n33
London, 88, 91, 101–3, 162–5
  All Hallows, Lombard
    Street, 188
  All Hallows Staining, 165
  Archdeaconry court, 165
  Beech lane, 101
  black population in eighteenth
    century, 195n16
  Borough, 187

Brentford, 190
Bridewell, 137
Brixton, 187
Field Lane, 101
Fleet Street, 137
Gray's Inn Walks, 181
Holborn, 183, 184
Hyde Park, 181
Minories, 183, 184
New Compter, 183
Old Bailey, 189
Poultry Compter, 184
St Brides, 185
Thomas Street, 187
Turnham Green, 190
Tyburn, 189
Warwick Street, 182
Westminster, 192; archives, 98
Windmill Street, 187
Louis of Orléans, 54
Louis XI, 55
love, 24
  ancient Greek theory, 45
  between the sexes, 52
  and communities, 5–6
  courteous, 53
  and friendship, 46, 146–7
  linguistic shifts, 47–8, 50
  neighbourly, 162
  'profane' idea of, 50
  romantic, 53
  spiritual and carnal, 23
Luther, Martin, 155
Lyle, Robert, 125

MacCulloch, Diarmaid, *The
    Reformation*, 101
McNamee, William, 186
Maiden-Bradley, Wiltshire, 177
male bonding, 20
  and drink culture, 110–30
Mandeville, Bernard, *Fable of the Bees*,
    197, 209
manhood, 186
  and appetite, 112, 126
  and drunkenness, 115, 122
Marlborough, Sarah, Duchess of, *see*
    Churchill, Sarah (Duchess of
    Marlborough)

marriage, 5, 132, 139, 146–7
and *amicitia*, 52
delay in, 5, 124
and drinking, 118
European patterns, 5
and friendship, 17, 139–42, 146
Thomas Aquinas on, 52
Marx, Karl, 211
Mary of Modena, Queen, 146
Mary Stuart, Queen, 10, 142–6
masculinity, 4, 10, 190–1
and affect, 28, 179
and charity, 182, 192
and class divisions, 180–1
literature on, 194*n*3
Masham, Abigail, 132, 138
Masten, Jeffrey, 4, 90
Matthews, William, 181–2
Maxwell, William, 189
Melville, Herman, 191
Mendelson, Sara, 7
Mendelssohn, Moses
To Lessing's Friends, 208
quarrel with Jacobi, 207–10
relationship with Lessing, 11,
    200, 201–3, 208–9, 212,
    213–14, 215
Middle Ages, 6–7, 32
friendship in, 45, 49–57
Miélot, Jean, 46
migration, 157, 167
molly houses, London, 16, 25, 88,
    91, 101, 104–5*n*3
monasteries, 6, 94, 96–8
dissolution of, 157
Montaigne, Michel de, 4, 9, 56, 132,
    140, 197, 211
More, Hannah, 142
Morley, Thomas, 124
Mosaic law, 151
Muldrew, Craig, 163

Nazism, 206
neighbourhood, concept of, 150
neighbourliness, 157–8
Bible on, 150–2, 158–61
neighbourly love, 162–3, 167
and exclusion, 164–5
in legal records, 164

neighbours, 66–7, 150, 160–1
'good neighbour', 70–3
Hebrew word for, 151
litigation amongst, 163
murders of, 161–2
Neville, Sir William, 6–7
New Forest, 116
Newman, John Henry Cardinal, 23,
    38*n*44, 92
Newton, Thomas, 91
Nicolai, Friedrich, 201
Nietzsche, Friedrich Wilhelm, 211
North, Lady Anne, 139
Norwold, Richard, 97
Novalis (Friedrich Leopold, Freiherr
    von Hardenberg), 210
Nowell, Alexander, 160

O'Donnell, Katherine, 28
Oppenheim, Moritz, *Lavater and
    Lessing Visit Moses Mendelssohn*
    (painting), 201, 217*n*17
O'Rourke, Michael, 28
Orgel, Stephen, 90
Oschema, Klaus, 8
Oxford, 92, 135

Paris, university of, 15
parish, the, 157–8, 162, 164–5, 166,
    175*n*105
patriarchy, 29, 77, 183, 185
Patye (butcher), 111
Paulinus of Nola, 48
Pearce, Edward, 125
Peazy, John, 184–5
Penner, Egina, 81
Penrith, 136
periodization, issues of, 18–19,
    31–4, 36*n*17
Philip II Augustus, King, 9, 50
Philippe de Commynes, 55
Philips, Katherine, 139
philosophers
ancient, 45–6
Enlightenment, 198, 207, 208, 209
philosophical friendship, 198, 199,
    207–10
Pierce, James, 122
Place, Francis, 186, 191

Plato
    Phaedrus, 45
    Symposium, 45
Pößl, Magdalena, 71, 72
Pole, Geoffrey, 99
Port Royal, Jamaica, 191
Porzin, Peter, 81
Potter, Israel R., 190
Poulter, Amy, 22
poverty, 157, 165
    duty to the poor, 115–16, 159
    poor women, 139
    see also beggars
prayerbook, 164; Edward VI's second,
    159
Premierfait, Laurent de, 46
'profane' idea of love, 50, 55–6, 57
    and sacred, 44
prostitution, 137, 192
Protestantism, culture of, 89, 151, 152
    see also C.B., *Puritanism*;
    Reformation, impact of
Puff, Helmut, 71
Pulford, John, 125
Puritans, 88–9, 101–3, 110–11, 121

queer theory, 21, 31, 34
Quest, 91

Rabel, Barbara, 75, 76
Raleigh, Sir Walter, 114
Randall, Nicholas, 190
Reformation, impact of, 6, 89, 93–7,
    146, 151, 157, 166–7
    see also Protestantism, culture of
religion, 157
    and beggars, 186–7, 193
    and homosexuality, 88–109
    see also under individual faiths e.g.
    Catholicism; Judaism; C.B.,
    Puritanism
Rey, Michel, 3, 15, 78
Richard 'the Lionheart', 9, 44,
    50–1
Rocke, Michael, 2, 179
Roger of Howden, 50, 51
Rogers, Margaret, 137
rogue literature, 193–4*n1*
Romans, carnival at, 80

Romanticism, 179, 182, 210
Rome, English College at, 99–100
Roper, Lyndal, 78
Rottinger, Michael, 70
Routon, Mary, 137
Rowse, A.L., *Homosexuals in
    History*, 2
Ryarius, Petrus, 94
Rye, Sussex, 121

sacred, the, 44
St John, Ambrose, 23, 38*n42*, 92
Samford, Thomas, 136
Schaumberg, Prince-Bishop Martin
    von, 67
Schnell, Rüdiger, 52
Schrad, Anna, 81
Scott, James C., 188
Scottish Enlightenment, 157
Seckendorf, Herr von, 81, 82
Sedgwick, Eve Kosofsky, 26, 28,
    90, 125
service
    casual labour, 183–4
    literature on, 195*n14*
    servants, female, 20, 131
sexual intercourse, 23
sexuality, 18, 20
    history of, 26–7
Shakespeare, William, 'Sonnet 20',
    25–6
Shannon, Laurie, *Sovereign Amity*, 20,
    36*n27*, 137, 138, 142
Sharpe, Jim, 163
Shaw, Thomas, 183, 184
Shepard, Alexandra, 9, 70, 78
Sherlock, Richard, 159–60
Sichar (nobleman), 49–50
Silbereis, Georg, 78
Sixtus IV, Pope, 94
slander, 119–20, 163, 175*n94*
    and women, 163
sleeping together, 2, 50, 54,
    100, 134–5
Smith, Bruce, 30
Smith, Joan, 137
social tension, 66, 157, 166–7
Society for the Reformation of
    Manners, London, 16, 88

sodomy, 15, 16, 36*n13*, 71, 77, 90,
93–5, 133
and drunkenness, 119
and friendship, 19, 20, 21–2, 24,
25, 26
meanings of, 2, 88
and monasteries, 96–7
and Catholicism, 89, 92–3, 94–100,
102, 104
Sodomy Bill (1534), 96
Somerset, 125, 165
The Spectator, 181, 182–3
Spinoza, Baruch, 11, 198–200,
215–16
as Jew, 200, 201, 205–6, 211–12
'Spinoza Quarrel', 207–10, 215
Spinoza societies, 211
'Spinozism', 199, 203, 207, 208, 210,
215
Staffordshire, 140
Stanivukovic, Goran, 88, 87, 100–1
state formation, 158
Steele, Richard, 182–3
Steiner, Rob, *When Harry met Sally*, 43
Stevens, Samuel, 101
Stewart, Alan, 9
Stigeliz, Hans, 78
Stone, Lawrence, 4, 5, 146, 166
Stuart, Lady Arbella, 30, 135
Stubbes, Phillip, 115
Sutcliffe, Adam, 11
Swallowfield, Berks., 150, 168*n3*
Swindon, 123
sworn brotherhood, 28, 30, 66,
112, 136

Tadmor, Naomi, 4, 10
Talbott, Robert and Thomas, 123
Taunton, 164
Tawney, R.H., 166
Ten Commandments, the, 47,
102, 156
on neighbourliness, 150–1, 153,
158–60
Theirmayr, Anna, 70
Thimelby, Katherine, 140–1
Thomas, Keith, 166
Tillotson, Elizabeth, 140
Tlusty, B. Ann, 78

Traub, Valerie, 3, 8, 90, 112, 113, 133,
139–40, 141, 146
*Renaissance of Lesbianism in Early
Modern England*, 27
tribadism, 76–7, 133, 147
Trip to St James's, 186
Trometerin, Thoma, 70

Upway, Dorset, 123

Varnhagen, Rahel, 214
Venantius Fortunatus, 52
Visitation, the, 8, 14*n28, 29*
Vockher, Jesse, 71, 72

Walch, Sabina, 81
Ward, Ned, *History of London Clubs*,
189, 190
Warminster, 178
Warwick, Countess of, 134
weddings, 73–6, 77, 81–2, 83
Weißenkirch, 74, 76
West Dereham, 97
Westerstetten, bishop Johann
Christoph von, 67, 68, 80
Westmoreland, 162
Weymouth, Lord, 177–8, 188
Whately, William, 117
Wiber, Dorothy, 136
Wiesner, Merry, 179
Wigglesworth, Michael, 4, 28
William IX of Aquitaine, 52
William of Orange, 142, 143
Willison, Mrs, 136
Windsor Forest, 166
Wisbech, 98, 100
witchcraft, 66, 67–8, 84*n1*
and agrarian crisis, 66, 68
in Eichstätt, 66–84
witches' sabbaths, 79–83
Wölch, Walburga, 75–6,
86*n34*
Wolff, Christian, Freiherr von,
207
Wollstonecraft, Mary, 43
women
and drinking, 121–2
and kissing, 136
and slander, 163

women's friendship, 7–8, 10,
    30–1, 131–49
  and marriage, 139–42
  political role, 132, 138
  in the Tudor age, 132
Woodward, G.R.O., 96
Worcestershire, 122, 124, 125, 161

Wrighte, Margaret, 137
Wrightson, Keith, 116, 162
Wyclif, John, 10, 153, 154

Young, Thomas, 114, 115, 116,
    118, 119
youth culture, 123–4